# RAWLS AND RIGHTS

# Rawls and Rights

• REX MARTIN •

UNIVERSITY PRESS OF KANSAS

© 1985 by the University Press of Kansas
All rights reserved

Published by the University Press of Kansas (Lawrence, Kansas 66045),
which was organized by the Kansas Board of Regents
and is operated and funded by Emporia State University, Fort Hays State
University, Kansas State University, Pittsburg State
University, the University of Kansas, and Wichita State University

Library of Congress Cataloging in Publication Data

Martin, Rex.
Rawls and rights.

Bibliography: p.
Includes index.
1. Rawls, John, 1921–     . A theory of justice.
2. Justice. 3. Civil rights. I. Title.
JC578.R383M37   1985        320′.01′1        84-27044
ISBN 0-7006-0266-6

Printed in the United States of America

Regan

# CONTENTS

PREFACE vii

1 THE BACKGROUND 1
 *1. Rights and the General Welfare 1*
 *2. The Basic Structure and the Original Position 11*

2 A THEORY OF JUSTICE AND RIGHTS 21
 *1. Rawls on Rights and Their Justification 21*
 *2. Natural Rights and the Basic Structure 31*
 *3. Global Justice 41*

3 EQUAL BASIC LIBERTIES 45
 *1. Some Liberties Are Basic Ones 46*
 *2. All Basic Liberties Are Equal Ones 52*

4 FAIR EQUALITY OF OPPORTUNITY 63
 *1. Establishing Inequality as Just 63*
 *2. Opportunities 67*
 *3. Three Interpretations of Equal Opportunity 70*
 *4. Collective Asset 76*
 *5. Basic Rights to Opportunities 82*

5 THE DIFFERENCE PRINCIPLE 87
 *1. The Maximin Interpretation of the Difference Principle 89*
 *2. Pareto Efficiency and Egalitarianism 91*
 *3. Pareto Efficiency, Egalitarianism, and Justice 97*
 *4. Pareto Efficiency and Egalitarianism versus the Maximin
  Interpretation of the Difference Principle 101*

6 THE PRIORITY OF LIBERTY                                    107
  *1. Arguments for the Priority of Liberty   107*
  *2. An Argument for the Priority of Rights   114*
  *3. Basic Rights under the Difference Principle   120*
  *4. Equal Basic Rights: A Summing Up   124*

7 ON THE CONFLICT OF RIGHTS                                  129
  *1. The Scope and Weight of a Right   130*
  *2. Stages of the Policy Process   137*
  *3. A Criterion of Coherence   141*
  *4. The Problem of Internal Conflict   148*
  *5. A Family of Rights   152*

8 RAWLSIAN ECONOMIC JUSTICE                                  157
  *1. The Market   157*
  *2. Just Returns   162*
  *3. Contribution and Ownership   169*

9 JUSTICE AND WELFARE                                        175
  *1. The Problem of Needs   175*
  *2. The Welfare of Those Unable to Work   181*
  *3. Self-Respect: A Postscript   191*

APPENDIX                                                     197

NOTES                                                        203

SELECTED BIBLIOGRAPHY                                        235

INDEX                                                        240

# PREFACE

John Rawls's book, *A Theory of Justice* (1971), is already something of a classic, for it is widely regarded as an important and seminal treatise on some of the main topics of moral and political philosophy. It is, of course, too early to say anything definite about its long-term prospects, but the book may well come in time to have a prestige and influence comparable to that of John Stuart Mill's *Utilitarianism* (1863) or even his *On Liberty* (1859). In any event, Rawls's book says much of significance about contemporary political culture and would be a valuable book for this reason alone.

The book, as might be expected, has engendered intensive and widespread commentary. Indeed, several books have been devoted to Rawls's *Theory of Justice*. These can conveniently be divided into systematic studies (notably Barry, 1973, Wolff, 1977, and Schaefer, 1979) and anthologies of essays (principally Daniels, 1975, and Blocker and Smith, 1980). The systematic studies have tended to be rather general accounts of Rawls's theory and have been uniformly unsympathetic and critical towards his project. The anthologies are, by their very nature, relatively unfocused and do not lend themselves to a systematic development or appraisal of Rawls's theory. Also, two of the more prominent books (Barry's and Daniels's) were published relatively early and, thus, were unable to take account of the considerable writing that Rawls himself has done (see the bibliography) in response to various discussions of his book.

One further point: Rawls's book is widely believed to have significant bearing on the philosophy of rights; but Rawls, though he frequently uses the language of rights, nowhere discusses rights as his main topic. His book contains, for example, no section devoted to rights, no entry for 'rights' or for 'human rights' or for 'moral rights' in its justly celebrated index (but there are three page citations under 'natural rights'). And though the discussion of his views has been copious, few articles have been concerned principally with Rawls on rights (among these few are Michelman, 1973; and Nelson, 1974). Even the books devoted to Rawls are notably reticent as to his views on rights specifically, though there are two anthologized essays (Hart, 1975; and Bowie, 1980) on the related topic of liberties. It is, perhaps, not surprising that incidental discussions in the literature have revealed a considerable variety of opinion about what Rawls has had to say on basic rights and their justification.

The place of rights in Rawls's theory has largely been an uncharted area. Accordingly, I thought that a study of the topic would be in order. In undertaking it, I found that matters of considerable philosophic interest were revealed, sometimes in unexpected lights, by my explorations. So my study grew to book length. And it has become more than a monograph. For, if my expectations are fulfilled, it will prove to be not only an examination of the philosophy of rights in Rawls's theory of justice but also something more general: a short, reliable guide to understanding that theory.

In my book I attempt to get at Rawls's theory on its own terms and to criticize it internally, on grounds already embedded—and acknowledged, if only implicitly—in the structure of the theory. In particular, I attempt to interpret Rawls's theory in the light of contributions and clarifications he has made subsequent to the book. In these respects the book has largely an exegetical purpose.

More important, my book is intended to be a systematic study of an important but hitherto somewhat neglected aspect of Rawls's theory, his account of rights. My object here is not merely to bring out Rawls's notion of rights and to afford it whatever systematic appraisal it deserves, though this needs to be done. My main concern, rather, is to use Rawls's account of rights to help restructure his entire theory. For I think the theory can increase its systematic power and reach with such treatment; and so doing allows one to deflect certain criticisms made of it, in particular, of Rawls's doctrine of the priority of liberty.

A second significant thematic feature of my treatment is an emphasis on the *application* of Rawls's theory. In the usual study, considerable attention is given to the framework developed by Rawls for deciding about the principles of justice in the so-called original position. In my account the emphasis is moved from this decision apparatus to the substantive *arguments* that would be generated and have weight within this framework. My procedure, then, is to trace these arguments beyond the original position to consider their effect on what Rawls calls the "basic structure" of a society and even on legislation and other transactions that would go on in a Rawlsian well-ordered society. Thus, rather than set the original position apart as a favored arena for philosophical discussion, I attempt to unify these main stages in Rawls's account into a single, coherent perspective and to identify the dominant arguments that are continually being elaborated within this perspective. These arguments, then, become the thread that connects the abstract formulation of principles of justice in the original position with the working out of the principles, first, in the basic institutions of a society and, then, in its day-to-day operations.

In the development of this program, my book falls naturally into three main segments. The first two chapters are devoted to background matters. In the first of these I attempt to sketch out the theory that Rawls is mainly concerned to dispute—namely, the utilitarian theory—and to indicate its bearing on rights. After that I examine two of the main features in Rawls's alternative theory of justice: the idea of the basic structure of a society and that of the original position. I turn, in the next chapter, to the nature of rights and, especially, the character of their justification in Rawls's theory. Particular attention is paid here to Rawls's idea of natural rights.

The succeeding four chapters are concerned with reformulating Rawls's theory by bringing to the fore the account of rights embedded in it. The centerpiece of Rawls's theory goes under the name of "the two principles of justice." In his standard statement of the two principles, the first is said to require that "each person is to have an equal right to the most extensive total system of equal basic liberties compatible with a similar system of liberty for all" (*Theory of Justice,* p. 302; see also pp. 60 and 250). The second principle, however, is characteristically rendered in somewhat different terms: "Social and economic inequalities are to be arranged so that they are both: (a) to the greatest benefit of the least advantaged, . . . and (b) attached to offices and positions open to all under conditions of fair equality of opportunity" (*Theory of Justice,* p. 302; see also pp. 60 and 83). Rawls argues as well that the first principle has a certain priority over the second (see, e.g., pp. 302–3) and this priority is grounded, ultimately, in what he calls the priority of liberty (see *Theory of Justice,* sec. 82, in particular). These chapters, then, concern the main arguments for the crucial features identified here: (1) equal basic liberties, (2) fair equality of opportunity, and (3) the benefit of the least advantaged. Then I turn, using Rawls's theory of rights, to a restatement and defense of his notion of the priority of liberty.

The book concludes with three chapters that apply this reformulated theory of justice to problem areas that Rawls himself has not examined closely. One chapter deals with the conflict of rights, with special attention paid to the role of the courts. And the other two take up issues concerning the main economic institutions of a well-ordered society. Here I examine such matters as the open and competitive market, the ownership of productive property, and, last of all, society's proper response to the needs of those who are unable to work. I have chosen to focus on these economic matters, in particular, because this part of Rawls's theory is especially tangled and has not been well presented or well understood.

There has been, as I have mentioned, sustained and painstaking discussion of Rawls's theory in the last dozen or so years since his book appeared. It is not likely, then, that any entirely new idea or interpretation could be unearthed after such extensive tilling of the field. Indeed, any interpretation of undue novelty would be met with suspicion and would, very probably, be unsound.

Even so, I would claim that some features of my treatment are distinctive. I have in mind two chapters in particular, the one on the benefit of the least advantaged ("The Difference Principle") and the one titled "The Priority of Liberty." I think the things said there will serve to put these elements of Rawls's theory in a substantially different light and should have, I believe, an effect on the interpretation and reception of his theory. But I cannot claim great originality even here, for I am conscious of many debts—of collaboration, of influence, and more generally of support and encouragement—which I am very happy herewith to acknowledge.

The studies that eventually took shape as chapters 5 ("The Difference Principle") and 8 ("Rawlsian Economic Justice") had their origin in work that I did, during the spring semester of 1979, when I served as Humanist in Residence in the University of Kansas School of Business (under a grant, on business and the humanities, to the school from the National Endowment for the Humanities). Chapter 5 is based on a paper which Prakash Shenoy and I jointly wrote and which was published, in a shorter version, in *Theoria*. The Appendix to the present book, which originally appeared in shorter form as an appendix to that article, is entirely the work of Shenoy. The ideas contained in chapter 5 germinated during a series of discussion sessions on Rawls's *Theory of Justice* between Joseph Pichler, Prakash Shenoy, and myself during the spring of 1979. Some of the leading ideas in chapter 5, in particular the formalism, were set out in much shorter compass in Shenoy (1980).

Chapter 8 had its origin in public lectures that I delivered during my stay in the School of Business in the spring of 1979. The final draft of the article on which chapter 8 is based was written at the Villa Serbelloni, Bellagio (Lake Como), Italy. I want to thank Roberto Celli, the staff, and the Rockefeller Foundation for the hospitality that I enjoyed there and to thank Eric Mack for his written comments (1981) on this article.

The studies that eventually took shape as chapters 3 ("Equal Basic Liberties"), 6 ("The Priority of Liberty"), and 7 ("On the Conflict of Rights") had their origin in a happy juxtaposition of appointments: on work I did, first, as visiting professor of philosophy at the University of Auckland (New Zealand) in July and August of 1981 and, then, as intrauniversity visiting professor in the School of Law of the University of Kansas in 1981/82.

I want to thank Krister Segerberg and members of staff at the University of Auckland for the hospitality I enjoyed—and especially Christine Swanton, the lecturer normally in charge of classes I taught there, for helping me to think through some of the ideas in chapters 3 and 6. Much of the writing of the article on which these chapters are based was done while I was in the School of Law. I want to thank Dean Michael Davis and faculty of the school, in particular, Philip Kissam and Robert McKay, for my extremely kind reception there and to thank the Exxon Foundation and the College of Liberal Arts and Sciences, University of Kansas, for making this particular visit possible.

The writing of the present book was completed during tenure of a sabbatical leave grant from the University of Kansas and a Rockefeller Foundation Humanities Fellowship. I am deeply grateful for this support.

My work on the book has also been aided greatly by reading groups on Rawls that I have participated in and by the comments and support of friends and colleagues. I am especially indebted to Karen Bell, Norman Bowie, Robert Hall, Dan Hausman, Donna Martin, Diana Meyers, and John Rawls (for many helpful comments, in particular, on the idea of collective asset in chapter 4, section 4, and on the presentation of some points in chapter 9). I also want to thank Susan Daniel, Cindi Hodges, and Pam LeRow. The assistance of all these good persons is acknowledged with heartfelt appreciation.

Acknowledgment is made to the publishers below for permission to use portions of (or quotations from) my own articles, as follows:

"Human Rights and Civil Rights," *Philosophical Studies* 37 (1980): 391–403, for use as a source, in particular, of chapter 2 (sec. 2). Copyright ©1980 by D. Reidel Publishing Company, Dordrecht, Holland.

"Human Rights and Equal Basic Liberties," in *Human Rights,* edited by D. L. Gruender, selected papers from the Tenth Inter-American Congress of Philosophy (forthcoming), for use as a source, in particular, of chapters 3 and 6.

"On the Justification of Rights," pp. 153–86 in *Philosophy of Action,* edited by G. Fløistad, vol. 3 of *Contemporary Philosophy: A New Survey,* Chronicles Series of the International Institute of Philosophy (The Hague: Nijhoff, 1982), for use as a source, in particular, of chapters 1 (sec. 1) and 2 (sec. 1). Copyright ©1982 by Martinus Nijhoff Publishers.

"Poverty and Welfare in Rawls's Theory of Justice: On the Just Response to Needs," in *Economic Justice: Private Rights and Public Responsibilities,* edited by K. Kipnis and D. T. Meyers, (Totowa, N.J.: Rowman & Allanheld, 1985), for use as a source, in particular, of chapter 9.

"Rawlsian Economic Justice and the Proper Bounds of Government Regulation," pp. 114–32 in *Ethical Issues in Government,* edited by N. Bowie, (Philadelphia, Pa.: Temple University Press, 1981), for use as a source, in particular, of chapters 2 and 8.

"Three Conceptions of Equal Opportunity." The 1983/84 Byron Shutz Award Lecture for Distinguished Teaching on Economic Systems (Lawrence, Kans.: University of Kansas, 1984), for use as a source, in particular, of chapter 4.

Prakash P. Shenoy and R. Martin, "Two Interpretations of the Difference Principle in Rawls's Theory of Justice," *Theoria* 49 (1983): 113–41, by permission of Shenoy and of the managing editor of *Theoria,* for use as a source, in particular, of chapters 1 (sec. 2) and 5 and the Appendix.

I also want to thank Harvard University Press for allowing me to quote portions of John Rawls's book, *A Theory of Justice,* which they published. (Copyright ©1971 by the President and Fellows of Harvard College.) Reprinted by permission.

# · 1 ·

# THE BACKGROUND

In this chapter and in the study as a whole, I am concerned principally with rights of two main sorts: basic moral rights (under which I include human rights) and constitutional rights. Many people have thought that utilitarians cannot provide an adequate account (or justification) of such rights. This, indeed, is Rawls's view and forms the backdrop of his theory of justice. But some philosophers have challenged this prevailing view and have argued that a utilitarian theory of rights drawn from Mill might prove adequate. In the present chapter I want to examine this attempt by recent thinkers to construct a justification of rights on utilitarian grounds. I conclude that there are deep problems with any such proposed utilitarian justification. This sets the stage for a Rawlsian nonutilitarian model of justification.

The remainder of this chapter and the entire next one concern the justification of rights in Rawls's own theory of justice. I begin this account by sketching out some of the leading features of the theory, concentrating on the claim that the basic structure of a society is the primary focus of a theory of justice and on Rawls's innovative idea of an original position. Briefly, his idea is that we can formulate principles of justice, which are both objective and agreed upon as reasonable, by identifying and observing certain constraints and simplifications which any argument about such principles would have to observe.

## 1. Rights and the General Welfare

The capacity of utilitarianism to provide a normative grounding for moral rights or for constitutional rights is open to some doubt. Historically, the utilitarian tradition has not been especially hospitable to the notion of basic moral rights, in particular those that can be held by individuals against governments. Jeremy Bentham characterized rights of this sort—so-called natural rights—as nonsense,[1] and utilitarian philosophers have tended up to now to follow his lead in dismissing or, more commonly, downplaying the notion of basic moral rights. Thus, the very comprehensive survey by Dan Brock of recent work in utilitarianism (written circa 1973) indicates a notable lack of interest in the topic of rights and their justification by utilitarian philosophers. Indeed, Brock's only significant mention of rights comes at the point where he sketches two arguments, one by Rawls and the other by Ronald Dworkin, to the effect that utilitarianism cannot accommodate the notion of basic rights of individuals.[2] A similar contention has recently been advanced by H. L. A. Hart.[3]

One typical response by utilitarian philosophers has been to accept such a contention but to deny that it bespeaks a grave defect in utilitarianism. A standard move here has been to give rights a subordinate place in utilitarianism by arguing that all valid rights can readily be explicated in terms of a more basic notion—that of enforceable duties—which can itself be accounted for by reference to such superordinate values as aggregate benefit or general welfare (i.e., "the greatest happiness of the greatest number," in Bentham's phrase).

The question remains, though, whether utilitarianism can take *basic* rights seriously. A plausible case can be made for saying that utilitarianism cannot accommodate such rights. Let us begin by sketching this case.

One difficulty with traditional Benthamite utilitarianism, often cited, is that it does not allow for rights that are independent of actual (i.e., official or popular) enforcement; hence one could never argue *from* rights to the conclusion that one or a few rights should be respected and enforced. I will set this particular difficulty aside, for it may well be a difficulty peculiar to Bentham's own views (and the way he conceived rights) and not one that is intrinsic to utilitarianism as such. We can turn, then, to raise a more substantial point.

The duties that utilitarian philosophers emphasize—whether rights attach to them or not—are not independent of considerations of general welfare. Typically, they are thought to be supported by such considerations in the following way: if all persons conform to a certain policy restricting their conduct (say, by paying their debts), then the consequences of following that policy will be more nearly in accordance with "the greatest happiness of the greatest number" than will those of alternative policies. However, there will always be cases where *deviating* from the specified policy will have a greater utilitarian value. In such cases the duty of following the policy can be set aside, or so it is argued; an exception can be made, which will serve the greater good, on that occasion. It could be contended that the exception

2

should be made (the deviation from established policy taken) even if the marginal improvement is very slight.

So we see that duties and the rights which sometimes attach to them, in being so dependent on and responsive to considerations of general welfare or the public good, can never give us a self-standing reason for acting in a certain way—one that is independent, or relatively so, of such considerations. Thus, rights having weight against such considerations cannot be justified on utilitarian grounds.[4]

The more serious problem, then, is that in the Benthamic approach considerations of general welfare ("the greatest happiness of the greatest number") are thought to exercise an absolute monopoly in justificatory arguments; it would follow that, in any given instance, one could not use the notion of basic rights as having any independent effect in matters of justification, as having any special normative force. For there is no way in which such a right could be allowed to block, let alone override, a sound welfare argument, even one that suggested but a minimal increase in general well-being.[5]

Now, those who have traditionally advocated basic rights—whether moral or constitutional ones—have had in mind, precisely, rights that are able to withstand, up to a point at least, appeals to the greatest happiness or the public good. Such rights provide a guarantee of specified benefits to individuals independently of fluctuations in the general welfare; they assure benefits to individuals even on those occasions (or some of them) when the weight of welfare considerations would dictate a different path. Accordingly, it could plausibly be said that utilitarians cannot account for basic rights.

It is possible, however, to move away from the standard utilitarian doctrine of rights, and recent work by utilitarian thinkers has constituted an interesting exploration of the possibilities for such a move within traditional utilitarian theory. Characteristically, they do not argue that basic rights are an essential part of utilitarian theory or that they are in any way presupposed by it; rather, they intend only to establish the weaker thesis that utilitarian foundational values, such as the general welfare, are compatible with the possession of basic moral or constitutional rights.[6]

One main device in this reconstructive account is to shift the focus of attention from Bentham, who did not countenance the idea of basic moral rights, to J. S. Mill, who did. A notable feature in this shift from Bentham to Mill is the contention that a moral theory is primarily concerned with judgments of (moral) right and wrong. It is then further contended that such judgments are, conceptually, a function of (moral) rights and obligations. And rules enter the picture in order to provide a suitably general statement of such obligations and the rights that attach to some of them. Thus, it follows from the logic of the moral concepts that utilitarianism as a moral theory is principally concerned with rules—specifically, rules that establish moral obligations and, in the case of some obligations, attendant rights. In saying this, these utilitarian thinkers are contending, presumably, not only that morality is correctly conceived in this way (by perceptive moralists of all philosophical persuasions) but also that it is the best or proper way for utilitarians to think about morality.[7]

On the view we are examining, the rules that specify moral rights and obligations are modeled on "ordinary" social rules; that is, they are conceived as relatively simple rules which take into account and thereby incorporate not just the utility of the course of conduct to be regulated (either to be promoted or to be prevented, as the case may be) but also the costs of such regulation, subject only to the proviso that these costs are justifiable.

Sometimes legal sanctions (the most costly in terms of the negative utilities involved) can be justified, but sometimes only public disapproval can be or, in the least costly case, only pangs of conscience. Thus a utilitarian, following Mill, finds out whether a given act is *morally* wrong (as distinct from legally wrong) by calculating whether internal sanctions for such an act could be justified on utilitarian grounds. Hence, a type of harmful act is morally wrong and one is obliged not to do it if a coercive social rule—that is, one which invokes guilt feelings and, perhaps, other nonlegal sanctions against it—would be warranted.

Now, it is crucial that these rules individually be kept simple,[8] so that they can be readily understood, easily followed in the usual cases, and applied more capably in the difficult ones. It follows from this—from the simplicity of moral rules as modeled on real social rules—that most of these rules will be merely happiness producing but not happiness maximizing. Thus the gap between morality and the maximizing of utility, already there in principle, is widened and made permanent.

But the gap here is not fatal to the project of a utilitarian morality. Morality is more narrowly conceived than is general well-being (as an end) or than expedient action (as action maximally instrumental to such an end). For morality is concerned with rules or policies of conduct (specifically, rules that set obligations by reference to sanctions or that make for obligation-protected benefits—i.e., rights—for some definite and qualified individual or class of individuals).[9] Morality does set requirements for action. And appropriate conduct in the individual case is, if it is moral conduct, always responsive to the dictates of these rules.

But would rights of the sort we are interested in—basic moral rights, including constitutional rights having moral force—never yield to the general interest, to rights-infringing conduct dictated by the highest principle, that of utility itself? It could be replied that in a particular case the point of applying the principle of utility is merely to contribute to an ongoing cumulative

4

ranking of "the opposing obligations" and is not to determine directly the choice among alternative actions on that occasion. "Our conception of the moral obligations would be refined," and it is this resultant clear ranking of obligations cumulatively which directly determines the proper course of action to take in a given case.[10] At most, then, a given welfare argument—one that brings the consequences of action under direct inspection in the light of the principle of aggregate benefit or general welfare—would *help* to establish the stringency of a given rights-rule (or, alternatively, a rule of mere obligation) in relation to other such rules.

There is, in sum, no direct requirement for action superior to the moral rules, nothing that one *must* do as a utilitarian moralist. So, the rules function as a sort of shield against direct welfare arguments (arguments posed in terms of expediency). Hence it is possible for rights to block a welfare argument since the latter has no direct moral standing as such. Certainly we are not *morally* required to let an obligation go, or to let a right down, even when doing so would yield a greater net benefit. To think otherwise is to confuse what is *required* with what is *desirable*.[11]

Thus, it is sensible to say, on the one hand, that rights and duties are attached to rules which can be justified on utilitarian grounds (as rules in the most desirable moral code, when justified from the perspective of long-term utility) and to say, on the other, that rights can withstand direct welfare arguments. Here we can say both that basic rights have independent moral force (since they can control conduct even in cases in which deviation from the rule would be expedient and certainly in cases in which the deviation would be of only slight advantage) and that basic rights are compatible with the utilitarian goal of general welfare (since, though founded on the general welfare, they cannot be required to be overridden by direct appeals to utility).

This reconstructive theory of "indirect" utilitarianism is an interesting one and would, if sound, support a thesis of compatibility, as I have tried to show. Thus, it merits careful attention. There are, however, serious flaws in the theory which, I believe, incapacitate it for that job.

As both Bentham and Mill argued,

> the criterion of utility can [be applied] to diverse objects—to traits of human character and individual acts, for example, as well as to rules and institutions. There is nothing in the idea that human welfare is to be promoted that restricts its application *either* to individual acts *or* to social rules. So, a thoroughgoing utilitarian cannot ignore direct utilitarian arguments, cannot regard them as irrelevant or out of place when considering what is to be done.[12]

Neither a primary focus on acts (occasions of conduct) nor a primary focus on rules is intrinsic to utilitarianism; what is intrinsic is to prefer the greater good—the greater amount of general happiness—to the lesser. Presumably, then, the committed utilitarian would range over all the relevant considerations and would select that one which best promoted human welfare, everything considered. He could not, consistent with his acknowledgment of utility as the single master principle, do otherwise. It would be irrational for him, given this commitment, to choose to do something that achieves a lesser well-being, as following the rule on that occasion would, instead of a greater, as a deviation from the rule would. Nor could he recommend such a choice to others. So he would deviate from the rule and do the thing that, everything considered, produced the greater good on the occasion in question. And he would make such a deviation, would have to, even when the margin of improvement is only very slight.

The utilitarian recognizes, of course, that there are costs in breaking an established rule; expectations may be disappointed, and there may be, as well, costs in social cohesion or in the habit of conforming to moral norms. Such subtractions from general welfare are specifically included (under the heading of "everything considered") in his calculations, and a sound welfare argument goes through, everything considered, despite these costs.

If this perception of utilitarian rationality is sound, then rules of obligation—whether moral rules or legal rules having moral force—could provide no justificatory or argumentative threshold at all to withstand sound welfare arguments. They could not function as screens against direct appeals to utility. And even minimal accretions to the general welfare could outweigh any right, be it legal or moral, basic or nonbasic.[13]

It is difficult to see that this conclusion could be avoided. One might, for a try, turn to the claim that rights and obligations are *conceptually* basic to morality. Thus, it might be argued that one could never be *morally* obliged to flunk all his moral obligations, as he would do whenever he made *direct* appeals to utility and thereby determined his conduct so as to violate a rule of obligation. But the claim that morality is essentially a matter of rights and obligations is itself highly doubtful, as Hart has pointed out.[14] And even if we were to allow this rather dubious point about morality to stand, the utilitarian could still say that he is normatively required, by the master principle itself, to act in a way that would violate his moral obligations. Note that he does not claim here that he is *morally* required so to act (for that would probably be a senseless thing to assert) but, rather, that he is *normatively* required.

There is only one way I see in which this point about normative requirements could be turned. For it could be contended that the normative requirement here mentioned may not, in fact, be a requirement to *act* in a certain way. So the issue of whether there is a requirement to act at the level of the principle of utility itself becomes the exact point in dispute. And here we come to a deep element in the reconstructive theory of "indirect" utilitarianism: the view that the peculiarity of moral rules is that they, unlike the goal of general welfare, set requirements for action.

Now, presumably, this requirement for action is a conceptual feature of any schema of morality in which obligations and attendant rights are involved. The question we need to answer, then, is whether anything intrinsic to utilitarianism provides a reason or basis for selection and incorporation of a schema of precisely this sort.

A standard utilitarian answer would be to link the requirement for action found in moral obligations to a prior requirement for action built right into the theory of general welfare itself. The argument here, the crucial one for our purposes, goes something like this. It starts with the claim that there is for utilitarians a requirement that one is to do that act or to follow that expedient course of action, among equally viable alternative ones, which has the best long-run net effect in terms of benefits (or which reduces disbenefits, if that is the issue). The requirement here is not one of morality; rather, it is a requirement set by means/end reasoning. For where the state most highly prized by utilitarians (i.e., the best long-run net effect, etc.) can be brought about by human conduct and where that state can be most effectively achieved by an individual act $A$ or by a course of such actions, an action or a course not otherwise ineligible, then one does, or *should* do, $A$. The requirement in question is that of a hypothetical imperative and belongs ultimately to the theory of the practical syllogism.[15] This requirement for action, the argument continues, is transitive to the theory of morality. And this is how a requirement for action finds its way, at least on utilitarian grounds, to a rules morality in the first place.

In short, the requirement for action from which we started initially—that found in a certain theory of morality (where the ends are identified as rights and obligations)—is here viewed as being generated by a prior requirement, namely, that we are required to act so as to serve the end of general welfare. Indeed, it must be viewed in this way if we are to retain a utilitarian perspective throughout and thus *explain* the requirement in question by reference to the principle of utility. (But let us allow here, for the sake of argument, that we are not required to *maximize* general welfare but, rather, merely to promote it.)

If this is so and if utilitarianism is a consequentialist theory (in which consequences of conduct can be directly appraised as to their bearing on aggregate benefit), I do not see how one can avoid the view that welfare arguments can sometimes override rights altogether. For by allowing that utilitarianism is a theory of action, that it does set normative requirements for action—a point seemingly necessary to any full and satisfactory account of rights and obligations within utilitarian morality—we have removed the

7

linchpin of "indirect" utilitarianism and, with it, the principal reason for saying that arguments from welfare cannot directly override rights.

Of course, it may be that the utilitarian principle of general welfare is merely evaluative, merely a principle of appraisal; but then we have no basis in utilitarianism itself for adopting a morality of rights and obligations. Thus, the two points—(a) that a utilitarian theory of moral obligations and rights is possible and (b) that the principle of general welfare can set normative requirements for action—stand or fall together.

One refinement here is, perhaps, in order before we proceed. For it could be said that moral rules (in particular those that define rights) are, in effect, parts of happiness or of well-being and cannot be separated out from it and then measured and possibly overridden by reference to the standard of general welfare, as the analysis seems to allow. The response has merit, for it may well be true that utilitarians have in fact reached the standard of general welfare, or understood it, by starting from existing rules.

Nonetheless, one could still say that the master principle has a certain independence from the moral rules. For utilitarians have traditionally held that the principle of general welfare could be proven to be true or appreciated as sound on its own, so to speak. (And all the great utilitarian moralists of the nineteenth century—Bentham, Mill, Sidgwick—held such a view.) Here the crucial claim is not that the principle of general welfare is genetically or even conceptually independent of moral rules but, rather, that it can be understood without reference to any particular moral rule and that, so understood, it can be seen to be a reasonable principle. It can count, then, as an independent standard of appraisal. As long as the independence of the master principle is so affirmed, as it has been traditionally, then the argument that I have conducted can go through. Although it may not be possible to set aside moral rules altogether, it is possible (using this principle) to justify exceptions to any one of them.

Ultimately, then, utilitarianism must be regarded as a mode of reasoning about conduct in which normative appraisals are made from a certain distinctive perspective. We take it that the principle of considering aggregate benefit—under which the greater benefit is to be preferred to the lesser—counts as both an independent standard of appraisal and as the master principle in all determinations, normatively, about conduct. Here it is the consequences of conduct that are to be appraised. And in doing so, the master principle can range over the consequences of acts of conduct, of rules for conduct, of states of character, and of motives for acting. These are the sorts of things whose consequences are to be considered. In each case the master principle is capable of identifying what ought to be done, of setting normative requirements for conduct. It may do so sometimes directly with regard to individual pieces of conduct (on given occasions) and sometimes indirectly, for

8

these same actions, with regard to rules or states of character or motives. What determines conduct is what most conduces to general happiness, everything considered.

The theory of indirect utilitarianism, as advanced, for instance, by David Lyons or as systematized by John Gray, does not deny the point just made about the general happiness. Rather, it asserts that, everything considered, direct appeals to general welfare are self-defeating and that putting standing constraints on that principle—such as by installing a system of moral rules—is in fact productive of the greater well-being. Even here, though, the indirect utilitarian does not assert that such rules should never be overridden; for he allows that where rules conflict, direct appeals to the principle of general welfare are in order. And presumably, it is always the case *then* that the idea of promoting the general welfare, as decided by direct appeal to the master principle, will have determinative effect, to some important degree or other.[16]

The point I have raised, in challenge to this view, is that direct appeals should not be limited to cases of conflict of rules. For the same standard that would allow a utilitarian solution to conflict of rules would underwrite making exceptions to rules on other kinds of occasions as well. The indirect utilitarian has given a good reason why, everything considered, there should be intermediate rules and why there should not be direct appeals to the principle of general welfare in the standard case. But he has not given a good reason why such rules should not be overridden when, everything considered, conduct that violates (or infringes) a rule will better serve the general welfare. Indeed, the argument that I have developed suggests that there is no good reason, at least not within utilitarianism. And I do not see how the indirect utilitarian can resist this argument.

It is always required that the utilitarian moralist prefer the greater good achievable by doing some particular act over following a rule that would not allow this act to be done, if in fact this act could be expected, all things considered, to be the better course. By the same token, he must always prefer the general welfare over any right that conflicted with it on any occasion.

It is not likely, then, that the thoroughgoing utilitarian would opt for the inclusion either of exceptionless rules or of basic rights in his moral or in his political system. Rights, in particular, resist utilitarian calculation and are not easily accommodated to it. For as guarantees of benefits to individuals—arguably to all individuals—basic rights establish what is to thoroughgoing utilitarianism a defective or substandard pattern in which individual benefit can stand on some occasions against the general welfare—certainly when the latter advantage is marginal. Thus, the utilitarian moralist, as a partisan of promoting the aggregative general welfare, will want to eschew them.

When the utilitarian moralist reasons in order to reach a decision about the best course of action, he follows the maxim "everybody [is] to count for one, nobody for more than one.''[17] Thus, the net benefits/disbenefits of each person who is affected by the course of action are taken into account; no one is left out, nobody is given more weight than is warranted by the simple value of that one relevant consideration in his case; and a total or aggregative sum is thereby reached. Supposing this sum to be greater than those of viable alternatives—sums established in the same way—we reach the determination of what is normatively required by the principle of utility. If we restrict ourselves (for the sake of simplicity) to particular acts and to rules for action, there is always a sense in which the best utilitarian solution to the problem of what to do is reached *at some point* by making such calculations.

But when the utilitarian considers, in the aftermath of that decision, how to *distribute* to individuals the appropriate effects of this aggregate sum of well-being, there is no analogous maxim that he follows. The effects of utilitarian-prescribed action on individual persons—whether that action is prescribed under a moral rule or directly under the master principle is here immaterial—are not determined or even affected by any independent principle of distribution. Rather, the relevant distribution simply follows the course that has previously been determined to promote the aggregate total of well-being. This may involve treating people quite unequally, even to the point of helping some while hurting others. In any event, it is quite uncertain how a given individual, picked out at random from among those who are affected, will in fact be treated.

The matter is quite different with rights, in particular, basic moral or human rights. Rights always involve some sort of distributional principle and, on top of that, some sort of mechanism for assuring that distribution.

It is clear, then, that the standard of aggregative general welfare would not support the assignment of rights—guaranteed benefits—to individuals in respect of interests that they have, even ''vital'' or ''important'' interests (such as the constant and common interest that each person has in security or autonomy). That is, it would not assign rights to each and every individual in advance and across the board—if, in effect, such across-the-board rights were meant to tie the utilitarian's hands (as it is in indirect utilitarianism) against using the master principle of general welfare to make subsequent relevant determinations. Thus, it is unlikely that basic rights could ever have a place in or be grounded (justified) in theories that are recognizably utilitarian. And we reach the conclusion that utilitarianism is incompatible with basic rights.

On reflection, we should not find such a conclusion surprising. For, as Hart says, ''in the last resort there is an unbridgeable gap between pure utilitarianism, for which the maximization [or the promotion] of the total aggregate general welfare or happiness is the ultimate criterion of value, and a philosophy of basic human rights, which insists on the priority of principles protecting, in the case of each man, certain aspects of individual welfare and recognizing these as [at least] constraints on the maximising aggregative principle of utilitarianism.''[18]


## 2. *The Basic Structure and the Original Position*

There is legitimate concern, then, about whether utilitarianism, certainly as traditionally conceived and even in its contemporary ''indirect'' form, can provide an adequate account of rights. In this section we shall begin the examination of one of the main alternatives to utilitarianism, that provided by John Rawls.

Rawls is very careful to identify and explicate certain nonutilitarian elements in his theory and to link it with the contractarian tradition, especially with the later form that the tradition had assumed in Rousseau and Kant. That tradition has a long and rich association with the philosophy of rights; contract thinkers have historically been in the forefront of explicating and championing the idea of basic human rights—often called, in the idiom of an earlier day, natural rights.

Not surprisingly, then, Rawls's work has been widely acclaimed in part as a ''substantive contribution to the search for an adequate basis for a political philosophy of rights.''[19] But there is some difficulty, as I pointed out in the preface, in drawing a full-scale theory of rights out of the body of Rawls's work.

One point, though, is universally agreed on: Rawls holds that utilitarians characteristically regard basic rights as ''a socially useful illusion'' and subject them to ''the calculus of social interests.''[20] Thus, Rawls believes utilitarianism would allow the sacrifice of some people's rights to liberty or opportunity if doing so would raise the level of (total or average) well-being in a society. One important motivation for Rawls's theory of justice, then, is to provide a secure grounding for basic rights.

We might get a clearer initial sense of how Rawls proposes to do this if we were to note some of the main ways in which he took his theory to differ from utilitarianism. I will discuss two points in particular: the basic structure and the original position. Then, after we have examined these necessary background matters in appropriate detail, we will return in the next chapter to the theme of rights.

Rawls sees utilitarianism as a blanket theory: the same principle applies regardless of the unit of analysis. Whether we are talking of the goodness of ends or the rightness of actions or the desirability of states of character, whether we are normatively appraising an individual's conduct or the transactions of a group or the institutional arrangements of a whole society, all these matters are indifferently brought under a simple fundamental principle, that of the greatest happiness (or general welfare). Rawls is unwilling to make such an assumption; it seems likely to him that there may well be, for example, different basic rules for the conduct of the international community, for the internal organization of a single society, and for the behavior of individuals towards one another. Thus, the principles of justice that are chosen for the well-being of a society will not necessarily duplicate those that govern the relations between individual persons (or between persons and animals). In Rawls's theory the predominant focus, though by no means an exclusive one, is on what he calls the basic structure of a society.

By and large, what counts as the basic structure of a society is determined by social scientists and theorists. Thus, we are told that every society has certain social and economic and political institutions (some seemingly more fundamental than others). The main political institution for Rawls is the constitution, which lays down the form of government; associated with it are a number of background institutions, such as procedures for campaigning, voting, and organizing the government. The main economic institution that he envisions is the supply/demand market (a system for allocating resources, pricing, coordinating demand, etc.); associated with it are background institutions which serve goals such as antitrust regulation, full employment, equal opportunity, and transfer or welfare payments.

Of course, when philosophers talk about institutions in the basic structure (regarding what ought to be), the accounts that social scientists provide are restated and institutions are redescribed, say, in terms of requirements of justice or general benefit (if one is a utilitarian) or what have you. The philosopher reinterprets, under some superordinate moral conception, the social scientist's account—often with the object of criticizing some main social institution(s). A philosophical theory of the basic structure is a normative one. Clearly, what Rawls has to say about the basic structure of a society is of this nature.

One might wonder, though, why Rawls has made focal a concern with the basic structure. The most straightforward answer is that people live in societies. They have not, characteristically, lived as hermits or solitary on islands (like Robinson Crusoe).

The societies involved have, depending on the state of technology, been fairly large, fairly complex, and reasonably long-lived. It is rather difficult to specify exactly how *A* is one society and *B* another. But in all cases there is a political dimension: *A* has its system of rules and internal political organization, which effectively exercises power and coerces people there; and *B* has its. Thus, in characterizing the societies that people live in and that Rawls has in mind, we draw especially on this salient fact: such societies are political states, independent states.

12

The fact of living in such societies means, for any given individual, that he cannot escape being dependent, for good or ill, on the actions of others. Rawls describes this fact under the heading of "cooperation." But it is a misleading term, for it identifies only one of the ways in which people affect one another's prospects for well-being. A more general and apt characterization would tell us, simply, that the well-being of each person in a society is affected at many points, and differentially so, by the way in which that society is set up, by his place there, and by the way in which others are expected or encouraged to act in it. As Rawls says, "The social system is not an unchangeable order beyond human control but a pattern of human action."[21] And we can use the term "interaction" as a way of referring to this complex feature.

All societies have the feature of interaction; and since all are internally organized and relatively self-contained, it would be reasonable for people to consider the best arrangements that could be made, within practical limits, for their living together—their interaction—in a given society. This means that they would have to think carefully about the best arrangements for the main institutions of that society: what these institutions are or could be, how they knit together into one system, and what effects their accumulated operations could be expected to have on the well-being of individuals in it.

To think seriously about this matter is to take the basic structure of a society as one's subject. Rawls apparently believes that the public or social dimension, as I have described it, has probably the greatest weight of influence, among the controllable factors, on human well-being; accordingly, he is willing to describe it as the *first* subject of justice.

We would expect the principles of justice that resulted from deliberation on this first subject—where we were concerned with a complex, relatively permanent thing like a society—to be different from those that might emerge, or be expected to govern, in the ethics of a lifeboat situation (or a case of private charity or of parental discretion) or in the first meeting—if only by wireless—of two previously isolated Robinson Crusoes.

But the principles of justice thus developed are not restricted merely to the basic structure. Rather, Rawls conceives a sort of natural sequence in which varying topics of justice could be taken up. For example, one sequence would be, first, to establish principles for a just basic structure; then, to consider principles of justice for subordinate or secondary institutions (such as industrial corporations or universities) in a society; finally, to take up the idea of justice in individual roles or positions within these secondary institutions. Another sequence—not so obviously plausible as the first—would involve moving from the idea of principles of justice for the basic structure of a society to that of principles for a just international order (or community of nations).

13

The important point is that the principles that are chosen at one stage continue to govern and are presupposed at later stages. Thus, the principles of justice for the basic structure would regulate and constrain conduct in other contexts as well (for example, in personal morality).[22]

How are these controlling principles to be determined? Here we shift to the second main point that I want to discuss in this section, the Rawlsian idea of the original position. We start with the claim that the principal subject of justice is the basic structure of a society, that is, the arrangement into one scheme of major social institutions insofar as these institutions determine the division of advantages from social interaction. Now, we need some relatively abstract way in which to represent these advantages to our thinking. For, first, it is necessary to simplify as much as possible an incredibly complex situation, and second, it is necessary to think about societies in a very general way when we are determining principles of justice for the basic structure of any society. Even if we were to restrict ourselves to a single society (such as contemporary America), it would be necessary to utilize similar simplifying abstractions in order to assure ourselves that we were indeed determining principles of justice: we would need some way to help filter out merely parochial or ideologically eccentric views and to associate our thinking with that of others who have thought about justice in other times or in other societies. Such simplifying abstractions are characteristic of all philosophical thought about public justice—that is, about the principles of justice for the basic structure of a society. Witness, for example, the utilitarian's treatment of complex and otherwise disparate phenomena under the simplifying heading of benefits/disbenefits and his principle of maximizing the net sum (or the average) of these.

So Rawls hits upon the idea of *social* primary goods as such a simplifying device.

> [Let us] assume that the chief primary goods at the disposition of society are . . . liberties, powers and opportunities, income and wealth. . . . [Later on he adds self-respect.] These are the social primary goods. Other primary goods such as health and vigor, intelligence and imagination, are natural goods; although their possession is influenced by the basic structure [of society], they are not so directly under its control.[23]

These social primary goods are things any rational person wants and will want regardless of his plan of life or his place in the social scheme. No one of them is dispensable.

We can set the Rawlsian problem of justice, then, in the following terms. What we want to determine is the proper or just distribution of *social* primary goods. To do this we need a procedure for determining the principles that are involved (for there are no antecedent or independent standards for such a

14

distribution). Accordingly, we create a hypothetical bargaining situation (called the original position) in which certain significant constraints operate. These constraints include those required to discount or bracket off all special, peculiarly personal, or circumstantial facts and biases and those embedded in objective circumstances (such as relative scarcity) or in our psychological orientation (such as mutual disinterest in one another's life plans). And as well there are a number of presumed formal constraints (that the principles agreed to are to be public, that they constitute the ultimate or foundational standard, that the principles are to be chosen once and for all, that they are to be chosen unanimously, that each participant is to imagine that he will live his entire life in a society governed by the principles selected, etc.).[24]

As Rawls says, "The idea of the original position is to set up a fair procedure so that *any principles agreed to* will be just."[25] (This is probably what is meant by his phrase "justice as fairness.") In short, whatever principles emerge from the original position, they are the principles of justice for the organization of the basic structure of society.

His contention, then, is that under the constraints involved in the original position (constraints imposed in order to make for a fair and realistic bargaining situation), it would be reasonable to define two principles for the distribution of social primary goods and to rank these two principles (as a set or as a unified conception of justice) above alternative principles or sets of principles (on a short list of such principles).[26]

The short list would include well-known "perfectionist" theories of justice (such as that of Plato or Aristotle or Nietzsche) and the utilitarian theory—in two distinct versions: one that emphasized the maximizing of *total* utility and the other, of *average* utility.[27] But the principles chosen would be, presumably, the Rawlsian two principles, in the following order:

1. Liberties are to be arranged so as to achieve the most extensive justifiable set of equal basic liberties for each and everyone.
2. Social and economic inequalities are to be arranged so that
   a. they are structured by social roles and offices which are open to all under conditions of "fair equality of opportunity" and such inequalities in wealth, income, and position serve
   b. to improve—ideally, to maximize—the life situation of the least advantaged group.[28]

The Rawlsian two principles, when emerging as a set from the original position, will have what Rawls calls a "lexical" order[29]—that is, a serial order of importance: $1 > 2a > 2b$. This is meant to suggest both an order of consideration and an order of satisfaction. It suggests permissible trade-offs, and it rules out impermissible ones. We can, for example, sacrifice aggregate wealth or personal income at each of several levels to achieve greater liberty for all or to help level out some of the natural or social contingencies that work against "fair equality of opportunity." But we cannot trade off a lesser liberty or an unequal liberty to achieve a greater overall standard of wealth.

What we have not yet considered is an account of the deliberations that went on behind the veil of ignorance[30] and of the substantive arguments that carried the greatest weight in the original position. For it is important to see that the controlling arguments, and ultimately the principles of justice themselves, are not simply given by the constraints of the original position. One does not literally deduce the principle(s) of justice from a description of the original position. For such a program would be at cross-purposes with Rawls's contention that the desired outcome of the deliberation is a *ranking* of eligible conceptions of justice. A logical deduction of the two principles from a description of the original position would not count as ranking them ahead of competing conceptions, such as average utility; rather, it would count as rendering those other conceptions wholly ineligible. Indeed, if the Rawlsian two principles were to emerge deductively from a description of the original position, then Rawls would legitimately be open to the charge that he had built the two principles into that description in the first place.

Rather, the original position is properly conceived as a framework or an arena for a fair agreement. But it is the arguments which go on there that actually determine the content of the principles of justice. Successful arguments in an untroubled and universalizable and fair context have an undoubted authority when the object is to determine principles of justice. And principles so supported—as would be, characteristically, those that emerged from the original position in the front rank—could be commended as rock-bottom reasonable. But such principles would lack authority either if they followed deductively from some descriptive feature of the original position (here the charge would be "packing")[31] or if any such feature had the effect of simply ruling out one of the alternative, competing conceptions of justice (the charge here would be non-neutrality).

We should not, however, restrict this important methodological point simply to the original position, for there are other initial or starting-point elements present in the theory as well. There is, for example, the doctrine of social primary goods. And there is, of course, the mode or standard of reasoning that is employed to make the decision about principles of justice. And finally, there is the short list of candidate principles.

The matter is more complex even than this. The participants in the original position would necessarily have a certain reflexive understanding of themselves. They know, or would come to know, that justice is being determined for persons and that they are persons. But in order to conform to the constraints of the original position, persons, like everything else in the original position, have to be represented quite abstractly. Persons would, of course, have to regard themselves as rational—that is, to the degree required to be participants in the original position; accordingly, they are rational within normal limits. More to the point, persons are understood (and would understand themselves) in the original position to be free and equal moral beings.

By moral we mean the opposite of nonmoral; thus, we mean here, first, that persons are beings who are capable of having goals and achievable excellences in mind—that each is capable of having a plan of life which might be different from, and even conflict with, the plans of others—and, second, that persons are capable of a sense of justice, that is, of being motivated to conform to agreed-upon or reasonable principles of just interaction.[32]

The idea of equality here also calls for special comment. When it is said that in the original position persons are equal, we do not mean that they adhere to some *normative* principle of equality. There can be no such principle as part of the initial furniture of the theory.[33] Rather, we mean that the participants are "symmetrically situated and subject to the veil of ignorance."[34] Accordingly, we start from the mere fact that persons occupy an *equal status* in the original position, and then we reason from there, if we can, to the two principles—or to whatever the favored theory of justice is. To do so, arguments are needed. We cannot go, straight from the gun, to conclude a principle of equality from the mere fact of equality.

The idea of freedom must be interpreted along analogous lines. The freedom of participants in the original position is, by and large, simply their ability to engage in deliberations about justice—to contribute proposals and to follow the arguments wherever they lead and thereby to reach a rational conclusion—unencumbered by strong psychological inhibitions (such as egoism or altruism) or by individualized ethical or value precommitments or by any sort of social pressure.

Now, the participants realize that their job is to formulate the principles of justice for the basic structure of a society. Accordingly, they will be sensitive to notable issues that could arise in the difficult project of coupling the rather abstract principles of justice, as determined by rational deliberation, with the basic structure of society, as determined by empirical social science. This theme is taken up by Rawls in his discussion of the well-ordered society, the general name that he gives to a society whose basic structure conforms to principles of justice. Two features are emphasized here in particular: (a) that a public sense of institutional justice would emerge in such a society and (b) that a society with the preferred public sense of justice would achieve stability.[35]

A well-ordered society would exhibit, or would come to exhibit, an explicit sense of justice. Hence, the sense of justice of the various persons in it either would be identical or would overlap significantly. This element of publicity or public consciousness is to be expected, given the high degree of

17

explicitness that Rawls requires in the formulation of principles of justice and in the design and criticism of the institutions of a society's basic structure. But it is not his main concern. Rather, the main concern is that the institutions of society conform to and actually operate on accredited principles of justice. Thus, it is the issue of institutional conformity that is crucial; and Rawls believes such conformity is most likely in a situation where there is a public charter or public consensus respecting the arrangement of institutions in the basic structure. Hence, the theme of institutional justice links up with the criterion of publicity, and a public sense of institutional justice results. Of course, any society is well ordered to the degree that it has a public sense of institutional justice, but the participants are particularly concerned with establishing one that incorporates the favored principles of justice.

Any such society should be stable—for we are concerned with the basic structure of a continuing society under conditions that we could reasonably expect in the real world. A stable society allows for effective interaction and for coordination of efforts. It would do no good, then, to devise principles that could not be understood or intelligently applied in a wide variety of situations, or to posit principles on the fortuitous conjunction of unlikely circumstances, or to make them depend on extreme, rarely achievable states of character or dispositions, or to settle on principles for a basic structure which would be undermined by attitudes that we knew people actually or unavoidably to have.

Accordingly, the accredited insights of social science would have to be called into play on this point of stability in particular. And assessments of relative stability would become an important factor in the ranking of the candidate principles of justice in the original position. But since social-scientific knowledge is developmental and varies over time, we could only ask that the participants, in their deliberations about justice, rely on the best knowledge available at that time. Thus, we should regard their conclusions as subject to scientific or public scrutiny then and thereafter and as revisable in that light.[36]

It follows that a certain interpretation will have to be put on Rawls's notion that the decision about principles of justice is to be made "once and for all." For it must be interpreted as specifying a decision that is taken for all persons alive at a given time (or during the time covered by several successive generations) but not for all persons, actual or possible, at literally all times. This interpretation is explicitly endorsed by Rawls when he says that the preferred interpretation of the original position is the present time of entry (i.e., "any time . . . for living persons").[37] But the rubric under which this particular interpretation is introduced into our account—namely, that in the deliberations about justice, participants would rely on the best knowledge available at the time—is, nonetheless, prefectly general and contains no bias towards any particular cultural formation or body of knowledge.

All the things that we have been discussing—in particular, the idea of persons as free, equal, and rational moral beings and the notion of a well-ordered society—are included as initial elements because they seem to be indispensable to making a reasonable, objective, relatively secure decision about principles of justice. They codify the way anybody would, on reflection, think it proper to reason about principles of justice for the basic structure of a society. All these initial elements, the social primary goods included, are things that could exist in the original position construct; for there is nothing personally or culturally peculiar about them. And none of them allows us to prejudge the competition between the alternative theories on the short list. Thus, utilitarianism—interpreted as a theory about the proper distribution of social primary goods—could, in principle, emerge as the favored conception of justice.[38]

The original position is only a part of the complex range of elements which we take to be given or provisionally settled in a deliberation about principles of justice. The original position "model" (as Rawls comes to call it) is best conceived as the intersection or point of mediation between two other principal models, that of the person and that of the well-ordered society.[39] Onto this mediating model a host of other considerations are grafted as well. What is distinctive about the original position construct is that it organizes the deliberation about justice; all of our starting points are situated by reference to it, and the main constraints on reasoning are explicitly specified in it. It comes to take on an appearance of finality and completeness, but only because some things must be taken as relatively settled so that principles of justice can be decided upon.

Rawls's intuition is that these diverse factors are necessary to a full and careful decision about principles of justice but that such factors are, whether singly or together, not dispositive. This range of materials represents a more comprehensive set of considerations than has usually been called on in support of utilitarianism. For example, compare Rawls's overlaid account of justification of principles with the much shorter and simpler "proofs" of the utilitarian principle of either Bentham or Mill. This greater, but carefully ordered, complexity is more adequate to the framing of the problem of justice; and while the set of initial considerations may dispose the dispassionate inquirer to adopt a different set of favored principles, they do not preclude a utilitarian solution to the problem.

A crucial point to bear in mind here (as I argued in the first section of this chapter) is that utilitarianism is a mode of reasoning which includes, but is not limited to, the principle of utility itself. In this respect, then, the original position can be viewed as a setting in which one tries to see not merely whether the principle of greatest happiness (of promoting general welfare) would be preferred over others on the short list but, more generally, whether utilitarian

19

rationality, in which that principle is interpreted and applied, could be endorsed as the most reasonable way to think in matters of justice—at least where we are concerned with the first subject of justice, the arrangment of the basic structure of a society.

So, the theory of justice is put on a very strict, a very narrow path by Rawls. That theory must provide a range of initial elements, including the original position construct itself, sufficiently rich to suggest and at the same time to constrain interesting arguments for (and against) various candidate principles and modes of reasoning. But the theory must not allow decisive arguments, or normative principles of justice, to derive deductively—as a matter of strict logical entailment—from a mere description of these elements. In this respect the initial elements are "weak" vis-à-vis the competing principles.[40]

What we are looking for, instead of deductive short cuts, are those arguments that would be developed in the deliberations of the original position in order to support such principles. Of course, these arguments—even the ultimately successful ones—are merely *begun* in the original position. All we look for there are the chief considerations that would tend to support the choice of one principle or set of principles from among the short list of those available. One should not look, then, for absolutely decisive arguments—for the knockdown inference that would settle the matter once and for all. Rather, if some of these considerations, on balance, seem weightier than others, then the original choice problem is sufficiently resolved. But the arguments that are involved here have to be continuously developed and amplified as we move beyond the original position to consider the fuller specification and the further bearings and application of these principles. Here it is good to bear in mind the idea of a sequence of stages. What unifies these stages and affords the development of a coherent perspective from which judgments about justice can be made is that these same arguments, progressively developed, control throughout.[41]

It is now time to turn to the sequence of rights in Rawls's theory of justice. I will do so in the next chapter in a schematic way. This will provide us with an initial opportunity to review the matter briefly and to fix our attention on main points.

# • 2 •

# A THEORY OF JUSTICE AND RIGHTS

In this chapter I will first identify the various levels or stages at which Rawls has found talk of rights to be significant (i.e, rights *in* the original position, rights emerging *from* the original position in the principles of justice formulated there, etc.). I then go on to show how Rawls would regard rights at these various levels to be justified. The focus of our discussion will be on rights as embedded in the basic structure of a society. I will try to provide an interpretation of Rawls's claim that such rights are natural rights. Then, last of all, I will consider the implications of this conception of natural rights for global justice.

## 1. *Rawls on Rights and Their Justification*

We could conveniently divide Rawls's theory here into a four-part structure. The first and topmost part concerns the so-called primary goods. The second part concerns the formulation of the principles of justice and the choice of a particular set of such principles over alternative ones. (Rawls's preferred set, which he calls the "two principles of justice," would, he thinks, be chosen in the original position.) The next part concerns the institutionalizing of the (two) principles of justice in what Rawls calls the "basic structure" of a society. The last part, then, concerns the actual workings of a society so organized and, in particular, some of the institutions and subordinate arrangements that would crop up in such a society—or, at least, in any such society under modern conditions. Interestingly, Rawls refers to rights at each of these four levels.[1]

The primary goods, as we might recall from chapter 1, are goods which, presumptively, any rational person would want, whatever his plan of life or value orientation might be. These goods, abstractly stated, are divided by Rawls into (a) the *social* primary goods—liberty, opportunity and powers, income and wealth, the bases of self-respect—and (b) the *natural* ones—health and vigor, intelligence and imagination.[2] As I suggested in chapter 1, we can view the deliberations of persons in the original position respecting justice as an attempt to define and select preferred principles for allocating or arranging the *social* primary goods among individuals. It is interesting to note that sometimes Rawls includes rights among these primary goods,[3] but sometimes he does not.[4]

In my judgment the listing of rights at this level is confusing and should be dispensed with. Rawls is obviously rather casual on this point. The matter may call for more attention than he has given it, however; for there are two quite distinct reasons why rights as primary goods would be a problematic notion in Rawls's theory of justice.

First, we had established in chapter 1 that the original position, as an arena for the formulation of the principles of justice, could have no features which in and of themselves would be strong enough to generate a principle of justice. For we wanted the eligible principles to follow, not deductively from any descriptive feature of the original position (or any elements initially included in it), but from the arguments that were deployed there. But rights, unlike the other primary goods, are overtly normative entities; moreover, a conventional principle of justice would assert that rights should be respected or that rights should not be violated. Thus, insofar as rights are among the social primary goods, we could generate a strong—albeit conventional— principle of justice almost immediately out of the primary goods. And there would be no need, then, for the elaborate mechanisms of the theory of justice to allow for the construction of some such principle in the original position. This would violate the constraint that there should be no normative elements of justice introduced into the theory prior to the construction of the preferred principles of justice.

Moreover, rights appear to be a moral category with which utilitarian thinkers have difficulty, as should be evident from chapter 1. So, if rights were to be included among the social primary goods, then this would strongly prejudice the deliberation in favor of a specific sort of moral theory. We would also simultaneously prejudice the event against a utilitarian solution, if it is true that utilitarians have a problem in accounting for basic rights. So, on grounds of the desired normative weakness—or nondeductivity—of the original position model and of the moral neutrality of that model with respect to the competing principles of justice, we should attempt to expunge rights from the list of social primary goods.

This brings me to the second point. To treat rights as primary goods is to regard them as both pretheoretical (i.e., as prior to the theory of justice) and as noninstitutional (since they would antedate the basic structure of a society and, for that matter, all other social institutions). But this seems to beg important questions about the nature of rights, which need to be expressly decided (a point that we shall return to in the next section).

Fortunately, Rawls's inclusion of rights among the social primary goods does not appear to represent anything deep-seated. It is relatively offhand and, apparently, relatively easily set aside. Let us treat rights as effectively purged from the list of such goods, although there is still the interesting question (to which we will return later in this section) of why Rawls would tend to include them.

This takes us to the second stage of our analysis in this section. Rawls argues that in the original position, under conditions of extreme uncertainty in which there are no objective bases for judging probabilities, the two principles would be formulated and selected as the preferred principles.

The important thing, for our purposes, is that the first principle is usually stated by Rawls as itself identifying a right. For example, in his standard statement of the two principles, the first is said to require that "each person is to have an equal right to the most extensive total system of equal basic liberties compatible with a similar system of liberty for all."[5] I would suggest, then, that on this reading the Rawlsian first principle states a basic moral right. And whatever justification attaches to the two principles, as justification through a choice procedure that is both fair and rational, attaches ipso facto to this basic moral right.

The second principle, however, is not formulated by Rawls as a right. Rather, it is characteristically rendered in somewhat different terms: "Social and economic inequalities are to be arranged so that they are both: (a) to the greatest benefit of the least advantaged . . . and (b) attached to offices and positions open to all under conditions of fair equality of opportunity."[6]

The two principles, as they emerge from the original position, are exceedingly abstract. Just as the primary goods belong to what Rawls calls a "thin" theory of the good,[7] so the two principles constitute a "thin" theory of justice. They require to be embodied. Justice is, or should be, a virtue of society, specifically of its basic structure. The object of the two principles is the design or the normative analysis of the basic structure of a society. Included in that structure is a society's political system and its economic system. Each of these, in turn, would be made up of a set of structural elements or institutions (as we saw in chapter 1), with some being described as main institutions (e.g., the political constitution or the supply/demand market) and others as background institutions (e.g., antitrust regulation as a control on the market).

23

The idea is that a just society would conform to the two principles by building them into its basic structure: institutions are set up which, when operating together, give results that tend to satisfy the two principles over time. These institutions, then, represent a set of middle principles standing between the two principles and the actual operation of a society. The background institutions check tendencies in the main institution which might over time take it away from its original seated disposition; they not only keep the main institution on track—and it, them—but also they remedy its deficiencies, as regards justice. The result is that the "ongoing institutional processes are . . . constrained and the accumulated results of individual transactions continually adjusted."[8]

Rawls repeatedly talks of the two principles, in particular the first one (Equal Basic Liberties), as *assigning* rights and duties.[9] But this is inexact. The two principles assign rights and duties by means of the basic structure. Rawls thinks, for example, that the inclusion of a bill of rights within the constitution is one important way in which the first principle of justice could be institutionalized in a given society. So, the constitution (or some other feature of the basic structure) assigns determinate rights to individual persons; what the first principle does is to "govern"—or better, to *justify*—the business of assigning equal basic rights to individuals.[10] Basic structure rights, in particular those attaching to the main institution(s), are conceived by Rawls as analogous in a variety of ways to natural rights.[11]

The last level in Rawls's theory of rights concerns the legitimate expectations of individual persons. We can assume that these expectations would include those established at the higher levels, as secured by justice. Thus, constitutionally protected political and personal rights as laid down in the basic structure of a society would be legitimate expectations of individuals in that society. And as well, other legitimate expectations would grow up in and around the operation of the various institutions in the basic structure (e.g., the highly detailed list of rights that have grown up around the institutions of trial by jury or of private ownership of property or of equality of opportunity).

But the basic structure is also a framework for the transactions of individuals and associations. Now, individuals do not merely interact (and associations—such as labor unions or corporations or universities—do not merely interact) with the embodied principles and subsequent workings of the basic structure. Individuals also interact with one another and with associations. (The same is true for associations: they interact with one another and with individuals.) Accordingly, rules and practices that are characteristic of these sorts of transactions could be formulated as well. Thus, we could follow a line of devolvement away from the institutions of the basic structure. And here we would encounter a vast variety of subsidiary institutions and practices, of private associations and cooperative ventures. Nonetheless, expectations would attach to the operation of these subsidiary elements and, insofar as the institutions and practices in question were compatible with justice or loosely derivative from it, the expectations would be legitimate ones, as secured or enframed by justice. Thus we can speak of subsidiary rights, as distinct from basic structure rights, of many sorts: rights under this contract or that, of particular organizational structures, of individual family life (e.g., the Martin family), and so on. In general, Rawls encompasses these rights under the heading of fairness or fair play.[12] They are all institutional rights that are justified primarily by their relationship to elements in the basic structure, rather than directly by the two principles of justice themselves. In the absence of reasonably just institutions, we would, of course, have to turn to the two principles; but these could cover only the clear cases (i.e., practices that were grossly unjust, such as slavery, or obviously fair, such as a nonexploitative and voluntary cooperative arrangement or agreement). Since my concern in this study is with basic moral and constitutional rights and their justification, I will have little to say about these subsidiary institutional (or practice) rights.[13]

I have schematically represented Rawls's method of justification as proceeding from the top down. Thus, the top level (deliberation in the original position about the rational and fair distribution of social primary goods) is used to justify the basic moral right that is stated in the first principle of justice; and the first principle of justice is used in turn to justify the constitutional rights that are built into the basic structure of a just society; and these, in turn, play a role of sorts in the justification of all subsidiary rights. But Rawls adds an important control on this procedure by requiring that the justifying principle or theme be matched with certain considered judgments (either in the form of maxims or of paradigm cases) which exhibit or help to exhibit the moral character of that which is to be justified (the "subject" of justification). For example, determination of the constitutional right of persons to be free from the injuries of "cruel and unusual punishment" would involve not merely the first principle of justice and its grounds (the primary goods of liberty and opportunity and of self-respect—i.e., the bases of self-respect) but also considered judgments about punishment and practices that have been associated with it historically (including such matters as mutilation as a form of corporal punishment, public execution and other forms of capital punishment, harsh treatment of those who have not been judged guilty or of those who have been judged insane, the aims of punishment, relevant maxims as to what is legally just, etc.). Rawls calls this matching procedure the method of reflective equilibrium.

In the application of this method a certain amount of to-ing and fro-ing normally results, with adjustments being made in the initial formulation of the justifying principle (or in its range of extension) as well as in our considered judgments. The goal of the method is to bring the two levels—that of justifying principle and that of the practice to be justified (and the material relevant to it)—into alignment.

We can put this point more precisely now by distinguishing between a narrow reflective equilibrium and a wide one. Briefly, a *narrow* reflective equilibrium means that the justifying principle of justice (e.g., the first principle) is matched, more or less on its own, with the considered judgments. A *wide* reflective equilibrium, by contrast, involves matching these judgments not merely with the principle itself but also with the various elements that went into its construction. From chapter 1 we are familiar with these elements as the ones that are organized around the original position ''model'' in the Rawlsian account of the deliberations about the principles of justice for the basic structure of a society. It is this peculiar sort of coherence between principles and their theoretical backdrop, on the one hand, and considered judgments, on the other, that satisfies the standard of justification in matters of justice and, hence, of rights.[14]

Rawls's account of the justification of rights is subject to most of the criticisms that can be made, more generally, of his theory of justice. Some criticisms, however, can be made specifically of this theory of rights.

Rawls's conception of rights is opaque. He does not attempt an analysis of the concept, and though he uses the term 'rights' freely, he does so without explication. The context is usually unhelpful. Rawls's failure to deal with the analytic issues poses an obstacle to his program as a justification of rights.

Oddly enough, the best place to look for guidance is in Rawls's discussion of what I earlier called subsidiary rights and practices. Thus, although this material may be relatively unimportant to our main project (that of developing a Rawlsian theory of basic moral and constitutional rights), it may, nonetheless, have important implications for what Rawls conceived rights to be. Then, if we can assume that he consistently has meant by 'rights' the same thing throughout, we can extrapolate this discussion to more interesting contexts and thereby have the beginnings of the Rawlsian theory we seek.

I would suggest, then, that a right for Rawls is an individual's legitimate expectation as to what he would receive in a just institutional distribution of social primary goods.[15] The justification of a right, then, would involve establishing the legitimacy of the expectation within the framework of higher-to-lower-level justification under conditions of reflective equilibrium that have already been described, albeit briefly, in this section.

On this reading, liberties as social primary goods could be called rights—not in the original position but, rather, under institutional arrangements imposed by justice. One of Rawls's standard pairings of primary goods—the pairing of rights and liberties[16]—would conform to this usage, though the pairing is confusing since it mixes those things that are primary goods *in* the original position (liberties) with things that could be included there only prospectively (rights). The pairing, then, is anticipatory (and should not be taken literally). It is also revealing—suggesting, as it does, a close tie (almost a conceptual one) between rights and liberties in Rawls's thinking, as if only liberties *could* be rights.

At the same time the reading gives us a reason why Rawls was not inclined to treat the *second* principle of justice as itself a basic moral right or to regard the pattern of just distributions of wealth and social position as a pattern of rights. The reason is this: though specific liberties can be secured to a determinate degree to *any* given individual (since all share in the basic liberties equally), specific economic or social standings cannot. In economic matters, individuals float between an upper and a lower limit (both of which are determined by the difference principle, the principle that inequalities of wealth and social position must be arranged so that the prospects of the least-advantaged group are maximized). Thus, no given individual has a legitimate expectation of receiving any particular distributive share and, hence, cannot be said to have a right to a particular share. Even the minimum *level* established by the difference principle does not define the legitimate expectation of any given individual (not even those who form the group of the least advantaged); rather the expectation is that of a ''representative,'' or ideal-type, individual.[17] Accordingly, Rawls characteristically withholds the term 'rights' in his discussion of the second principle and its applications. And Rawls's approach here is markedly different from his handling of the first principle and its applications.

But what, exactly, does this Rawlsian conception of rights amount to? I would suggest that two main ideas are determinative here: first, the idea of something distributive or individuatable[18] and, second, the idea of something the distribution of which can be guaranteed.[19]

When it is said that something can be distributed, one means that it can be assigned or parceled out to the individuals in some target group or class. Thus, the towels in a locker room would be, in this sense, distributable to the members of the club, though probably the acoustical properties of the room would not be. Rawls is interested in universal rights, that is, basic moral and constitutional rights; so, the things that someone can have a right to in such cases would have to be things that could be distributed to everyone: that is, the same things to each and everybody in the relevant class (e.g., persons, citizens).

Now, the sand on the beach on some out-of-the-way Pacific island would thus be distributable (assuming that no one owned it), but there is no readily available mechanism to achieve such a distribution; more important, there is no way to guarantee it. This is one reason—probably only one among several—why no one would be inclined to say that people had a right to grains of sand from this beach. Something is, or becomes, a right only when its distribution (we assume it to be a benefit) can be guaranteed, or at least reasonably assured within practical limits, to the individuals who are relevantly said to be the recipients.

Thus, when Rawls speaks of legitimate expectations, he can be interpreted to mean not only that an individual's claims are valid but also that they are reasonable *expectations:* the individual's receiving his share or his due can be counted on because it is built into the structure of things and, we might add, because it is normatively independent of the usual considerations (the public good or the general welfare) that might be urged against it. Rights, for Rawls, are not free-floating claims, of the sort often called moral. They are, rather, details of an institutional arrangement in which the claim and the means for delivering on it are linked closely together.

But at this point we begin to sense a certain amount of tension in Rawls's theory. I will try, in concluding this section, to make this unease explicit.

Some have claimed that Rawls has no place in his theory for moral rights.[20] But the judgment here is hasty, since the first principle, the principle of equal basic liberties, seems itself to be a right in Rawls's account. And since the first principle is developed in the original position, as a principle for the design of the basic structure of a just society, it is prior to any society; the first principle itself cannot, then, be regarded as an institutional right but rather as a prescription for institutional or political rights. And as a prescription, it is moral in character; or so it might be argued. Thus, if the first principle is a right at all, it must be a moral right.

Let us say provisionally, then, that the first principle states a basic moral right: namely, that each person ought to have available the most extensive system of equal basic liberties compatible with a similar system of liberty for all other persons. Having such liberties in a well-ordered society is the legitmate expectation of each person. But what are these liberties?

Now, one could reply that the first principle does not actually specify the liberties in question; it speaks merely of "equal basic liberties." The initial specification of liberties occurs at the point when the basic structure of a society is designed (perhaps with the help of the method of reflective equilibrium). But this is to suggest that the first principle has no essential content of liberties, leaving the determination of "equal basic liberties" to time and circumstance. The first principle becomes, then, merely formal; it says, in effect, once the basic liberties have been determined in the constitution, they are to be equal for all citizens. But if the meaning of "equal basic liberties" cannot be fixed initially, then the first principle offers inadequate guidance as to precisely what liberties are to be institutionalized. The first principle—and with it, the original position—ceases to be the "Archimedean point'' (the phrase is Rawls's)[21] for the critique and design of the basic structure of a society.

The issue that I have been examining is, I think, a serious one for Rawls's theory of equal basic liberties as rights. For if some or even a few basic liberties are by and large specified at a further stage—say, at the design of the basic structure—then the first principle to that degree lacks essential content and stability.[22]

Let us put this point somewhat differently. If the liberties on the list lack specificity or, even worse, fundamental identity, then it is difficult to say that one could have a *right* to them. Rights are, for better or worse, fairly determinate things. There comes a point, as we relax and let go of detail and then of substance, when one can no longer be said to have a legitimate expectation. The thing loses the name of right and becomes something else— an aspiration, perhaps. This line of reply, then, has obvious defects.

Accordingly, one could reply instead that Rawls's first principle of justice establishes a particular ''list'' of basic liberties; it identifies a specific set of liberties which are to be acknowledged as being held equally by all. (This particular reading has been suggested by Hart.)[23] It is, I think, the correct interpretation; this interpretation of the first principle as specifying a list of basic liberties is made clearer, Rawls says, in revisions that were made for the German edition of his book and in some of his later writings.[24]

The relevant liberties are, Rawls tells us, rights of citizenship and of the person: such things as the right to vote; freedom of speech and assembly; liberty of conscience; the right to own personal property; freedom from slavery, arbitrary arrest, and seizure; and so on.[25] They are standard civil liberties (or rights).

So the tension in Rawls's theory, to which I referred earlier, can now be stated. If, on the one hand, the liberties are specified too loosely, then there is no clear sense in which a person can be said to have a legitimate expectation respecting them. Hence, there would be no *right* to them as defined in the original position but, rather, presumably only in the more determinate institutional setting provided by what Rawls calls the basic structure of a society. On the other hand, were one to say that the basic liberties are rights (as one would be licensed to do, presumably, in the basic structure), then it would appear to be otiose to say of *these* rights that one has a right to them.

So Rawls's way of putting his first principle seems to fail under either option. If the basic liberties lack specificity (in the original position), then one cannot be said to have a legitimate expectation regarding them there; the legitimate expectation arises, so to speak, in some subsequent institutional setting (where they have, presumably, the requisite specificity). Hence, there is no *right* to the basic liberties that is stated by the first principle. But where the liberties have the requisite specificity—as they would have in the basic structure of a society—then they have become rights themselves (i.e., each basic liberty is itself a right), and it is redundant to speak of an additional or supervenient right to such liberties.

The dilemma appears to be that if we feed enough substance into the basic liberties to have a legitimate expectation concerning them, then there's no point in identifying a general right (= the first principle, as stated) alongside them; and if we don't, then we won't have a legitimate expectation, hence no right (regardless of what the first principle states). The first principle, then, seems doomed either to be pointless and trivial or to be inaccurate if taken literally.

The problem here is, perhaps, deeper even than this. In his theory of justice, Rawls operates with two distinct but related categories of analysis: the original position and the basic structure of a society. The original position is quintessentially *moral*. It can be entered by anyone at any time. When people are in the original position they are there, all of them, as free, equal, rational, and moral persons. They are societyless. The original position is a forum for discussion and the formulation of principles. It is a noninstitutional context. The basic structure of a society is quite different in these respects. It supposes a limited and finite population of people whose entire lives will be lived together and who will bequeath, among other things, a set of institutional arrangements to their children. The people here are all inhabitants of some *particular* society and, hence, are co-citizens with one another; as fellow citizens, they are under the *particular* political (and economic and social) institutions which go to make up the basic structure of that one society, their society. The basic structure of that society is an arena for application, for the building of principles of justice into the ongoing life of that one society in particular. The citizens' principal concern is with institutional design and criticism. The basic structure is necessarily an institutional context.

It is not clear, however, that the notion of rights can flourish in both contexts. Rawls, and many others, have all too easily assumed that it can. Rawls has made it sound as if talk of rights is fluid and can shift effortlessly from the one context to the other. What I have been delineating is at bottom not so much a difficulty that is internal to Rawls's theory (though certain tensions within that theory have helped bring it to light) as it is a fundamental philosophical difficulty in how one talks intelligibly about rights. I will begin the next section with that issue primarily in view, as our main topic for discussion there.

Before we move to that point, however, let me very briefly summarize the main results of our brief introductory survey of rights in Rawls's theory. We have determined that two of the ways in which Rawls talked about rights are dispensable: any listing of rights among the social primary goods was seen to be deeply confused and misleading, hence dispensable for that reason; any reference to rights that individuals might have (toward other individuals or associations) in virtue of legitimate expectations that arose through the workings of institutions that are subordinate to the basic structure (e.g., rights of parishioners or clergy in a church) was seen to be peripheral to our primary concern with basic moral or constitutional rights. That left two main areas for further discussion: (1) the supposed *moral* right stated in the first principle of justice ("each person is to have an equal right to the most extensive total system of equal basic liberties compatible with a similar system of liberty for all") and (2) the basic liberties themselves as rights. And I have suggested some reasons for saying that these two do not fit well together. If my suggestions were to be accepted—a point that depends on the argument of the next section—then we would drop the idea that the first principle states a right at all. We could reword it, for example, in language reminiscent of the *second* principle, to say that "political institutions are to be [or should be] so arranged that the most extensive justifiable system of liberties is to be available for each and all." We would concentrate then entirely on the idea that the basic liberties named, in effect, in the first principle are rights when embedded in the basic structure of a society. Our whole discussion of rights in Rawls's theory would lead out from that one point. We turn to the first stages of that project, then, in the next section.

## 2. *Natural Rights and the Basic Structure*

Rawls is one of the few contemporary philosophers who uses *natural rights* as his standard term (Hart is another). We will assume, though, that he means by natural rights roughly what others have meant by human rights. And I will treat these ways of talking as more or less interchangeable.

We can also assume that Rawls does not mean by natural rights what Thomas Hobbes and John Locke did; for them a natural right was any right that an individual had *in the state of nature*. Such a doctrine would have no appeal to Rawls. He rarely speaks of such a state, and when he does, it is, by and large, to distinguish his account of the original position from that of the state of nature in classical contract theory.[26] In Rawls's view, one would reach such a state only if the participants in the original position failed utterly to achieve a decision on preferred principles of justice and then decided, in effect, that no principle on the short list could be preferred to having no principle at all. A state of nature, rather like the one Hobbes envisioned, would result from that failure; it marks for Rawls the point of "no agreement."[27] There is a deep gulf, then, between natural rights in Rawls's theory, where they are identified by reference to the basic liberties that are listed in the preferred first principle of justice, and the idea in traditional contract theory that such rights are the rights an individual has willy-nilly in a state of nature.

Our main project in this section, then, is to provide an interpretation of what Rawls means by natural rights so understood. I will do this by sketching out an argument to show that the concept of rights (hence that of human or natural rights) implies certain practices or institutional arrangements; thus, the notion of a natural (or human) right as wholly noninstitutional, as logically prior to all practices of formulation and maintenance, is a mistake. It might appear from this that I am actually repudiating the Rawlsian idea of natural rights. But this is not so, for I do not believe Rawls's idea reproduces the traditional conception of natural rights at the crucial points where it breaks down.[28]

Now, supposing my argument to be sound, we are able to settle one important issue raised in the previous section: whether, in Rawls's theory, the notion of rights takes hold at the point of the abstract statement of the first principle in the original position or at the point of *applying* that principle to the basic structure of a society. For I think my argument forces the latter conclusion.

It follows that it is idle to describe the first principle of justice itself as a right (even though Rawls's text can bear such an interpretation). I do not, of course, mean to say that the first principle is thereby pointless but only that the term *right* is dispensable in its formulation. The first principle can be put differently, without using the term *right* at all, and suffer no loss of essential content whatsoever—something that has already been suggested in the previous section.

My argument is designed to show, in short, that it is only when basic liberties are built into the basic structure of a society that they are properly called rights in any significant sense. And this interpretation of natural rights in Rawls's theory—as basic liberties insofar as embedded in the basic structure—is one, I think, that can be gotten from Rawls's texts and that can be supported by sound arguments independently of those texts.

My main contention here is that basic moral rights—natural rights—are basic structure rights (and in that sense constitutional rights). And now to the argument.

Let us begin by turning to one of the main dimensions of what can be called legitimate expectations, that of claims *against* other persons. It is arguable such claims require there to be specific duties which fall on determinate or assignable individuals. Lacking these, claims-against could not take hold and would thereby be defective.

Rawls apparently concurs in this. For we note that Rawls frequently pairs rights and duties.[29] It seems, moreover, that he regards rights as always being correlated with duties—at least in the sense that all rights as legitimate expectations imply duties of second parties (i.e., of persons other than the rightholder).[30] And if this pairing—this correlation—were not in evidence, then the claim-to element (e.g., the claim to a particular liberty) would not in and of itself count as a legitimate *expectation* and, hence, would not be a right for Rawls.[31]

The filling in of the requisite background here need not, however, involve creating new duties (or what have you); it may involve simply hooking on to existing ones. In both cases, though, a fully legitimate expectation, hence a natural or a human right, will combine a valid claim *to* something (e.g., a liberty) with a valid claim on or *against* someone.[32]

Thus, a legitimate expectation includes these two elements (a morally justified claim-to and a morally justified claim-against); but can it be limited to them? The question is whether a legitimate expectation could be limited to being simply a valid claim (as defined by these two elements)—as that and nothing more—and still count as a legitimate expectation, still count as a right. Could one exist, in short, without any sort of social recognition or promotion whatsoever?

In order to answer this question we need to put a certain amount of logical pressure on the notion of a legitimate expectation. The existence of a legitimate expectation in Rawls's sense would probably require, in the simplest case, that there be duties actually incumbent on persons in a particular society and that these could be derived or endorsed in virtue of standards of critical morality. For duties that cannot be acknowledged in a given society—or that cannot be shown to follow, discursively, from accredited principles of conduct which are at least reflectively available to persons in that society—cannot be regarded as proper duties which could normatively bind conduct in that society.

Now, clearly, Rawls's theory is committed to the formulation and social recognition of principles of justice in the original position and to sound arguments, themselves certified publicly there, connecting the principles to goods such as specific liberties and thence to the duties of individual persons.

But we would not want to *restrict* these possible acknowledgments to the original position, for then we would lose all hold on actual persons and on their duties and obligations. There must be some requirement that the duties specified in critical morality (in the original position, for example) carry over into the real world of human action. One cannot have an obligation (or a duty) of which one literally cannot be aware. An actual person's conduct cannot be determined by duty (or obligation) if it is not possible for that person, even upon reflection, to be aware of that duty as a duty.

Now, where the beliefs that people have (including their moral beliefs) effectively block acknowledgment of something as a duty, or as a claim on the doing of their duty, then we have precisely the unawareness of which I am speaking. Thus, if a duty is removed or a supposed moral reason for performing one's duty is removed, in a given time or place, through such unawareness, then the legitimate expectation dissolves and loses the name of right. For rights imply a significant normative direction of the conduct of others, and that would be missing in the case at hand.

A parallel argument could be developed to show that if a certain claim-to (e.g., to a specific liberty) was similarly unavailable in a given society or could not be understood in that society as following from principles of critical morality, then it could give rise to no legitimate expectation there. Hence it could not be a right, nor could it constitute an element in a right.

So there is an unexpungeable element of "social" recognition built into the Rawlsian idea of rights as legitimate expectations. And I have argued that this factor of social recognition cannot end with the original position but must be extended into actual societies, insofar as they have any prospect of becoming well ordered. Accordingly, questions about basic rights must be addressed from this standpoint, as including both the original position and the basic structure of societies which are well ordered (or at least reasonably that way). This, of course, is Rawls's position; for he requires the elaboration of these would-be basic rights (or legitimate expectations) in the form of social institutions.

Now let us take this one step further, from recognition to maintenance. Here we will canvass the issue of what counts as an exemplification of a natural or human right.

Consider the case of innocent travel.[33] I would argue that the right to travel would be vitiated *as a right* if it were not protected or promoted at all. In such a case the right would be a merely nominal one, a right that existed in name only but not in fact. An ideal-type nominal right is in principle never an enforceable one; enforcement simply does not belong to its nature. Its permanent "recognition" could be assured (the liberty put in writing, enshrined in a declaration or in a bill of rights, honored by lip service), but its perpetual nonenforcement would be equally assured. Such rights do not, as some have suggested, constitute a special class of full-fledged rights. Rather, they constitute a limiting case; they are rights only on paper and nowhere else.

Now, to be sure, nominal rights are rights. The point is, though, that we regard the total absence of promotion and maintenance as infirming a right, as rendering it defective. Nominal rights are rights *in one sense only* (that of recognition), but they fail to function as rights. A merely nominal right gives no normative direction to the conduct of other persons in fact; such persons act as if the right did not exist even on paper. No one of them takes the nominal existence of the right as a reason for doing, or not doing, as the right directs. The right here has in actual practice no justificatory or directive force. Where social recognition effectively counts for so little, the rightholder is without any effective guarantee respecting that which has been recognized and formulated as a moral right. Such a right—when merely nominal—has failed in a crucial respect. It represents at best a marginal and precarious example of a right. On the assumption that any right under serious discussion here is not merely nominal, then, for any particular moral right, there would have to be certain appropriate practices of promotion, protection, enforcement, and so forth, on the part of society, including at least forbearance by (other) private persons. The determination of what is appropriate for a basic moral right then becomes the exact point at issue.

The great natural- and human-rights manifestoes were intended to impose restraints upon governments. Individuals were involved as beneficiaries of these restraints but, for the most part, were not the parties to whom the manifestoes were addressed. The right to a fair trial, which is often given as an example of a natural right (by Rawls and others), is a right that one has against governments in particular, especially one's own. The example is by no means atypical. Whether we look at details of specific rights, as we find them in the great declarations of rights, or at the theory of natural rights (including its actual history), we find that government is in fact the principal addressee.

Thus, I would want to argue that, insofar as the claims-against implicated in natural or human rights are addressed to governments in particular, we have to regard practices of governmental recognition and promotion as being the appropriate form that such social recognition and maintanence must take. To that degree, governmental practices are included within the notion of natural rights. They are (or have become) a part of the concept in question. A natural- or human-rights claim that lacks such recognition and promotion is still a valid claim, but it cannot qualify as a proper natural or human right.

And the issue of whether something is a natural right, or whether such rights "exist" or whether people "have" them, cannot be decided without consideration of the whole range of relevant practices, which include recognition in law and governmental maintenance of the claimed way of acting or of being treated. Such practices are ingredient in the very notion of what it is for something to be a natural or a human right, or so my argument is meant to show.

Now it may be, I would add, that for some universal moral rights the role of government is incidental or even nonexistent. These rights hold strictly between persons. The moral right to be told the truth (or at least not to be lied to) or the moral right to gratitude for benefits provided or, perhaps, the moral right to have promises kept are examples. Such rights differ from, say, the right not to be killed—even when we're talking about the latter right as held against individuals—in being rights that are maintained exclusively, or almost exclusively, by conscience. They are moral rights merely and in no way claims against the government. Interestingly, though, it is often in these very cases that while we are willing to call such rights moral rights, we would tend to withhold the name of human (or natural) right.

There is a sound basis for saying, then, that natural-rights norms (i.e., valid claims) are addressed to governments primarily. And natural or human rights can be distinguished from other universal moral rights in this very circumstance.[34]

There is an important reason, which needs bringing out, for precisely this restriction. In talk of specifically human or natural rights, it is assumed that human beings live in societies. The goods that are identified in claims-to are here conceived as goods obtained and enjoyed in a social setting. That is, such goods are conceived as provided peculiarly or especially through life in a society. They are not, in short, thought to be attained principally, if at all, on a mere individual-person-to-all-others basis. Here then, where the social context is emphasized, claims against others are for the most part addressed not to individuals as such but, rather, to individuals insofar as they exercise the powers of some assigned agency in that particular social setting. Such claims-against hold, not against everyone individually, but against an organized society; and it is of the institutions—or agencies—of that society that satisfaction is expected.

Admittedly, it is not so much governments as it is organized societies that are selected out by human- or natural-rights claims. The point, though, is that the basic structures of such societies are correctly regarded as being *politically* organized; and it is governments that typically play, and have played, a major role in such organization. Thus, government enters the natural-rights picture as the organizer, and as one of the major agencies, of the kind of society against which a natural-rights claim is characteristically lodged. Thus, the requirement that natural rights be lodged in the basic structure of a society, that their status as rights of this sort requires such incorporation, seems to follow naturally. And this I take to be the view that Rawls is advancing.

If my analysis is correct or even plausible, we have a reason for the central place that government occupies in our concept of natural or human rights; given this reason, we find it natural that recognition and maintenance by governmental action (the satisfaction principally sought in natural-rights claims) should be relativized to particular societies. For these claims, insofar as we have regard to their primary addressee, are satisfied by political devices (e.g., basic laws) having an appropriately universal scope within a particular society. Such a law would exist when, for example, a freedom to travel on the part of every citizen (or preferably, every person) was recognized in the law of that society and scrupulously enforced. We can call any such operative and universal right (i.e., universal within a given society) a general political or civil right—or, if you will, a constitutional right. The latter, which is the more conventional term, seems serviceable enough.

This particular notion of constitutional rights is easily inserted into Rawls's theory. The rights he has in mind are, on their claim-to side, universal and unconditional (in that a valid moral claim holds good for everyone, or at least for everyone who is alive at a given time—for the ground of the claim is simply a title to something or other that is given to all persons, merely in virtue of their being persons, in accordance with moral principles). This is how I would interpret Rawls's contention that the basic liberties, as determined in the original position, are natural rights. That is, on their claim-to side they are like natural rights in the traditional sense.[35] Such claims are explicitly accommodated in the basic structure of any well-ordered society; and they are, under the requirement of a public sense of institutional justice, not only formulated and acknowledged but also scrupulously maintained there by the particular government involved.

There is, I would note, though, an important asymmetry between the claims-to part and the claims-against part of a complete (or full) valid moral claim. The former may well be universal and virtually without restriction; yet it does not follow automatically here that the claim-against element will be similarly universal. For example, all human beings are, or were at one time, children and all have (or had) the appropriate claims to care and concern: to nourishment, upbringing, and so on. But these claims on the part of each child are principally addressed, not to anyone and everyone, but to that child's parents or guardians in particular. Rights that are thus restricted are called special (rather than general) rights. I want to suggest that something like this functions in the case of human or natural rights; they too are special rights.[36] The claim-to element is unrestricted: it holds for every person (or for every person who is alive at a given time). But the claim-against element is typically restricted: not all persons, but only some (namely, agencies of government), are addressed as principally having the moral duty in question. It is their job to arrange the basic structure so as to incorporate the substance of these claims-to for the benefit of their respective inhabitants.

Indeed, the term *basic structure right,* which I introduced in the previous section, seems to be singularly well suited to capture the peculiar sense of constitutional rights that we want to have in view. The turn to constitutional—or basic structure—rights reflects the fact that human rights typically are special rights and are claimed on moral grounds which hold good for all persons, simply in virtue of their being persons, against particular politically organized societies—specifically, against governments. (Or, as Rawls would probably prefer to say, against one's fellow citizens.) The question of whether a particular valid and universal moral claim has been appropriately responded to by government or by the members of one's society is answered by considering the class of active constitutional rights. Such rights, when molded under the influence of these claims, are the kind of right involved. Their existence is a necessary element in a morally valid claim's being (or becoming) a natural or a human right.

If a particular constitutional right is missing in a given country, then lacking this necessary ingredient, the incipient natural right will fail to jell or it will dissolve, for that country or for that time and place. And we are at best left with a moral claim (presumably valid) that something *should be* a constitutional right.

The basic contention, then, which forms the backdrop of this entire study is that natural or human rights necessarily have an institutional side and that, on this side, they would have in a given society the form of constitutional rights. We recognize, of course, that even in a well-ordered society there may be some constitutional rights which do not have the sort of direct backing, in a valid and universal moral claim as determined from the perspective of the original position, that we have been discussing. These would not, then, be called natural rights. Natural rights are confined to those constitutional or basic structure rights that have the appropriate moral support. I will restrict my discussion in what follows to things that are natural rights in this precise sense.

It is often asked what something that is otherwise a human or natural right would be in a society in which the relevant constitutional right was lacking. The answer is that it would be merely a morally valid claim there. Or to be exact, it would be a valid claim that holds, insofar as practicable, for each and every person in that society, against the government there (and in many cases against private persons also). The claim would hold simply in virtue of its following from accredited moral principles. And the claim would be that the thing identified as the claim-to element (e.g., a given basic liberty as specified in Rawls's first principle) should be established as an operating basic structure or constitutional right in that society.

Any such claim would have an important use insofar as it was or could be acknowledged by people in that society. (And it would most likely be if the conventional morality of that society is such that the first principle would be affirmed when that conventional morality was carefully reflected upon.) For it would provide a realistic and reasonable basis for criticizing the conduct of government or of people generally in that society. Thus, the government could be criticized for failing to promote and maintain a course of action, or a way of being treated, that was incorporated in law as something to be promoted and maintained. Or it could be criticized—that is, the society in question could be criticized—for having failed to take even the first step, that of incorporation into the basic structure and, hence, of authoritative recognition in law. These criticisms would be perfectly sound insofar as they followed from accredited principles (as developed in critical morality, e.g., in the original position) and insofar as they really could be made to connect up with the normative direction that was provided to people in that society by their existing morality or by their system of law.

Thus, for instance, on the assumption that there are morally sound arguments (in the original position, as incorporated in the first principle) against the practice of slavery, we could say that slaves (in the United States in the late eighteenth or early nineteenth century) had a morally valid claim to personal liberty despite what the United States Constitution said or implied (or despite what intellectual defenders of slavery, such as Aristotle, might have said). More important, there was a morally valid claim that this particular liberty should be embodied as a constitutional or civil right (specifically as a right not to be enslaved) for every human person in that society. The intended result of authoritatively acknowledging this claim in that society is that slavery would cease to exist there (but until it did so, the right established by that acknowledgment would be, to some degree, a nominal one). We could expect, then, that the personal liberty would become in time a proper or full-fledged right—that is, an active consitutional or basic structure right there.

The moral soundness of this criticism of slavery does not require that there be some right superordinate to conventional morality or to existing systems of law. Indeed, legally sanctioned slavery may violate no one's rights in those cases where the relevant liberties have not been incorporated as basic structure rights. Nonetheless, the crucial point remains that legally sanctioned slavery is always unjust (a point that I will argue more fully in the next chapter). But whether or not something is a right raises a somewhat different set of questions. Natural rights are not simply demands of justice, not even of distributive justice. Rather, as I have argued in this section, the crucial issue here is whether appropriate practices of recognition and promotion are in place for that kind of right. For without such social recognition and maintenance, whatever was said to be justified, on moral grounds, would not be a proper right.

There is, we see on reflection, an irreducible duality to human or natural rights. On the one side, they are morally validated claims to some benefit or other. On the other side, such rights require recognition in law and promotion by government of the claimed way of acting or of being treated. Neither side is dispensable in a human or natural right.

On its legal side a human or natural right would have the form of a constitutional right. If there are any natural rights at all, it follows that there are active constitutional rights in at least some countries. There will be such rights in all Rawlsian well-ordered societies.[37]

This concludes my line of argument and my use of that argument to interpret Rawls's notion of natural rights. One caveat is, perhaps, in order. Rawls says that "the liberties of equal citizenship must be incorporated into and protected by the constitution";[38] this is often interpreted as requiring their incorporation into a bill of rights. Thus, it might appear that Rawls's account requires, as a matter of justice, that a well-ordered society have a *written* constitution. But this is a considerable oversimplification. (Though we can say that, where there is a written constitution, it should incorporate the liberties that are listed in the first principle of justice.)

What Rawls's position requires, fundamentally, is the rule of law; with his emphasis on publicity it would follow that such rules will be explicitly formulated—or at least the more important ones are required to be. Among these important laws will be some that are regarded as basic (e.g., laws in a representative—parliamentary—democracy that set the term of a parliament, that identify the frequency of elections, that stipulate how or when a parliament may be dissolved, etc.). Thus, whatever counts as the basic laws in a society, those are to include laws that formulate and afford protection to the basic rights. Accordingly, a country like Great Britain, which has no written constitution, could incorporate universal political—that is, constitutional— rights into its basic laws and thereby conform to Rawls's requirement.

It is even possible to imagine nonlegal sources of constitutional rights. Their principal formulation could occur in a religious book or code or in a work of philosophy (such as Mill's *On Liberty*). Or it could occur in some political document (such as the Declaration of Independence or the *Federalist Papers* or Lincoln's Gettysburg Address) which lies largely outside the law. And it could occur outside the usual legal context of explicit constitutional provisions or valid statutes (as, for one example, the United States Supreme Court's assertion of a fundamental "right of privacy" does or, for another example, as does the considerable codification, by the Executive Branch, of rights to "affirmative action"). What is important is that basic rights be formulated, that some formulation be authoritatively recognized within the standard political and legal channels of a society, and that, within these channels, government bring its powers to bear so as to promote and maintain the rights that are authoritatively recognized. It is this kind of commitment to basic rights, which can control the political process and is never taken lightly by the political agencies, that Rawls had in mind. (And, we should hasten to add, many of these rights will also normatively direct the conduct of individual citizens as well.)

Rights that are so understood become, literally, a *part* of the basic structure. The way of thinking I have tried to portray here is very like the ancient Greek conception of a constitution (*politeia*) as that which concerns the principal parts of the *polis*—or of the state, as we would call it. If we keep in mind the Rawlsian idea that constitutional rights are basic structure rights, we will not depart too far from this fundamental conception.

This brings us back to the main contention that I have tried to advance in this section: namely, that for Rawls, basic moral rights—natural rights—are basic structure rights (and in that sense constitutional rights). And I have sketched out a rather complex argument, both to interpret Rawls's idea of natural rights and to support his insistence on the explicit formulation by government of rights in the basic structure and of the development there of attendant political institutions for the promotion and maintenance of these rights. I have argued that a theory of natural rights would fail insofar as it leaves out these latter features, of appropriate social recognition and protection, which are essential to any proper right. For without such measures, there could be no basic structure *guarantee* to an individual of what was justifiably claimed as his due, and he could not count on getting what was claimed. There would be no legitimate expectation, hence no true right as part of the basic structure, in the absence of such formulation and maintenance.

Admittedly, the basic liberties are understood as explicitly stated in the first principle of justice (though their formulation there is a rather loose one). This initial formulation does occur, and can only occur, in the original position. But there are no mechanisms for protection in the original position. It is merely anticipated that there will be some such devices. The original position exists simply so that the principles of justice can be *stated* (and can be seen, as stated, to be reasonable and well founded). Hence the liberties that are listed from the perspective of the original position can be, when in the original position, at best merely morally valid claims. Even if we were to waive the requirement of social recognition, letting the formulation of these liberties in the original position stand as surrogate, the rights there would still be analogous to constitutional rights that were merely nominal. This gives the reason, then, why it is empty to regard the first principle of justice, when merely formulated in the original position, as itself a basic right, or as listing basic rights, in any full and significant sense.

But the liberties, as listed in the first principle, can be built into the basic structure of a society, and when they are incorporated in the way I have specified, they become proper rights. They become constitutional rights, parts of the basic structure.[39]

## 3. *Global Justice*

For Rawls all natural or fundamental rights, insofar as they are rights, strictly conceived, are necessarily embedded in the basic structure of society—that is, of some *particular* society. The basic liberties are goods of all people, everywhere and at all times. But they are realized as goods only in society—and for any individual, that means in some specific society. Thus, when we look at basic liberties, not as liberties but as constitutional rights, there is an important sense in which they are not "globalized," not spread, as it were, to the four corners of the earth as a single blanket of rights covering all peoples. As proper natural rights such rights enjoy, and can only enjoy, a local existence, in the basic structure of a given society.

Why should this be? Because, as I argued in the previous section, Rawls apparently believes that the basic liberties are inadequately determined—not properly identified or distributed or guaranteed to individuals—in a setting that lacks mechanisms for defining rights: for setting their scope, for adjusting them one to another, for assuring that they will be distributed to actual individuals, for enforcing and protecting that distribution, and so on. Individual political societies—states—have such mechanisms. They are, given their relative independence and self-contained character, the largest such entities, and the most important ones, that do have the appropriate mechanisms. Thus, the same reason which underwrote Rawls's claim that the basic structure of a society is the first subject of justice also underwrites his housing of natural rights—basic liberties as constitutional rights—within discrete political societies.

The motivation is practical, not logical. The world itself could be the locus of natural rights if there were a world government. But there isn't. There is no basic structure—no political infrastructure—for the globe. The largest viable unit today is the nation state.

This does not mean that a larger, more inclusive political society would be inappropriate, nor does it mean that one should not work to achieve a larger framework. Indeed, if we take seriously the idea that the basic liberties should be rights of all people, then such a global framework might well be indicated. (Though, equally, it might be indicated that the liberties should be incorporated into the basic structure of every existing political society.) But the point is that the possibility of a global framework is very remote at present.

Suppose, though, that one wanted to work now to help globalize the basic liberties as rights at some future date. How should one best go about this? Rawls's answer seems to be—I am theorizing here—that a plausible procedure would be for individual states to strive (where their traditions and institutional development permitted) to conform themselves to justice in their basic structure. This might well constitute a necessary first step. After that, some further move might be possible—perhaps an international association of such states and the development of a new political infrastructure, acting directly on individual persons, within that association. Something like this further move is afoot in western Europe today, though what has resulted so far is much more like a confederation of states than like an individual state.

A good argument could be made, then, that direct moves to a global state—or to a large confederation of inevitably and radically unlike-minded states—from where we are today is not wise. Also, it would not be practical.

Nor would it be likely to help achieve anything like the end in view: the globalization of basic liberties as rights for all people everywhere.

All this is useless speculation, however, if we lose sight of the main point. Basic liberties cannot be rights except in a suitable institutional context. They cannot be effective constitutional rights except in the basic structure of a political society. We must confine ourselves, then, to consideration of such basic structures. Insofar as we are interested in institutional design that has any prospect of practical application, we must not outrun the range of existing or feasible basic structures. Thus, we are necessarily concerned with the largest viable political societies—independent states—and their basic structures. This precludes, for the foreseeable future at least, any serious program for designing a global or even an ambitious confederative scheme of basic liberty rights.

The same inhibitions that I have just described, as existing for the basic liberties of the first principle, will also exist for the other primary goods as determined in the second principle (under its two main headings, fair equality of opportunity and the difference principle). The operation of these two features are equally meant to be confined to the basic structures of particular societies. And for the same reason: namely, that today the necessary political infrastructure exists only in these societies and not globally.

It could, of course, be urged that *economically* there is at present a great mutual interdependence among peoples of the earth. But even if global economic interdependence is a fact, two points remain germane.

First, we can speak from the perspective of the original position. The parties there would be concerned about the well-being of persons in *any* society—hence in *all* societies, whether or not these societies and these persons were economically interdependent. The whole point of formulating principles of justice, it seems to me, is to identify areas of appropriate concern for the well-being of persons everywhere insofar as that well-being is a matter of basic fairness. The fact of economic interdependence on a global scale is quite irrelevant to this concern. It can become relevant, but only depending on what the unit of application is. If the unit of application is the existing market (or the multinational firm or capitalist society), then the fact of global economic interdependence is clearly relevant. But if the unit of application of the difference principle is the basic structure of a *political* society, then equally clearly it is not.

The perspective of the basic structure of society is the second one that we can take and must take in order to determine which unit of application is the appropriate one. Suppose the basic structure is as we've already described it (in the earlier discussion in this section of basic liberties); one would have to say in such a case that there is no world-wide political structure that answers to the global economic community. Accordingly, there can be no world-wide

43

application of the difference principle today. There cannot be; for that principle, in order to be applied, requires political mechanisms, not merely economic ones. The relevant political mechanisms exist, for now at least, only in independent national states (or perhaps in certain federations of these) but not globally, not in any single, all-encompassing political regime. And what is true for the operation of the difference principle holds also for fair equality of opportunity: the political mechanisms required for its application do not now exist, to any practical degree, except in particular societies, in independent states.[40]

So, the Rawlsian concentration on the basic structure of a particular society, which I have tried to bring out through my analysis of natural rights, limits the application of the preferred principles of justice in a very fundamental way. For direct global application is ruled out—once, that is, we take account of the actual character of the contemporary political world. And I will observe this limitation—in effect a limitation to the basic structure of some particular political society (or state)—throughout my discussion of the application of the two principles of justice.

In the analysis of this and the previous section, we have a setting for Rawls's discussion of basic liberties as rights. I will turn to a more exacting account of these liberties in the next chapter.

# • 3 •

# EQUAL BASIC LIBERTIES

In the analysis in the previous chapter, human or natural rights have two dimensions: on the one side, they are morally valid claims which hold good for all persons, and on the other, they are constitutional rights in at least some societies. The characteristic focal point in Rawls's discussion of natural rights was the basic structure of a society. The analysis was designed to show that this focus was well motivated and could be supported by sound argument.

One minor virtue of this analysis is that it provides a plausible reason for closely linking the constitutional (or design of the basic structure) and the original position stages in Rawls's theory. The work of these two stages is complementary; they are part of the same project: the transformation of morally endorsed basic liberties into basic rights. Rawls's way of talking about natural rights is more congenial to such a project than is the traditional way—where natural rights are identified with the state of nature, which is then sharply distinguished from civil society. But correspondingly, the distinction between the two stages is not watertight in Rawls's account; indeed, about all that one can say with any confidence is that the constitutional stage presupposes the choice of preferred principles of justice in the original position and further elaborates the supporting arguments which were started there.

The principal themes of the present chapter are taken up at this point through consideration, in close detail, of a particular class of morally justified constitutional rights: those that formulate basic liberties as part of a program of affording them special governmental protection and promotion. I proceed to identify the main perspective from which determinations about liberties as constitutional rights are made in Rawls's theory. This is the perspective of the interests of the so-called representative citizen. Working from this standpoint, we have a ground for deciding which rights are basic (and therefore should be fundamental constitutional rights), and we are able to generate the main arguments for saying that basic rights should be *equal* rights for each and all.

### 1. *Some Liberties Are Basic Ones*

As I indicated in the previous chapter, Rawls's first principle of justice is not a general principle of liberty: it does not establish liberty in gross or in the abstract. Rather, it establishes a particular "list" of basic liberties which are to be acknowledged as held by all. One problem would be to determine how *in the original position* these specific liberties could be established, in particular such institutional rights as the right to vote or to own property.

The solution to this problem, I suggest, is to distinguish between stages at which a formulation could occur. (And here I follow Rawls's own account of the main stages.)[1] At the stage of the original position, the "list" of basic liberties is selected; but the items on the list are broadly, even vaguely, stated, and no attempt is made to adjust these liberties mutually to one another. At the next, or constitutional, stage the individual liberties, already selected at the previous stage, are defined more precisely, and a first step is taken in the direction of their "definitional balancing," that is, towards limiting the scope of each in relation to that of the others.

Rawls's setting up of a tandem procedure here is in no way arbitrary. For the movement from the one stage to the other exhibits considerable continuity. The original position and the constitutional stage (especially when the latter is broadly conceived as the design of the basic structure of a society) are enough alike to constitute a single perspective. In each the significant restrictions on applicable knowledge are such as to screen out or disallow all individual particularity: for the veil of ignorance has been lifted only slightly, to let in general facts about the particular society whose basic structure is being designed, as we move from the one stage to the other.[2] The result is that the interests which are admissible—the only ones which are allowed behind the veil in either stage—are the general or universal interests of the so-called representative citizen. Those interests that everyone has, or presumably has identically under the relevant constraints on knowledge, are the interests that define, that justify and give substance to, the selected liberties.[3]

The basic liberties, then, are those that have been selected out from the whole range of liberties (of liberties as primary goods) in a determination made from the "everyman" vantage point of the representative citizen. They are called *basic* because they can justifiably be put on the list of preferred liberties in accordance with a principle—or a set of principles—that could be entertained within the perspective afforded, equally, by either the original position or the constitutional convention. In this regard I have stressed the

46

principle of universal interests; it is important, however, to recall that not all universal interests are contemplated here, but only those which could exist in the original position (i.e., in the original position as carried over, through the arguments and principles generated there, into the constitutional stage). It is those interests alone that identify which specific liberties, as fundamental ones, are intended for distribution to each and all.

A further clue to the nature of the selected liberties is given by the items on Rawls's list of basic liberties. These are, Rawls says, "roughly speaking, political liberty (the right to vote and to be eligible for public office) together with freedom of speech and assembly; liberty of conscience and freedom of thought; freedom of the person along with the right to hold (personal) property; and freedom from arbitrary arrest and seizure as defined by the concept of the rule of law." For there is a certain coherence here. They are, every one of them, liberties of assignable persons; they can both be "individuated" (parceled out to individual persons) and be said to hold without qualification for *all* people. They are, then, liberties of persons (i.e., of individuals viewed simply as persons), and they are justifiably on the list as liberties that are appropriate or essential to that status. Liberties that are not personal, that do not contribute to or are not required by individuals *as persons,* are excluded. Thus, to cite one interesting example, the ownership of personal property is a specified liberty under the first principle, but the ownership of productive property is not.[4]

There is one way, however, in which the list is a bit heterogeneous. Some of the things on it are straightforwardly liberties, and others are not. To see this, let us begin with a clear-cut case. Liberty of conscience means that *someone* (i.e., the representative citizen) is free *from* certain disallowed interferences (e.g., a state establishment of religion) in order to be free *to* think his own thoughts and to establish his own beliefs and practices on important matters of conscience (in the areas of religion, morals, philosophy, science).[5] A liberty always specifies, in the end, something that someone *does* or can do. But some of the things on Rawls's list are not of this sort. Thus, although the integrity of one's body may be described as a freedom from certain physical injuries or mutilations, it is not in fact a liberty, not principally something that the rightholder does or can do. We see, on inspection, that the list is made up of two kinds of things: (a) liberties in the strict sense and (b) the avoidance of certain injuries at the hands of others. So, when Rawls talks of basic liberties, we must take him to be referring, without distinction, to things of both these kinds.

This suggests that the items in the category of noninjuries (e.g., freedom from arbitrary arrest) are as important as those in the category of liberties in the strict sense (e.g., freedom to own personal property). They are important for the same reason: they are fundamental interests of all those who have the status of persons and would be seen to be essential to that status, for each and every person, from the perspective of either the original position or the constitutional convention. They are, accordingly, all of them rights of persons. It is this fact that warrants putting both kinds of things on a single list of basic liberties—or better, of fundamental rights.

The argument is, then, that certain liberties and noninjuries are basic or fundamental rights insofar as they are essential to anyone's being a moral person, that is, someone who is capable of moral life. Rawls attempts, in his later writings, to refine this argument.

Moral persons, in the sense intended, can be characterized (as they were in chapter 1) as having two capacities or powers. First, they are said to be capable of affiliation with certain excellences (like holiness or athletic prowess or scholarship) or, more likely, with some combination of these and of exhibiting a rational plan of life to achieve such goods. And second, they are said to be capable of having an active sense of justice (informed, in the best of cases, by the principles of justice that one would affirm in a reflective deliberation modeled on the original position); persons here are conceived as social beings, who are aware of social interaction and capable of cooperation on just terms. For purposes of thumbnail identification, we can call the first power that of having a determinate conception of the good and the second that of having a determinate sense of justice. Moral persons, then, are "moved by two highest-order interests to realize and exercise these powers."[6] So, the refinement that Rawls intends in the main argument is to associate the basic liberties and noninjuries, in a convincing fashion, specifically with these two highest-order interests.

Rawls also adduces what he calls a higher-order interest (as distinct from a *highest*-order interest). This is the interest that each person has in advancing his specific conception of the good. It is not clear to me exactly how we are to interpret this third interest. We could say that the interest consists principally in putting forward arguments for one's determinate conception of the good, in a competitive setting, in order to win approval or endorsement or even adherents for that conception. No doubt, this is part of what Rawls meant by *advancing* one's conception of the good, but it doesn't seem to tell the whole story. We would want to include that one advances his determinate conception of the good by doing the things indicated, as it were, in one's rational plan of life to achieve the relevant excellences.

In any event, the interest in question is not thought to be a highest-order interest because if it were, then it might be able to supersede the individual's capacity for justice; thus Rawls wants to emphasize, in calling the interest merely a higher-order one, that it cannot do so. By the same token, were the interest in advancing one's conception of the good an interest of the *highest* order, then it might be permissible, as part of realizing a determinate good for oneself, to supersede one's indeterminate but generous *capacity* for having conceptions of the good. Now, the scholar might let his commitment to learning usurp his waking hours and his energies to such a degree that he no longer had the time or the will to be a halfway-decent parent or stamp collector or dancer to "new wave" music. This might happen, true enough; but surely even the dedicated scholar would not want to lose altogether his capacity to *revise* his determinate conception of the good or to alter his rational plan of life. So, in order to underline this point, Rawls says that the *capacity* to have a determinate conception of the good is of the highest order; thus, it is a higher-order interest than even the interest one has in advancing one's own determinate conception of the good.[7]

But there is, in fact, virtually no difference between these two interests. Indeed, if we were to add the stipulation that the individual always be able to revise the determinate conception of the good that he is advancing, then the two would be identical. Thus, each person's interest in having and advancing a determinate conception of the good, when properly understood, would incorporate some such proviso.

Determinate conceptions of the good that might differ from individual to individual are not, as we saw in chapter 1, allowed in the original position model (nor in the constitutional stage, we could add). The parties—or their representatives—know that individuals actually have determinate conceptions of the good; it is merely that, in the deliberations there, they are not allowed to affiliate with any one conception in particular and to push it. Particular conceptions, then, are not admitted as such. So such conceptions are unable to figure in the deliberations there. For example, there would be no such thing as the scholar's rational plan of life (or anyone else's) admitted into consideration in the original position. The relevant highest-order interest there is simply the interest that each person has in advancing his own determinate conception of the good, *whatever it might be,* subject always to the proviso that any such conception can be revised. Only this interest and the highest-order interest in having a specific sense of justice—each of them an identical interest for all persons—can be given weight in the original position.

Actual determinate conceptions of the good are here represented abstractly by certain building blocks that they have in common—things such as liberties, opportunities, and so on. For these abstract building-block elements (i.e., the social primary goods) are all that remain of individualized determinate conceptions of the good when these conceptions are admitted, under the aegis of the relevant highest-order interest, into the original position. Thus, in the original position we do not directly consider determinate goods and excellences; instead, we consider them only as broken down into the building blocks of *any* such conception of the good. Or we consider what is needed, again as identified by the primary goods, to advance any determinate conception of the good. For the primary goods are building blocks both of these conceptions and of the instruments that advance them. We have regard here to what would be a just distribution of such determinate goods abstractly conceived or of the means to them.

In short, we consider the social primary goods exclusively and relate them to the two highest-order interests of persons. Or, to put the matter differently, it is the two highest-order interests that allow us to pick out and to characterize certain goods as primary goods. Accordingly, then, our project here is to see which liberties and noninjuries would be selected as basic—and under what descriptions. We do so by determining which liberties were required by the two highest-order interests of moral persons. And thus we would use the idea of the person to help account for the social primary goods.

The development of the idea of highest-order interests and the use of that idea to structure the social primary goods (and, ultimately, the basic liberties as a special case of such goods) is perhaps the single greatest change between Rawls's book and his later writings on justice. The important thing, for our purposes, is that it allows Rawls to differentiate between the basic liberties in an interesting way as to how, precisely, they are supported by the concept of moral personhood. Thus, at the risk of some oversimplification, we can say that *some* of the basic liberties are supported *principally* by the moral person's highest-order interest in advancing his own determinate conception of the good. And some are supported principally by the *other* highest-order interest, that of exercising one's capacity for living in accordance with a well-developed sense of justice. In his essay "Basic Liberties," Rawls calls these the "two fundamental cases."[8]

Thus, liberty of conscience is said to be associated principally with the first of the two highest-order interests (of moral persons). We might say that liberty of conscience is the idea that one should be able to advance his own determinate conception of the good, as founded on some definite ideas of religion or science or conventional morality (and subject to the proviso about revisability already given). Moreover, the parties to any original position deliberation would choose liberty of conscience so understood in order not to jeopardize their actual conception of the good, whatever it was, once the veil of ignorance had been lifted. Of course, they would have to pay the price for this (as specified by justice and enshrined in the first principle): that for each to have liberty of conscience, free from coercion by others, he must be willing not to coerce the conscience of others. Likewise, Rawls says, freedom from injury to bodily integrity, freedom from slavery, and freedom of personal association would all be supported principally by the highest-order interest that each person has in advancing his own determinate conception of the good.[9]

And if we turn to the other highest-order interest (that of having and being guided by an active sense of justice), we would find that certain of the basic liberties would be supported *primarily* by that interest. Thus, liberty of political speech and assembly would reflect one's highest-order interest in being able to shape and to express one's active sense of justice. Likewise, we would find that freedom of the press and the whole range of political-participation liberties (voting, etc.) would be supported principally by a single highest-order interest associated with the second of the moral powers, that of having a sense of justice.[10]

Of course, it is often the case that a basic liberty (like freedom of political speech), though it is primarily regarded as essential to or supportive of *one* of the highest-order interests in particular, is significantly related to the *other* moral power as well. Thus, its selection as a basic liberty would be accomplished by reference to both of the highest-order interests, and not merely to one of them.

Rawls's account of how certain liberties and noninjuries could be established as basic ones, by using the two highest-order interests as touchstone, is considerably more complex and more systematic than the one he developed in his book, *Theory of Justice*. And it does seem to me, clearly, more satisfactory to ground the basic liberties on something fairly specific, such as the moral powers under their description as highest-order interests, than on the much vaguer concept of a (moral) person. Such a procedure also allows Rawls to avoid the clumsy device of arguing to liberty of conscience from the rather vague notion of a person; and then taking that liberty as a sort of paradigm for *all* basic liberties, thereby generalizing his arguments for liberty of conscience pell-mell to all the other basic liberties (including such obviously difficult cases as the ownership of personal property or the possession of the franchise).[11] Thus, the line of argument that Rawls takes in his later writings is preferable, even though the arguments themselves are very sketchy. (However, this sketchiness is offset to some extent by the allowance that any argument developed in the original position may be amplified considerably at subsequent stages.)

The main refinement he has introduced, in sum, is that the various basic liberties are to be accounted for differently, by reference to two different highest-order interests. But this is the only change of any real moment. For the notion of two highest-order interests does not go beyond the notion of two powers of the person, an idea already found in his book; hence, the account of basic liberties found in his book already incorporated these powers as the foundation of basic liberties. The later writings mainly serve to make this foundation explicit.

So we can summarize what is fundamental in Rawls's account of the basic liberties, as follows. In the original position—and likewise in the constitutional convention—anyone would, upon reflection, affirm certain goods as being important for himself and for all the others. Each individual would conclude, then, that specified liberties and noninjuries ought to be constitutional rights—ought to be formally acknowledged and specially protected—because they are significant universal interests, interests of all persons when taken simply as persons. (And it would follow, too, from the analysis of natural rights developed in the previous chapter, that these important liberties and noninjuries, in actually becoming constitutional rights, would also gain the status of full-fledged human or natural rights.)

## 2. *All Basic Liberties Are Equal Ones*

The standpoint taken, when persons are considered simply as persons, is the standpoint of the original position; and the persons there, in being simply persons and in contemplating all others as themselves simply persons, occupy an equal status. Or if we regard the parties in the original position as representatives of persons, the same conclusion would be drawn: that *they* occupy such a status as representative of persons who occupy an equal status. Rawls's argument for equality in rights arises from this point.

In the perspective taken, that of the representative citizen, individuals do not know facts about themselves in particular. Hence, no one would know whether he himself would suffer an allowed-for inequality. Since the basic liberties are all essential to the status of being rational moral individuals with the same highest interests and since each individual in the original position (or in the constitutional stage) is such a person and each is, vis-à-vis all the others, equal in that status, then each would opt for a program in which the basic rights were equal for all. We can at least presume a tendency for the parties to act in this way, for they are not disposed to tolerate unnecessary inequality.[12]

The only argument in the original position which could prevail over this tendency would be one that alleged that a certain restriction on basic liberties—including therein a restriction that amounted to inequality—was necessary in order to achieve a more extensive system of basic liberties for all. Now, it is clear that, for persons in the original position, a greater but equal liberty, if justified, would be preferred to a lesser one; but it is not clear that an *unequal* liberty could ever be acceptable to the parties, and hence justified. This becomes, then, the precise matter under dispute. Let us take these considerations up in turn, addressing first the issue of restrictions per se and then the more problematic issue of restrictions that embody inequality.

Rawls contemplates two ways in which liberties might be restricted so as to achieve a greater justified system of liberties overall.[13] The first involves restrictions built into a political process on a more or less regular basis; the second, restrictions of an emergency nature.

Rawls envisions a basic constitutional situation in which the status of free and equal persons (a status held by all of the parties in the deliberations of the original position) translates into a process of political participation that has such features as one person/one vote, free and contested elections, majority rule, and so on. However, a political-participation liberty, such as majority rule, could be restricted if it threatened or could threaten the basic liberties. Thus, a kind of definitional balancing at the constitutional level might occur in which majority rule would be limited so as to prevent it from conflicting with or overriding basic liberties (such as liberty of conscience or freedom from the injury of violations of due process). Accordingly, a constitutional device is settled on that limits majority rule, by putting liberty of speech off-limits to congressional action and by adding the protection of judicial review, for instance, or by requiring an extraordinarily high proportion of votes or something like a special referendum to effect a constitutional amendment. The idea here is that the system of basic liberties of persons is more extensive, or is safer and more secure, than it would be if majority rule were not so restricted. Thus, majority rule could be delimited, Rawls argues, on the principle that a basic liberty could be restricted for the sake of basic liberties. Indeed, some such restriction on majority rule represents the paradigm case of what an argument for restriction, conducted in the original position (or in a constitutional convention), would look like.[14]

It should also be noted, however, that majority rule, in being restricted, would be restricted equally for everyone, because the constitutional rule that limits it makes no distinction of persons. So we retain the notion, as dominant, of *equal* basic liberties and the idea that such a system should be as extensive as can be justified.

The other main sort of restriction that Rawls contemplated was of an emergency nature. Thus, for example, freedom of political speech might be restricted in a time of war or other national emergency, to secure such values as national survival or "public order."[15] (By the same token, universal conscription might, while restricting liberties of individuals, be thought necessary in time of war in order to prevent the collapse of an entire social system.)[16] But national survival and public order are here only proximate and instrumental values. The more direct consideration is whether the failure of national survival or of an existing public order would virtually annihilate basic liberties or lead to severe restriction of them. Clearly, the failure of some governmental systems to survive could threaten basic liberties in the society in which that government existed, but in other cases (e.g., Nazi Germany) it probably would not. So the point remains that basic liberties can be restricted only for the sake of basic liberties. And some, but not all, such restrictions, of an interim nature in time of emergency, could be justified on that principle.

There are several important differences between the two cases. First, the restriction on majority rule was an institutional one; it was built right into the system, into the very rules that defined the various liberties and adjusted them to one another (in what we have called "definitional balancing"). But the interim restrictions that are imposed by emergency are not necessarily embedded in the defining rules. For example, it need not be part of the rule that defines freedom of speech to specify that this liberty can be restricted in the interests of national survival or "public order." It could, rather, be a matter of public understanding that *any* liberty could be restricted on an interim basis and for an acceptable reason, and it could then be left to the legislature or to the courts to determine the occasion and the degree of threat.[17]

Second, the restriction on majority rule represented a case in which one liberty (that of participating in a scheme of majority rule) was limited by another liberty (e.g., freedom of speech) or by several of them. Such a restriction, then, did not count as an exception to liberty in general or as a deviation from it; it did not represent the imposition of an extraneous value on liberties. But the interim restrictions that we have considered (e.g, conscription) were not themselves liberties or, in any straightforward sense, avoidances of injury. Conscription is not a right that one has. Such restrictions were, rather, deviations from liberty, exceptions taken to it. They represented an imposition from without, by circumstances; they represented the imposition of extraneous values (such as national survival) which were not in themselves part of the system of liberties—or of constitutional rights—even though they could, in some cases, be coordinated with it. The case of restricting a liberty *by* a liberty seems less problematic than restricting a liberty in the interests of a nonliberty; and I have tried to suggest that the latter might be justified in Rawls's account, if it were done for the sake of preserving or extending liberty and if it had a plainly exceptive and interim character, a point to which I will return.

Finally, the restriction on majority rule did not compromise the principle that the basic liberties should be equal ones. But the interim restrictions in time of emergency might require some such compromise. Conscription that fell short of universal service or that assigned some persons to more dangerous wartime tasks than others would appear to be inherently unequal.[18] And so would more severe restrictions on the speech of some than on the speech of others.

Rawls does not hold, as we have already noted, that equality is never to be deviated from. Rather, Rawls's general claim is that the achievement of a more extensive or a more adequate system of constitutional rights could allow for such a deviation. But this claim is problematic if we consider that the

54

ultimate goal is not merely a more extensive system of liberties but, precisely, a more extensive system of *equal* liberties (or, to be exact, of *equal* rights).

We can suitably simplify the issue if we consider deviations from equality only in the case of essential or basic liberties (i.e., basic rights). It is unlikely, let us note at the outset, that any such deviation is going to be included in the very rule that defines the right. For we cannot expect a rule to be acceptable to everyone if it states a basic liberty or a freedom from injury while explicitly excluding some persons from full participation under that rule.[19] The reason for this is simply that if we leave aside some classes (children, aliens, prisoners, and possibly convicted felons) as likely to be subject, justifiably, to restriction, the remaining class of citizens would probably require equal status under the rule in order for the rule to be passable (and hence justified) from the perspective of the representative citizen—that is, from the perspective afforded by the original position or by its analogue, the constitutional convention.

Of course, it is not possible to make the liberties equal in de facto value to each and every person. People differ too much in fact. Thus, the actual value of free speech will probably be unequal between given individuals (for instance, between a successful newspaper columnist, a university lecturer, and a rather inarticulate, poorly educated, politically uninvolved day laborer). This is because the value (or worth) of a basic liberty to a given individual respresents the ability of that individual to make use of the liberty, which, in turn, involves such matters as his inclinations (including willingness) and the necessary resources available to him. And even after adjustments have been made to eliminate any element of unfairness (by providing for fair equality of opportunity, for example), significant differences would probably remain in the value of free speech to persons in each of these groups.[20] To assure equal value, we would have to create a homogeneous class of persons—alike, for example, in vocational interests—and place them in similar circumstances. Since Rawls assumes throughout that there will be significant differences among persons in the real social world, it is no part of his program to achieve equality in fact for the actual value of liberties to various persons. The doctrine of equal liberties operates at the level of the rule that defines the liberty; but as regards the actual value to a given individual of a specific liberty, the main constraint Rawls allows is the working of the principle—which he calls the difference principle—that the economic gain of any one class is not to be at the expense of the least-well-off members of society and thus that, as those who are better-off improve their prospects, the situation of the lowest income group is constantly improved as well.[21] This constraint is a rather rough-hewn one, admittedly, but it does reflect the sound judgment that there is a relation between a person's income level and that person's ability actually to use the resources necessary to carry out what he has the liberty to do.

The general line of argument here confirms the earlier contention that the perspective of the representative citizen affords no grounds, once we entertain the principle of universal interests (especially those highest-order interests of moral persons) and have due regard to the free and equal status of the parties in the original position, for discriminating among individuals in the coverage of the defining rule. Accordingly, when a basic liberty is restricted, it must be restricted equally for all. This seems to be the only conclusion that we can draw as a general principle or guideline.

The point of the original position is to select the basic liberties and noninjuries, those that are essential to the status of being rational moral persons, under the constraint that the selecting parties are themselves free and equal. It follows, then, that an admissible inequality could never amount on the part of some people to a deprivation, as a person's lot in life, of one or more of these liberties. Thus, no representative social position could be defined, in terms of its reasonable expectations, as one that lacked wholly, or for the most part, an essential liberty—even if that deprivation actually attached only to some people. Hence, there can be no place for slavery in such a scheme.

Let me add, parenthetically, that Rawls consistently argues that slavery violates the principle of equal basic liberties, with one notable exception. There he asks us to ''suppose that city-states that previously have not taken prisoners of war but have always put captives to death agree by treaty to hold prisoners as slaves instead.'' He goes on to comment that such an arrangement ''seems defensible as an advance on established institutions [and hence is less unjust, he says], if slaves are not treated too severely.''[22] I would remark in turn that, true, the arrangement may well mark an advance and it would, no doubt, be preferred—psychologically—by the actual participants; moreover, it is not inappropriate to balance a basic liberty (freedom from slavery) against a basic noninjury (avoidance of being put to death) in a given system of rights. Nonetheless, Rawls's account of this arrangement is not acceptable. The agreement to allow slavery violates the principle enunciated in the previous paragraph, for it does envisage an institutional arrangement for sacrificing a basic liberty *entirely,* as one's lot in life. And it does allow this to be done selectively, that is, unequally, and permanently (for some people).

Such a representative position would violate the principle of universal interests of persons. It does not follow, however, that an inequality which fell short of total deprivation of a basic liberty would be inadmissible, because intolerable, by those who would suffer the inequality.

Rawls himself provides an interesting example of such an inequality.[23] He allows that one of the political-participation liberties—as captured in the slogan "One person/one vote"—could conceivably be restricted in an inegalitarian way in the interests of promoting a greater system of *other* liberties. Rawls had in mind a system of plural voting such as existed in Britain well into this century (and as was advocated by J. S. Mill in his *Considerations on Representative Government*).[24] In this system some individuals might have two votes, others only one. Those who had two votes might vote both as residents within a district and as members of a university corporation. Since the privilege of dual voting was extended here only to university graduates, it might be alleged that this inequality led to more enlightened decision making and, hence, in a Rawlsian well-ordered society, would lead to an enhancement of the *other* basic liberties. Thus, inequality at this point might make for a greater system of liberties overall, for everyone.

But could it make for a greater system of *equal* basic liberties? The problem could be easily resolved if we had reason to believe that voting, though a liberty of sorts, was not a *basic* liberty, a liberty essential to the status of personhood. One could even argue, for example, that "significant political participation" was the basic liberty, not voting per se. Indeed, in the original position some such phrase might be preferred. But in the design of the basic structure of a society whose constitution embraced electoral procedures and representative government, it is likely that voting would be specified as one crucial aspect of "significant political participation" in such a society. So, voting is a basic liberty in a constitutional democracy, and Rawls concurs in this. How, then, could the presumptive argument in favor of *equal* basic liberties be defeated in the present case? More to the point, how could one assert that an allowed inequality in a given basic liberty could be the means to a greater system of equal basic liberties for all persons?[25]

We assume throughout that the business of the original position is to define a solid core of basic liberties. Its job is to state an ideal or standard of such liberties, thereby constituting an "Archimedean point" (the phrase is Rawls's) for all political thought and for the design of every constitution. It affirms the basic liberties that are to be achieved; it sets the ultimate goal. Now, if we grant, as very likely arguable within the context of the original position, that these liberties should be not only the same liberties but also equal liberties for all individuals, then we reach the idea that such liberties and noninjuries ought to be *equal* basic rights. Hence, the ideal is that the basic constitutional rights are equal rights. It would seem to follow then that voting, insofar as it is a constitutional or basic structure right, would have to be equal. Otherwise we have failed to reach the standard set in the original position, which calls for a constitutional embodiment, in the form of equal basic rights, of the various specified liberties and noninjuries. It is not clear, then, that Rawls could say both that voting was a basic right and that it could be unequal, or at least that it could be unequal on a permanent and foreseeable basis as a matter of constitutional writ.

The argument here seems to me conclusive. But, perhaps, Rawls's claim is susceptible of reinterpretation. One way of taking his notion of an allowed deviation from equality, in the case of basic rights, would be to suggest that an inequality *now* could be a means to a greater set of *equal* rights *in the future*. In the case at hand, this would translate into saying that at some point in the future, individuals would have the *same* vote and an otherwise greater system of equal basic liberties than was had initially (i.e., before or without the system of plural voting).

Such a reading, however, would be subject to the same sort of criticism that I raised earlier. If each of the basic liberties is essential to the status of personhood and if the rule defining the liberty is to be acceptable to *all* persons from the perspective of free and equal representative citizenship, then there will be no *rules*—no acceptable ones—that allow for the total deprivation of any liberty (e.g., slavery) or that allow for discrimination among classes of persons (but for a few well-accredited exceptions). Hence, a principle of unequal voting would not be encoded in the *rule* developed in the original position or in the constitutional convention.

Indeed, in his later writings, Rawls emphasizes strongly that there should be not merely a formal equality (i.e., equality under the constituting and operative rules) in the political-participation liberties but, more especially, an *equal worth* or value of these liberties for all citizens. Rawls calls this requirement—in which the political-participation liberties are singled out—the requirement of "the fair value of the political liberties."[26] He had in mind here such familiar liberties as the universal franchise, one person/one vote, competitive and regular elections, relative equality of opportunity for office holding, and representative government in the context of these other liberties; and he meant that such liberties should be equal in fact, or as nearly equal as possible, for each voter. Accordingly, Rawls advocated, as devices to this end, measures such as limits on campaign spending by individuals, governmental financing of elections, and the public subsidy or ready and inexpensive availability of air time to candidates and political parties.[27]

Now, one might wonder why Rawls was willing to make an exception, in the case of the political-participation liberties, to his frequently affirmed contention that the basic liberties need be only formally equal in a well-ordered society. Among his reasons are the claim that the activity of legislation (actual laws made by actual legislatures) is of crucial importance in the application of the two principles in a society and the claim that wealth and preferred position can, in and of themselves, give disproportionate advantage to a comparative minority of citizens, especially in a situation where the means of public communication (newsprint, television, widespread travel) constitute a "limited space" which is open only to a few or only at considerable cost. Thus, without "fair value of the political liberties," the legislative stage would lack essential continuity with the earlier stages (the original position and the just constitution) and could not be counted on, as a matter of course, to protect, let alone to elaborate, the fundamental interests of the representative citizen. Nor would such a deficient legislative environment give rise to a *fair* political process—one in which individual persons had roughly equal opportunity to help determine the final legislative results (or to monitor the carrying out of these results by judges and administrators). Legislation that occurred in the absence of fair value of the political liberties would inevitably lead to distortions that gave undue advantage to special interests, interests indifferent to the public interest—to the universal interests of the representative citizen—and even hurtful of particular interests of some citizens. And these defects would be augmented, cemented and amplified, when the coercive powers of the state were put at the disposal of the economically well-off citizens in the service of their narrower interests.[28]

These are the reasons that Rawls had for thinking that the political-participation liberties constituted a special case among the basic liberties—in that more than mere formal or operative-rule equality was called for. Chief among these reasons, as I've tried to make clear, is the importance of legislative action for the application of the two principles, in particular the constitutional rights, in the ongoing life of a society—not only in the laws that are passed but also in the background institutions (i.e., governmental agencies) which are installed to embody and assure justice in that society. And this importance suggests as well why Rawls thought the fair value of the political-participation liberties had to be assured directly, by political measures, and not indirectly, through the operation of the second principle alone (because that principle, simply inasmuch as it did not rule out appreciable differences in wealth, did not provide the requisite "value" to these liberties).

Rawls's strong emphasis on the equal worth of political liberties serves to underscore the essentially political character of a well-ordered society (or at least of its basic structure) in his theory. Here his idea of the fair value of the political liberties requires these liberties to be equal not merely formally (by reference to equal rules) but also in fact. And we have explicit support from Rawls's texts for the treatment, in the present chapter, of voting as a basic liberty,[29] and, more generally, for the fundamental thesis of this chapter that the *rules* that define the basic liberties would not allow for any unequal basic rights for persons in a given society.[30]

In enunciating this fundamental thesis, we have not, however, ruled out all justifiable toleration of inequality in basic rights. Legislative and judicial exceptions are still possible. Some such discrimination as could be found, for example, in plural voting might justifiably be allowed, as an *exception* to the basic rule, if the discrimination extended the system of other equal basic liberties and if in fact the discrimination was itself ultimately replaced by a system of equal voting.

We say *ultimately,* but when is that? Is it that notorious Keynesian "long run, in which we shall all be dead"? I suppose, rather, it would have to be within the average life span of the participants. One generation cannot sacrifice the well-being of other generations either to itself or to some distant future goal. People can decide *now* to sacrifice for their *own* future good, but they cannot justifiably make that decision for others, that they will sacrifice their well-being for *someone else's* future good. Nor would it be rational for anyone to sacrifice his own or another's standing under a rule specifying an equal basic liberty for all persons in order to advance the well-being of yet others under this and similar basic liberty rules. If people understand correctly that something is a basic right, then equality is required. And the equality presumed there can be sacrificed only on an interim basis, to be regained within a lifetime, and only for a reason that would satisfy the perspective of equal citizenship—that it be for the sake of a more extensive or a more secure system of equal basic liberties for all persons in the society.

The main rationale—the root idea—behind these conclusions is that basic rights represent universal interests, that the rights are those of persons with identical highest-order interests, and that persons are or would be free and equal parties in a deliberative process of the sort described in the original position model. Hence, there are important constraints placed on the idea of deviating from equality in the case of any given basic liberty. (1) The deviation is not encoded—except for those concerning certain agreed-upon groups such as children or prisoners—within the original position or constitutional rule that defines the liberty; rather, it is a justified exception to that rule, legislatively enacted or judicially ratified, that occurs under the general principle that basic rights can be restricted only by basic rights so as to increase the overall system of equal basic rights. (2) The deviation is short-term. The inequality that is allowed does not affect the lot in life of the representative citizen (or any class of representative citizens). For the inequality is rectified within the life span of the representative citizen, or at least that is the reasonable intention behind the deviation, with the result that all persons are better-off with respect to equal basic rights. No one, no one class, is sacrificed in this regard. (3) The inequality, given these other constraints, would be acceptable to those who suffered it or, better, to anyone who took the perspective of representative citizenship.[31] Anything short of these constraints would violate the root idea.

The tendency of the doctrine of basic rights is towards equality. This tendency, never justifiably thwarted, can be justifiably diverted only on an exceptive and short-term basis and only for the sake of preserving or expanding the system of equal basic rights itself.

And just as exceptions to equality had to meet these constraints, so those interim restrictions on basic liberties that applied equally to all would have to meet them as well. The reasoning that supports the denial of inequality in the case of basic rights also supports the denial of restriction, on grounds extraneous to liberty, of those rights. Thus, a restriction on freedom of speech that applied equally to all in time of war or a program of universal conscription for wartime service would have to meet these same constraints. (1) The restriction is not encoded into the rule that defines the right except as an emergency and interim feature; for otherwise it would cease to be a deviation from the rule, and the rule itself would become, simply, a more restrictive general rule. Rather, the restriction—even when legislatively enacted—is regarded as an exception, as a justifiable ad hoc constriction, to a rule that otherwise does not include that restriction in the scope of the liberty or in its defining content and would not tolerate it there as a permanent feature. (2) The restriction is short-term, for otherwise it would count as a lifelong restriction on some (all those citizens alive in a certain period) in the interests of others (other citizens alive at some future date). Even if the restriction was willingly undertaken, it could not justifiably be undertaken, as rational, within the perspective afforded by the original position. (3) The restriction—already constrained as in (1) and (2)—would require the approval of those who are restricted, at least insofar as they occupied the standpoint of representative citizens, to the end that the restriction on basic liberties (even when done equally) serves to enlarge or, if need be, to preserve the system of equal basic rights.

Rawls's general principle, then, is that basic liberties, as part of a system of equal rights, can be restricted on a standing and regular basis—that is, permanently—only by basic liberties, only by the other elements in the system of constitutional rights. And any constitutional right, when so restricted, must remain an *equal* basic right. This general principle together with the constraints, as specified above, afford a unified perspective on the allowable restriction of equal basic rights. For the constraints govern the apparent exceptions to the general principle: covering both those that restrict equally (but on a principle extraneous to liberty) and those that deviate from equality. In effect, then, the general principle and the constraints spell out the preferred meaning of the motto that liberty is to be restricted by liberty and only for the sake of liberty.[32]

At this point, now that we have sketched in the idea of equal basic liberties (and noninjuries) as constitutional rights, we are ready to turn to other main themes in Rawls's theory of justice. Specifically, to his discussion of fair equality of opportunity, the difference principle, and then the priority of liberty.

# • 4 •

# FAIR EQUALITY OF OPPORTUNITY

Rawls's first principle of justice establishes equality; it does so with respect to one of the social primary goods, basic liberties (and noninjuries). The second principle establishes inequality; in so doing, it ranges over the *other* primary goods: opportunities, income and wealth, positions or powers (i.e., offices, social and economic roles, skills or vocations).[1] For simplicity we will view positions here largely in terms of the income and wealth that they generate (though this is, of course, a considerable oversimplification). The second principle says that inequality in positions (and the income and wealth that derive from them) is justifiable if two stipulations are met: (a) the positions are open to all under conditions of equality of opportunity and (b) the difference principle is satisfied.

In this chapter, I turn to the first of these stipulations, equality of opportunity; in the next, I will take up the second. I will be concerned throughout the present chapter to identify the basic structure rights that emerge in this account of equal opportunity.

## 1. *Establishing Inequality as Just*

Let us begin with what Rawls calls the general conception of justice. The general conception asserts that "all social values—liberty and opportunity, income and wealth, and the bases of self-respect—are to be distributed equally unless an unequal distribution of any, or all, of these values is to everyone's advantage." Or alternatively, "unless an unequal distribution . . . is to the advantage of the least favored."[2]

One plausible way to intrepret the "general conception" is to say that inequality in a primary good is acceptable only if it improves the situation of everyone (including the least advantaged) with respect to that particular good. Thus, liberty can be unequal if those who suffer inequality are better off than they were *initially* with respect to liberty; likewise, income and wealth can be unequal if those who suffer the inequality are better off than they were initially with respect to income and wealth.[3] And so on. What is interesting about this reading is that it covers the main relevant cases (it covers Rawls's own interpretation of each of his two principles of justice) while making no concession to the idea of "trade offs" between one kind of primary good and another. And it seems to provide a straightforward, indeed a literal, interpretation of Rawls's actual statement(s) of the general conception of justice.

This version of the general conception is concerned primarily with the issue of deviation from equality. Such deviation is allowed, within a single primary good (e.g., liberty or income), only if the deviation makes available a greater amount of that very same good to each and all. Similarly, restrictions other than those which deviate from equality would be allowed, within a single primary good, only if the restriction makes a greater amount of that good available for everyone. There is, in either case here, no consideration whatsoever of calculations that "cross over" from one species of primary good to another—that measure and allow, for example, decreases in the amount of liberty against increases in the amount of income and wealth.[4]

I do not want, however, to get involved in a lengthy discussion of whether this interpretation of the general conception is a better interpretation than the conventional one, which does allow for "trade-offs." For the problem is that the role of the general conception in Rawls's theory is never clear. There are, for example, no direct arguments for it in Rawls's book or in his later writings, and in the latter, even mention of it has diminished appreciably.[5] Nonetheless, the general conception has remained one of the staples, a fixed point, in the scholarly and philosophical interpretation of Rawls. So we need to provide some account of its role, especially since it would appear to figure crucially in the issue that we are currently addressing—the establishment for Rawls of certain inequalities as just.

The most important thing to note is that the arguments Rawls does develop are for the two principles of justice, either as a set or individually. The general conception seems to relate to these principles, once they are established, in the following way: it summarizes what they have in common; it shows that they share a similar orientation and, hence, can be regarded as principles focused on the same theme; in particular, it indicates the point of the second principle of justice. The relation is that of the general to the special case. Thus, Rawls refers to his two principles as a special conception of justice, that is, a special case of the general conception.[6]

But it doesn't follow from this that the general conception has any prior or independent standing *as a principle of justice.* It is general only in the sense that it sums up, in a single conception, what has been independently established, on other grounds, as just.

Consider an analogous case. One establishes through inspection of species (including our own) that mammals are sexual beings, that they reproduce through sexual contacts, and that such sexual congress is always between individuals of two distinct genders. Thus, we have a general conception of mammalian sexuality and can correctly regard human reproductive sexuality as a special case of that. But it would be senseless to *explain* human sexuality by treating it simply as a special case of the general conception. Similarly, we cannot *justify* inequality in the positions that generate wealth and income simply by reference to the general conception of justice, for that conception already presupposes such inequalities to be just on the basis of independent arguments. Hence, the general conception as a substantive conception of justice has no standing outside or apart from these arguments and can justify *nothing* on its own.

Again, we can never know from the general conception what trade-offs between species of primary goods are to be allowed. We would need, rather, an independent account of the priorities that hold between the primary goods, and it is this that would answer the question of trade-offs. Such an account would be wholly determinative; there is nothing that the general conception could add to it; and without such an account, the general conception would be wholly inert—it could justify nothing on its own. All that the general conception of justice could do is to register in a perspicuous general statement, if feasible, the whole list of independently established priorities. (Such a statement would be roughly analogous to the earlier one about mammalian sexuality.)

At most, then, the general conception can be said to orient these independent patterns of reasoning by indicating, in a general way, the path by which such inequality can actually be established. Understood in this way, the general conception is actually a principle of reasoning and not a substantive conception of justice at all. It asserts that a preference for equality would be irrational if it were believed that inequality in a particular primary good would make more of that good available for each and everyone.[7]

If my interpretation is correct, then the enormous literature about when the "special" conception comes into play in human history, taking over from the "general" conception, or about what trade-offs are allowed by the general conception, represents a waste of energy. For inequality in positions—or for that matter, trade-offs between primary goods—cannot be justified by reference to the general conception (inasmuch as the latter always waits on the issue, as determined on other grounds).[8]

Thus, we would need to turn our attention to the direct arguments for any such inequality. The main considerations in favor of inequalities in wealth and position seem to be these. (a) Such inequalities are probably inevitable. In any case, they are useful: (b) they have an incentive function. They also help (c) to cover the costs of training and education or (d) to attract people to places where they are needed. (e) Those inequalities that we would regard as advantages probably conduce to entrepreneurial enterprise and to effective management. All in all, then, such inequalities seem to lead to greater economic efficiency and (f) to make for a higher level—both qualitatively and quantitively—of productivity in goods and services.[9] Just as we want liberties to be as extensive as possible, so we want wealth and income to be, as long as this is consistent with those principles that it would be reasonable to agree to in the original position.

It seems that a higher aggregate of wealth overall should be preferred when it translates as a higher index of wealth and income for the representative persons at various income levels, say, by quartiles. It is reasonable, then, to agree to a principle that specifies and establishes inequalities in cases where inequality is beneficial all around.[10] We can tolerate inequality in matters of wealth, income, and position; and where a greater total of wealth is distributed to the advantage of each and all, such inequality is reasonable.

But is this just? Presumably, it would be if certain stipulations were added. The exact point at issue, then, becomes which ones to add as the main ones.

We could imagine the following characteristic line of reasoning. All the parties to the deliberation about justice might agree to the point about the reasonableness of preferring a higher index of wealth and income for representative persons at the various income levels. (Here they follow the line of reasoning that I earlier associated with the general conception of justice.) But each realizes that inequalities in position and attendant wealth will be involved. No one wishes to accept an inferior position for himself, even though it might prove to be for the common good in a particular society. For each person reasons that by so doing, he would be worse off in those circumstances than he would be if he had an average or a superior position in that society. Each sees, then, that it would be unfair for anyone to have to take or be forced to take an inferior position as his lot in life. So, granting that inequality in positions is both inevitable and useful, each would want those positions to be open to all on some principle of equitable competition or fair play. Moreover, each would realize that unless some such principle were instituted, then the distribution of positions might not in fact be productive of the benefit that was sought.[11] That is, the distribution might not achieve a greater aggregate of wealth available socially. The parties do not want to act in an unreasonable or indefensible way. Therefore, they concur in the stipulation that the wealth-generating positions be open to all on some reasonable principle of equality of opportunity. So the establishment, as just, of inequality in such positions requires this stipulation.

## 2. *Opportunities*

We speak here of *reasonable* equality of opportunity, but the notion is quite indeterminate. We will require additional argument to fix the idea of equality of opportunity more firmly in our view and to show that equality of opportunity, so understood, is reasonable. But before we do this we will need to do some preliminary work to determine what opportunities Rawls had in mind when he spoke of equality in opportunities.

Perhaps the clearest idea of what he intended can be gleaned from the canonical lists of primary goods in his later writings. There we find reference to "freedom of movement and free choice of occupation against a backdrop of diverse opportunities."[12]

The opportunities mentioned here are economic opportunities: opportunities to train for positions, opportunities to seek and to hold positions—where positions are understood, largely, as economic offices or vocations that generate income and wealth. Accordingly, we exclude some opportunities, or ways in which opportunities are characterized, from consideration. People speak of recreational opportunities ("If I live in Boulder, then I'll be able to ski more in winter") or of educational or spiritual ones ("If I read this book or spend time with this mentor or go on this pilgrimage, then I'll be a better person"). Such things are not unimportant, but unless they have fairly direct or forseeable economic impact (in one's prospects for, or performance in, an economic office), they are not under scrutiny here. They are not the sort of opportunities that Rawls had in mind when he stipulated of inequality in positions that these positions should be open to all under reasonable conditions of equality of opportunity.

Thus, the liberties mentioned in connection with these opportunities are themselves taken as having an economic focus. Free choice of occupation obviously has such a character. Freedom of movement, then, would have to be given an appropriate interpretation. We do not mean all movement but only that which is connected with such things as training for, finding, and performing a job or engaging in commerce or, perhaps, shifting resources from one productive use to another.[13]

We also exclude from view the freedom of movement involved in visiting holy shrines or art museums, petitioning at the seat of government, or emigrating from one state to another (where that emigration is, for the most part, politically motivated).[14] These things are not negligible; indeed, many

67

of them would be covered—more or less indirectly—under the basic liberties of the first principle. But they lack the requisite economic focus; so they are excluded from consideration under the second principle of justice, the principle that concerns inequalities in the positions that generate income and wealth, stipulating that such positions be open to all on terms of equality of opportunity.

The liberties that are mentioned by Rawls in connection with economic opportunity—freedom of movement and free choice of occupation—are, of course, liberties; hence, they are the right sort of thing to go under the first principle. But they are *functionally* different from the basic liberties enshrined there, for they are fundamentally oriented, unlike liberty of conscience or freedom of political speech and assembly, toward the economic dimension. Hence, they come more readily under the second principle and the restrictions appropriate to it than under the first principle.[15]

There are, of course, other liberties that Rawls mentions in the same family with the economic liberties already named. Most conspicuously, there is that part of the freedom to advertise which is concerned with notices about jobs or prices or about features of products and services for sale.[16] And there is the freedom involved in allowing "the decisions of households to regulate the items to be produced for private purposes."[17]

Some of the liberties that we have examined, such as the last one named in the previous paragraph or the freedom to move resources from one productive use to another, seem to be closely associated with a particular economic scheme (with a market economy or with capitalist ownership). Now, Rawls does presume some such scheme (if only for purposes of illustration) in his theory of justice; he assumes, as he calls it, a "property-owning democracy."[18] But it seems inappropriate to include among the social primary goods those which have a definite institutional character. At least we should avoid giving prominence to such goods independently of some account of the economic constitution of the society in which they figure.[19] Excluding or bracketing these would, of course, still leave many economic liberties as primary goods. And though we are not in any position to put these on a list analogous to the list of basic liberties in the first principle, we can certainly take some of the ones mentioned in this section as typical and, hence, as representative of those on any such list. Thus we could generate, for purposes of illustration, a short list: freedom of movement, free choice of occupation, freedom of information about jobs and prices. And we can treat these—and other liberties like them—as instances of those economic opportunities to which Rawls meant the stipulation of equality of opportunity to attach.

The question I want to ask now is whether the liberties on this list can count as rights. I am not asking whether the named liberties are basic liberties, for this raises a different issue (the issue of what is essential to moral personhood, the issue of whether a given liberty or noninjury figures among the universal and fundamental interests of the representative citizen).[20] I am asking simply whether these economic liberties are rights.

For Rawls, a right is an individual's legitimate expectation as to what he would receive in a just institutional distribution of social primary goods, where justice is determined by the two principles. Thus, the kinds of things that could be rights are the primary goods—liberties, opportunities, and so on. A particular right, then, must pertain to a particular primary good, such as liberty of speech. And it is characteristic of any right to a particular primary good, in order for it to be a legitimate expectation, that it specify with respect to that good a central content which can be *individuated* (parceled out equally to the individuals within a certain class) in some *determinate* amount or to some determinate degree, under publicly recognized rules, and that it *guarantee* this distribution to each and every member of that class. Indeed, it is primarily this distributive feature and the fact of a guarantee that distinguishes Rawls's position on justice from the utilitarian one and that creates a natural affinity between his account of justice, on the one hand, and basic rights, on the other.

Now, just as the basic liberties—as liberties—can be individuated to some determinate (and equal) degree and guaranteed, so can the economic liberties. Of course the principal line of reasoning in support of this scheme of distribution will differ from the one main case to the other: for (1) the fundamental liberties and noninjuries of the first principle are supported by the argument from moral personhood, while (2) the economic liberties of the second principle will be supported by the argument for reasonable equality of opportunity offered earlier in this chapter. But simply because the main lines of argument differ, we can sidestep the question of whether these economic liberties are *basic* liberties. For regardless of whether or not they are, we must conclude that they are rights.

Indeed, they are basic structure rights. For the argument supporting the relevant specification, determinate and equal individuation, and authorization for protected status of these liberties can be developed in the original position, and the conclusion can be reached there that guarantees to them should be built into the economic constitution of any just society. Thus, we can expand our list of constitutional or basic structure rights to include both the fundamental liberties and noninjuries of the first principle and the economic liberties of the second.

But what about the *other* opportunities—the "backdrop of diverse opportunities"—that Rawls means to include among the social primary goods? Are there rights to these, individually or as a group? We cannot say now. For the notion of a "backdrop" of such opportunites is too vague to bear the conceptual pressure introduced with the idea of rights. In order to answer this question and to further elaborate the notion of a reasonable equality of opportunity, we will need to specify the concept of equal opportunity more precisely and to develop additional arguments, as appropriate.

Accordingly, we turn to consider three interpretations of equality of opportunity, provided by Rawls, and try to determine, on the balance of reasons, which is best.


## 3. *Three Interpretations of Equal Opportunity*

Suppose a situation in which people of diverse talents, backgrounds, and so on live together in a relatively fluid social setting. They are free to get on with their projects, subject only to limitations imposed by their basic natural endowments or by their social circumstances. In particular, they are unhampered by any legal or institutional barriers, restricting one class or a kind of individual, that would prevent them from exercising their talents or seizing opportunities up to the limit of their own abilities. The economic liberties, of course, hold good in the society in question. We would have here, then, a situation of "perfect liberty" (in Adam Smith's phrase), a sort of "free market" in opportunities.

What result could we expect in such a market? The ultimate distribution of income, wealth, and position would probably reflect, more or less, the initial distribution of natural abilities and social advantages (one's family, one's social class) of the various individuals involved. If we assume people to be basically rational, then the ideal limiting case of any such arrangement would be given in the economist's notion of efficiency—a state of affairs in which resources are so allocated that no one's condition can be further improved unless someone else's (at least one other person's) is worsened.

One could say in defense of any such arrangement: people aren't equal; the final results shouldn't be equal for them either. It's a fair race if people line up at the same starting line and have an unfettered crack at the same range of opportunities. The best ones will win out.

Here we have the old nineteenth-century ideal of "careers open to talents."[21] Two distinct themes are involved in it. One is that reasonable equality of opportunity is achieved when there are no official or rule-book restrictions on the taking of opportunities. The other is that, on principle, nothing should be done to disturb the pattern, whatever it might be, that results from the free market in opportunities. The "correct" final arrangement is one that results from the actual use of aptitudes and talents by individual persons under conditions of *formal* equality of opportunity. This account, then, provides one interpretation of reasonable equality of opportunity. It is called by Rawls "the system of natural liberty." Or it could be called, in honor of Adam Smith, the Smithian system of liberty.[22]

Would such a system appeal to persons in a deliberative discussion on the order of the one in the original position model? I think not, because they would probably reason as follows. The system of natural liberty gives too much weight to one's social connections and to one's established position. These are things that one is born into as a member of a certain family or of a certain class. When these things are included in the picture and are allowed to give initial advantage or disadvantage, it's not surprising that people end up unequally. We fool ourselves if we think that *only* talent and ability account for the resultant inequality; factors such as class or family are also involved, though these are largely irrelevant to one's basic abilities. Of course, such social factors do help to develop (or to retard) one's fundamental aptitudes and talents. But there often comes a point at which the social factors will go beyond helping a talent develop and will simply give it undue advantage, over what similar talents can command. Or even worse, they actually hurt the development of aptitude and can sometimes destroy its exercise altogether. One's external circumstances, the accident of birth into a particular family or class, should not be determinative of one's success in life or of one's development and use of talents to the degree that is allowed in the system of natural liberty. Moreover, a society that operates on the principles of such a system would deprive itself of untold assets by letting social circumstances have unimpeded sway; for the very best people would not be rising to the top. Thus, the system of natural liberty is sometimes bad for individual persons in it and always bad for society as a whole. It would be unreasonable, from the perspective provided by the original position, to opt for such a system if another system could correct this most obvious defect.

Now, social circumstance and expressed aptitude are intertwined; there's no way to untangle the lines entirely. Moreover, whatever is done about social circumstances will also affect the development and use of one's natural endowment. Nonetheless, something can be done to reduce the difference in advantage that accrues to individual persons simply in respect of these social contingencies. For example, taxation on inherited wealth or the provision of public education for all at no special cost to the individual or to his family would be effective toward such an end.[23] The implicit ideal here is that *social* advantages (or disadvantages) should be "cut" or mitigated up to the point that people of roughly equal *natural* ability and motivation have roughly equal opportunities and can reasonably expect, over the course of a lifetime, to hold a roughly equivalent range of positions (jobs, roles, etc.) and to have roughly the same income and wealth, as attached to these positions.[24]

Such an ideal would commend itself to the persons in the deliberative situation. It remedies the obvious defect in the system of natural liberties. And since these persons are symmetrically situated towards one another (behind the veil of ignorance) and since no one is allowed to shape things so as to favour his own peculiar social circumstances or their effect on his development and use of aptitudes, each person so constrained would prefer that the advantages and disadvantages accruing from social contingencies be mitigated in the way indicated. Through such mitigation, using the sorts of measures suggested above, a society—and the individuals in it—would be able to conform to the recommended ideal.

Thus, the second proposal for reasonable equality of opportunity differs from the first (the "careers open to talents") in that it attempts to make for a *fair* equality of opportunity by going beyond the mere formal equality of the system of natural liberty, by rearranging the social contingencies so as to mitigate the undue advantage or disadvantage that accrues to individuals from social circumstances. But beyond this, the second proposal sticks with the basic laissez-faire approach of the original liberty system. It reasons that once this basic rearrangement is achieved, respecting the social contingencies that play on one's formative years and that can continue to give undue advantage even after that, then the resulting distribution of positions (and income and wealth) is the correct one—for every individual and for the society—and should not be disturbed. Rawls calls this second proposal the "liberal interpretation" of reasonable equality of opportunity.[25]

Even so, it could be contended, the individual's natural endowment (with whatever stimulation or encouragement it gets from social circumstances) still has too much sway. Why is it fair, one asks, to factor out and then attempt to reduce the gap between people as regards their social circumstances (and the undue advantage/disadvantage this brings) but to ignore such a gap in the case of their *natural* endowments? For the two sets of factors—one's social circumstances and one's natural endowment—seem to be equally "arbitrary from the moral point of view."[26]

It is, I would add, relatively difficult to work directly on the natural endowment of individuals. Few examples of direct rearrangement come to mind, and these are highly controversial, such as benign procedures of genetic engineering that are designed to eliminate subsequent birth or health defects. The more promising strategy is to work *indirectly* on natural endowment, usually through rearranging those social circumstances that are known to influence that endowment. Thus, for example, prenatal care might be utilized or general measures that provide for public health and a safe environment and that would dramatically cut the incidence of childhood diseases and other forms of disablement.

The point of these measures, whether direct or indirect, is not merely to rearrange the natural endowment itself. Rather, the point is to reduce the gap in advantages that accrue to individuals as a result of differences in their natural make-up—their genetic endowment, the bodily constitution that they are born with, their general health, and the intelligence, personality, and imagination that are developed during the formative years of each of them.[27]

Let me add with respect to these matters (in particular, the latter grouping—intelligence, etc.) that Rawls is not suggesting any sharp separation of the social from the natural factors. He seems, rather, to be suggesting merely that the factors identified—genetic endowment, initial bodily constitution, and overall health—have some influence on one's talents and abilities and on one's standing in life: one's vocation, one's prospects for income, one's long-term economic well-being. He seems, however, to be committed to no particular view as to the relative proportion of influence that holds between the social and the natural.

Rawls's argument does suggest, though, that traits such as intelligence, imagination, or certain features of personality or character may be directly traceable, to a degree, to genetic endowment or to bodily constitution. In a way this doesn't seem controversial. The fact that people—human beings as a biological species—are intelligent, surely, has something to do with genetic endowment. Moreover, when individuals are intellectually retarded, this often has to do with the prenatal health of mother or child, with accidents before birth or during it, or with environmental factors. It is also possible that genetic factors could have a differential effect on individual persons. But none of this, even if true, would lead us to draw any conclusion about differences in intelligence, for example, or courage between races or between the sexes. Rawls's argument supposes that there are no such differences of any significance. His argument recognizes, moreover, that the usefulness of a particular natural talent is a relative thing, depending not only on the incidence of that particular talent (or complementary talents) among one's fellows but also on one's social setting. (Thus, mathematical ability of a high order probably would be more useful in a society that has computers than in a society where counting does not even exist.)

The important point here, when all this has been said, remains that it is extremely difficult, often impossible, for a society directly to do much, if anything, about the actual natural endowment of the individuals in it. The prospects for dealing with social contingencies, sometimes indirectly affecting natural endowment in the process, are somewhat better. And sometimes it is not the attempt to influence natural endowment that is contemplated but, rather, measures to deal with the gap in advantage between individuals once the effect of natural endowment has settled in. Thus, the ready access of handicapped persons to buildings and places of business and their ability to move about comparatively easily might be facilitated by laws and ordinances affecting building design, street construction, and so on.[28]

Thus, we conclude that something can be done about natural endowment, often indirectly and sometimes after the fact. But we must also admit that, using such measures, we cannot achieve an absolute equality of opportunity. Or for that matter, even come close—where the issue is one of natural endowment.

Nor is it clear that we would want to achieve such a goal, of absolute equality of opportunity. For it would be foolish and self-defeating to nullify or remove the differences of people in respect of natural endowment and social circumstance (and there probably is no other way to reduce to zero the gap in resultant advantages short of making people absolutely alike, were that possible). Human diversity is desirable in any society, and to have such diversity will almost certainly require this very unlikeness of natural endowment and of social circumstances in the development and use of aptitudes which, when realized, makes people different and, in the end, unequal.[29]

Hence, we settle for doing what we can, by *reducing* the inequality in advantages among people that accrue to individuals from the two sources. But simply because we can achieve only a passable equality of opportunity with measures that are acceptably available (or foreseeably available), some further remedial steps are required to deal with the resultant inequality that remains, or ensues. The presumption here is that the gap can be further counteracted by seeing to it that the difference in realized aptitudes between persons is not allowed to work to the further disadvantage or harm of those individuals who were initially disadvantaged by the two main sources—namely, by one's natural endowment and by the social circumstances that one is born into.

If this is so, then the laissez-faire approach that is common to liberalism and to the system of natural liberties must be abandoned. It is necessary, given our inability to remove the inequality afforded by the initial sources of advantage and disadvantage, to disturb the results that ensue. They are not to be treated as final. So, neither mere formal equality of opportunity nor fair equality, when construed narrowly as by liberalism, is enough. Rather, fair equality of opportunity, conceived more generously, must be combined with some non-laissez-faire principle to achieve the fullest possible measure of reasonable equality of opportunity.

The third interpretation of reasonable equality of opportunities differs, then, from the second or liberal interpretation in two important respects. First, it recognizes a broader set of opportunities over which fair equality is to be ranged by requiring consideration of important differences in *both* social starting points and natural endowments. And second, it replaces an approach that lets the results lie, after a conscientious effort has been made to "cut" the gap in initial advantage, with a non-laissez-faire approach that further sorts these results. Rawls calls this third approach the "democratic interpretation" of the notion of equal opportunity. It is the approach he favors.[30]

I have no desire to maintain suspense. The recommended non-laissez-faire approach is, of course, the operation of the difference principle. Thus,

Rawls says, "The acknowledgment of the difference principle redefines the grounds for social inequalities as conceived in the system of liberal equality."[31] And I will characterize the difference principle rather narrowly here (along the lines found in section one and set forth in the principle of reasoning associated with the general conceptions of justice) as requiring merely that everyone is to be made better off than he would have been—in respect of the income and wealth that attach to positions—by the inequality that exists in such positions.

In sum, just as liberal equality builds on and incorporates the notion of formal equality of opportunity, so democratic equality builds, in turn, on both the liberal conception and the Smithian one. The democratic interpretation combines fair equality of opportunity—conceived now as the taking of remedial steps, conscientiously, to reduce the *initial* inequality in advantages accruing to individuals from two main sources—with the difference principle (the principle of everyone's benefit), which further reduces the *resultant* inequality between them. The object of this two-step procedure is to minimize the gap between persons by taking account of both starting points and end results.

Thus, the democratic interpretation provides a natural account of the second principle of justice (the principle that is concerned with inequalities in social and economic position and attendant inequalities in income and wealth). It makes clear that it is a principle with two parts, that the parts are connected and make a coherent whole, and that one part, fair equality of opportunity, has priority over the other, the difference principle. For the difference principle appears in the democratic interpretation primarily as a device necessary to *complement* the idea of fair equality. It helps to do what fair equality of opportunity, even when conscientiously applied, cannot do by itself. These two components, then, make for a reasonable equality of opportunity, and in so doing they make the gap in initial advantages and the ultimate inequality in positions (and what results from that inequality) acceptable from the perspective of justice.

The difference principle does not, of course, have to be linked with fair equality of opportunity. We could imagine a situation in which natural endowment and initial social circumstance and the results that ensued were left untouched except by the operation of that principle.[32] But it would be considerably less effective and less fair than the procedure that Rawls prefers.

So, although the two main elements of the second principle are connected in the way that I have indicated, each is a distinct element. In order to preserve this distinctness and to avoid any confusion, I will characterize fair equality of opportunity as the conscientious striving to take feasible remedial steps *other than the operation of the difference principle* to reduce the gap in natural and social advantages among individuals.[33]

75

I will turn next to the main argument and set of considerations that would induce people in the original position to adopt the democratic interpretation of the second principle of justice.

### 4. *Collective Asset*

The main argument begins with the fact that people have different natural endowments and are born into and grow up in different social circumstances. No one can be said to be responsible for—hence, to deserve—these factors in his own case.[34] Nonetheless, such factors powerfully affect a person's life prospects, advantageously for some and disadvantageously for others. And these particular results cannot be said to be deserved either. But what can be done?

Rawls says:

> The natural distribution [of talents] is neither just nor unjust; nor is it unjust that men are born into society at some particular position. These are simply natural facts. What is just and unjust is the way that institutions deal with these facts. . . . The basic structure of [some] societies incorporates the arbitrariness found in nature. But there is no necessity for men to resign themselves to these contingencies. The social system is not an unchangeable order beyond human control but a pattern of human action. In justice as fairness men agree to share one another's fate. In designing institutions they undertake to avail themselves of the accidents of nature and social circumstance only when doing so is for the common benefit.[35]

Since these initial differences are both morally arbitrary and undeserved on the part of the individual involved, each person could agree that the initial social circumstances and the natural endowment of each can and should be developed to benefit everyone. This might not be a view that we could expect individuals to take in the everyday world, but it is a view that it would be reasonable to take in what Rawls calls the "original position." The original position is a conjectured arena for discussion and for making decisions about principles of justice in which all individuals, by hypothesis, bracket off a vast number of prejudicial facts, pertaining to themselves and others, including, in particular, such things as their natural endowments and actual social circumstances.[36]

In short, society can be arranged (and should be, from the perspective of the original position) so that no representative individual is hurt and none unduly helped by his own "luck" in the natural "lottery" (as measured by his initial draw of natural endowment and social circumstances). Rather, all are to use their natural assets and to exploit their social circumstances not merely for their own advantage but also for the good of everyone.[37] Rawls's point, then, is that it is reasonable in the original position for persons to regard "the distribution of natural abilities as a collective asset" and to constitute society accordingly, such that "each person can participate in the total sum of the realized natural assets of the others."[38]

Here I think it is important to note briefly three crucial points. First, it is the *distribution* of natural talents, and not the talents per se, that is said to be the collective asset. Thus, there is no claim to the effect that the talents of individual persons (or their natural endowments and bodily parts) literally belong to society as a whole. The point, rather, is that the differences among persons—the sheer variety of talents and the differences in level of achievement for a given talent—should constitute common good fortune, to be used to mutual advantage. Second, in saying this, we are not describing a natural fact but, rather, affirming as reasonable an agreement to regard the distribution of talents as a collective asset. We thus occupy a normative perspective here. Or to be precise, in the original position the collective asset idea is a normative attitude that attends and follows upon prior considerations of justice. This brings us to our third main point.

People do not first hit upon the idea of collective asset and then argue from there to fair equality of opportunity. Rather, they first establish the requirement of a reasonable equality of opportunity, and then the collective asset idea arises from reflection on that. If one accepts fair equality, one also accepts collective asset. The idea of collective asset is the Rawlsian solution to the problem posed by differential starting points and by the fact that these unmerited initial differences can never be reduced to allow for more than a passable measure of equality of opportunity.

Of course, what actually makes the distribution of talents a common asset is its deployment in accordance with the doctrine of fair equality. Or to put the point differently, the distribution becomes a common asset when it is used to the advantage of everyone. The idea of collective asset must be translated into a particular basic structure, one that yields a mutually advantageous society.

The notion of a cooperative society designed to secure mutual benefit is not inconsistent with the notion that the parties in the original position are mutually disinterested. Mutually beneficial cooperation is not ruled out by the assumption of mutual disinterest but, rather, is endorsed by it in some circumstances. Persons in the original position are not, as Rawls says, "attracted by this idea and so agree to it," nor are they "moved by the ethical propriety" of the ideal of a society in which the distribution of natural assets is a collective asset; but there are "reasons for them to accept this [ideal]."[39] They are *not naturally* disposed to it, but they will accept the idea, nonetheless, in the original position—after suitable argumentation has taken place.

Let me summarize now the main results of the agreement to treat the distribution of natural assets and initial social starting points as a collective asset. Here we consider only the implications for the argument of the previous section.

First, the idea of collective asset and the considerations that led up to it provide a rationale for including natural assets within the scope of fair equality of opportunity. Since no individual could be said to be responsible for having the natural endowment that he has, no one could be said to deserve that endowment; its possession is unmerited. This does not imply, of course, that one's natural endowment is contrary to desert but merely that it is neither deserved nor against desert. (Thus, no notion of redress or of retributive redistribution is warranted.)[40] Initial social circumstances are unmerited for the same reason. Natural endowment and social circumstance are not negligible; they have a significant impact on the subsequent holding of positions and on the derivation of income and wealth from them.

The idea of collective asset provides, second, a rationale for allowing discounts on the earnings and wealth of some (or all) in order to pay for measures that will diminish the disparity in opportunities. Thus, in a given society, if public schooling or benign genetic engineering or measures for public health (such as clean air and water, inoculation against diseases, labeling and other qualitative controls on food and drugs) are necessary or highly effective ways of providing fair equality of opportunity, then the costs of providing them—including the expenses of relevant training, of research and development, of supervision—must be borne by the public. I do not mean that all the costs must be channeled through government but, rather, that the body of citizens, not the recipients of the benefit alone, must provide the funds. And those citizens who have advantage from their unmerited natural and social assets, and who have considerably higher earnings as a result, should be expected to contribute more.

Surely it is possible, always, to do more for equality of opportunity. But to what purpose? It cannot be merely to make the opportunities for holding positions *equal*—or as nearly equal as possible. Measures for equality of opportunity that narrowed the gap in advantages in such a way that the general social system generated less wealth overall and reduced standards of living across the board (or made the least well-off even less well-off) would be unreasonable. For the idea of fair equality refers to opportunities to hold positions that generate income and wealth. And it would be unreasonable, given the argument in the first section of this chapter (concerning the general conception of justice), to extend measures for providing opportunity to the point of counterproductively diminishing such opportunities. The issue here is not *equality* of opportunity but, rather, the extent of things over which it would be reasonable for measures to secure fair equality to range. It is not, then, equality per se that controls the idea of reasonable equality of opportunity. It is, instead, the notion that under conditions of inequality, in starting points and in the positions that generate wealth and income, measures for equality of opportunity in the holding of these positions should be initiated and carried through to the limiting point where the prospect that representative persons have for income and wealth from such positions (including, in particular, those in the lowest quartile) would be worsened.

Thus, the idea of mutual benefit not only motivates the democratic interpretation of fair equality but also sets a limit on that quest for equality. The notion of such a limit, then, is the third main result, for equal opportunity, of the idea of collective asset. In saying that there is a limit, I do not want to suggest that this limit is ever actually approached in the world of nations. I want to suggest merely that it is the proper control on the idea of fair equality, and not any abstract ideal of equality per se. And when a frenzy for equality in the abstract takes over, as it did in Cambodia under Pol Pot, one can see the point of insisting on this proper control.

It follows from the perspective in which this proper control has been identified that fair equality of opportunity should operate, in general, not by reducing the advantage in talents of more-favored individuals, but by improving the situation of less-favored ones. For if the gap in advantages were reduced in the first way, it would not be as productive of benefits, for everyone, as would the second way. The point of Rawls's idea of fair equality, if we can paraphrase the words of one of the British idealist thinkers of the last century, is to "hinder the hindrances" on opportunity.[41]

Here we have also the substantial reason for Rawls's unwillingness to countenance the elimination of the nuclear family, which he acknowledges to be a potent source of inequalities in opportunity. The reason is not so much that families nurture the development of talents as it is that differences of family are generative of that very versatility and diversity of talents which is itself productive of the greater well-being of all, including those who are least well-off. This reason is to be contrasted with the one that Rawls actually cites: namely, that we need not be too concerned about the family, as a source of inequality, once the operation of the difference principle is in place. But Rawls's reason will not do, because that same reason would stay us from acting against *any* particular hindrance to equal opportunity and, hence, would make pointless any idea of fair equality as a distinctive consideration.[42]

So the idea of a *desirable* limit on fair equality of opportunity, as given in the superordinate notion of collective asset, is a powerful one in Rawls's theory. And it is quite distinct from the other limit on fair equality—namely, *feasible* limits.

We turn, then, last of all, to the relationship that holds between the idea of a collective asset and the difference principle. That idea can be said to lead to the difference principle, once we acknowledge the inability (through lack of knowledge or an inadequate social technology or a concern to forestall undue intrusiveness) adequately to reduce the gap in advantages from the two main sources. At least it leads to that principle in the form we have given it in this chapter. We noted, at the very beginning of this chapter, that there will always be inequalities in the positions by which aptitudes are realized and employed. And I suggested that such inequality would be reasonable and, hence, possibly justifiable if the income and wealth attached to these positions were higher overall, for the representative persons at various income levels, than it would be in that society under a condition of equality in positions. This yields, one might say, the first or primitive form of the difference principle.

Now, under the influence of the idea of collective asset this principle can be given a more precise statement. Society must be arranged so that everyone is helped by this inequality in positions: everyone's circumstances are improved in the relevant way(s), and no one's life prospects are further worsened. Thus, the gap in advantages remains, but everyone benefits from it, even the least-advantaged individuals. (Or to be precise, everyone is to benefit from the distribution of positions implicated in a particular scheme of differential advantage.)[43]

Here we get to the significant point. As some people improve their situations, others will benefit; they too should *continue* to improve, to become better-off. No one should be hurt or left behind without recourse. Mutual improvement is a continuous process. This is the understanding of the difference principle—the principle that concerns the distribution of resultant benefits—that we have reached so far by deploying the idea of collective asset as a justification and rationalization of inequality.

We do not, of course, assume that the desired result—continuous mutual improvement—will be achieved automatically. For just as positive measures are required to ensure fair equality of opportunity and must be paid for by discounts on the earnings of individual persons, so positive measures (of income transfer or negative taxation or provision of services to those who are less well-off) are required to ensure conformity with the difference principle, and these, too, must be paid for through additional discounts, especially on the part of those who are better-off.[44] The justification for such transfers and discounts is provided by the idea of collective asset.

Thus, that idea provides a rationale for the main features of Rawls's second principle of justice in its establishment of a justified inequality in positions. The idea of a collective asset underwrites both fair equality of opportunity, in its ''democratic interpretation,'' and the difference principle, in the rather simplified version that we have used in this chapter.[45]

But the development of the underlying idea of collective asset and the spelling out of its role in this section in no way affects the distinctness of these two elements of the second principle, or the priorities that are involved. Conscientious efforts to secure equal opportunity, insofar as reasonable, have the priority, for they are designed to reduce the initial inequalities among persons, both natural and social, and are to be carried through so far as possible. The operation of the difference principle complements these efforts by reducing the inequalities in results which remain even after reasonable efforts have been made and which stem from differences in aptitudes and inequalities in positions. The two elements together give the result that the collective asset idea seems to require.

There is still one point, though, that gives pause. We have taken for granted throughout that the people who are initially advantaged (in respect of their natural endowment and social circumstances) end up in the better positions, those with greater income and wealth, and that the people who are disadvantaged in these respects end up less well-off. The idea of collective asset does not so much rationalize this connection as merely presuppose it. So we can't move from the first point—the rationale for fair equality of opportunity—to the second—the justification for income transfers on a principle of mutual benefit—*solely* by reference to collective asset. That idea gives us no reason to make this particular inference; instead, it merely *assumes* a connection to exist between one's starting and one's ending point and goes on from there to provide a rationale, first, for fair equality of opportunity and, then, for the difference principle as supplementing fair equality.

Now, curiously, we know this assumption to be incorrect in given individual cases. For example, a person who has suffered a disabling childhood illness or who has come from very poor circumstances could end up in a favored position, which yielded a better than average income. Another person, seemingly favored by factors of health and family wealth, might do less well and fall below the average, far below his starting point. How, then, can we support the assumption in the face of these counterexamples?

The assumption rests, we could say, on a fundamental law of social science: that there is a *statistical* or probabilistic connection between a person's having been initially disadvantaged (in terms of natural endowment or social circumstance) and his ending up in a lower income group or a less-satisfying or less-skill-requiring job. Correspondingly, there is a probabilistic connection between a person's having been initially advantaged and his ending up in a higher income group or in a more-satisfying or more-skill-requiring job.[46]

Once this connection is made, the link-up of the difference principle with the idea of fair equality of opportunity is complete, and the internal connection of the two parts of the Rawlsian second principle of justice is laid bare. The ultimate justification consists, then, in two distinct features: in a law of social science *and* in the idea of a collective asset.

## 5. *Basic Rights to Opportunities*

Now that we have a clearer understanding of the interpretation of fair equality of opportunity, we can again ask whether Rawls's account endorses the idea of basic structure rights to opportunities other than to those listed as economic liberties.

There is, I would suggest, no right to fair equality of opportunity in itself. For that idea, put so broadly, is too indeterminate to admit of rights status. Fair equality of opportunity becomes a suitably determinate notion only when we can specify particular practicable measures as necessary or as highly effective, in a given society, toward the end of reducing the gap in advantages that accrue to individuals from differences in natural endowment and in initial social circumstances. So we would need to follow a strategy like the one we followed earlier with the basic liberties. We would need to specify measures for fair equality of opportunity and inquire of these whether rights status was assignable in given cases. We can stick for simplicity to those cases that have already been specified, by way of example, in this chapter. Thus, it might be claimed that there is a right, for each individual (up to a certain age), to free public schooling.

It is possible, but not likely, that such a right could be decreed in the original position. For one doubts that the requisite knowledge of the level of development and of the determinate needs of a society, or of the individuals in it, for public schools could be ascertained there. Nonetheless, such knowledge is available at the constitutional stage, at the point of the design of the basic structure of a particular society. Thus, it is conceivable—even likely—that a case could be made for such a measure as public schools, in order to ensure fair equality of opportunity in a particular society, and, thus, for a basic structure right to (public) education in that society.

Ascertaining rights status in any such case would involve, principally, two stages. First, the connection of a certain feasible measure or policy to the securing of fair equality of opportunity would have to be established. Then, second, a central or *core content* of the policy would have to be specified; this core content would have to be something that could be *individuated* (parceled out equally to all individuals within a certain class) in some *determinate* amount or to some determinate degree, under publicly recognized rules, and devices would have to be put in place for *guaranteeing* this distribution as a *benefit* to each and every member of that class.

If the latter stage of analysis—the main features of which I have italicized—had been satisfied in a particular society, then the policy in question could be said to produce a right for individuals in that society. If the requisite specification, and so on, had occurred in the constitutional domain, then the right would be built into the basic structure of that society as a permanent feature of one of its main political or economic or social institutions. The right would then be a basic structure right and, in that sense, a constitutional right. If the requisite specification, and so forth, had occurred or could only occur at some *later* point (e.g., the legislative or the administrative), then the policy in question would yield a right, but not a basic structure right.

Now, it could be argued that public schooling is important because it increases the "fair value" of the political-participation liberties (in particular, the right to vote on a one person/one vote basis) or because it increases the value of such rights as freedom of speech. This, no doubt, is true. But it is not the point I am making. Rather, my claim is that public schooling would be a right in itself, an independent and self-standing one, if certain rights-making features were satisfied. And I have suggested, further, that the policy of public schooling would likely yield a basic structure right, at least in some societies.

Could we make a similar case for measures of taxation on inherited wealth? I think not. The reason for this denial of rights status is not that the payment of taxes is required or coerced and, hence, could not be a right. That reason would also rule out public schooling as a right, since it is usually required of individuals. The main reason for denying rights status to the requirement for paying inheritance taxes is that it is, unlike the case with education, not thought to be for the good or benefit of the individual being taxed. Hence, it is not said to be his right. Clearly, people do not normally regard the receipt of a tax bill as an individual's right. Thus, not all policies that are designed to achieve fair equality of opportunity will yield specific rights of individual persons.

If we turn to those policies that are designed to provide fair equality by reducing advantages that result from differences in natural endowment, we find additional inhibitions on granting rights or basic rights status. Genetic engineering—benign or otherwise—is still in the experimental stages, safe procedures do not exist, and controversy rages about the advisability of allowing such procedures. We could not, then, expect that society, through deliberation in the constitutional stage, would assign high priority to such a policy, thereby yielding basic structure rights to individuals under such a policy.

Some of the other policies named—for example, the provision of clean air and water or the labeling of food and drugs (and, more generally, the control of quality in such matters)—cannot be individuated (i.e., parceled out to individual persons on a one-on-one basis) so as to count as rights, let alone as basic structure rights. And still others, such as policies concerning prenatal care or immunization against childhood diseases or architectural and engineering designs for the handicapped, seem to require a rather specialized knowledge which is inappropriate to the stage of constitutional design. They are more properly the objects of legislative action.

I do not deny that such policies would yield rights in a society in which they were legislatively (or judicially) invoked. What is in doubt is that the rights so generated would be basic rights. I want to suggest, in these circumstances, that legislatively produced rights, under a policy of fair equality of opportunity, would count as basic structure rights only if they were to specify ways of acting or ways of being treated that deductively follow from or are direct applications of a basic structure right. Since fair equality itself—the ground of such policies—is not a right, it would follow, then, that these legislatively produced rights would not count as basic structure rights.

So we conclude about opportunities, under the category of fair equality, that some of them, the economic liberties, would almost certainly be basic rights and that others, such as the right to free public schooling, *could* be basic rights. But it is not likely—for a variety of reasons, such as nonindividuation or indeterminacy or controversy at the constitutional stage—that still others would count as basic structure rights. (Though it is possible that some of these could be rights attached to policies having a legislative origin.) Thus, unlike the case of the basic liberties and noninjuries, where *all* of them counted as basic structure rights, only *some* of the opportunities under the heading of fair equality would count as basic rights.

Those that do, though, are permanent features of a particular society. For the conditions—respecting of the two main sources, natural endowment and social circumstance—that bring about the need for such policies are never wholly resolved in favor of equal opportunity. These conditions are constantly being renewed, albeit in differing guises, for each generation. Thus, *each* generation must overcome the gap in advantages from the two main sources through policies of public education, taxation on inherited wealth, the provision of clean air and water, and so on. And some of what is done in the way of these standing, permanent countermeasures will, I have suggested, count as basic rights. Indeed, if they did not have this character of permanence, they could not be basic rights.

Rawls also includes among the devices for fair equality of opportunity some that might be called affirmative action measures: "policing the conduct of firms and private associations and . . . preventing the establishment of monopolistic restrictions and barriers to the more desirable positions."[47] It could be contended that the practice of discrimination (on grounds, say, of gender or race) is unreasonable and, assuming employers to be rational economic persons, would be overcome in a situation in which the second principle of justice was duly operative.[48] This may be true, but we should not count on it. We should not assume more rationality (on the part of employers

84

and others) than is required simply to achieve reasonable measures for fair equality and the satisfaction of the difference principle.

Thus, there might be a place for antidiscrimination laws in any well-ordered society. But it is not clear that other measures of affirmative action, such as busing or so-called reverse discrimination (in hiring programs or in admissions policies for law and medical schools), would be equally appropriate. At least, such measures do not follow simply from the principle of fair equality itself. Rather, it would be required as well that the society in question have a history of proscribed discrimination and that this discrimination—directed, say, at people in virtue of their race or gender—had left members of such groups at a competitive disadvantage, a disadvantage whose effects were still being felt and, hence, still needed remedy.

Accordingly, there may be a need for policies of affirmative action even in a society that conforms to the second principle of justice. Hence, there may be rights to affirmative action in such a society. But they will not be basic structure rights merely insofar as they follow from the principle of fair equality of opportunity; for that principle is not itself a right. Moreover, we cannot presume a policy of affirmative action to be permanently required in a just society. And this is the main consideration. Thus, we could not accord the status of basic rights to rights to affirmative action in such a society, even though they might be effective there, under circumstances that could be envisioned, toward achieving free choice of employment (which *is* a basic right).

This completes my brief survey of basic structure rights to opportunities, under the principle of fair equality, in Rawls's theory of justice. I have not, however, addressed the question of whether there are basic rights under the difference principle. In this chapter that principle has been given a minimal specification and treated merely as an adjunct of the principle of fair equality of opportunity. In order fully to answer the question of basic rights here, we would need to fill out the characterization of the difference principle, along the lines of its usual formulation, and to discuss the difference principle when it is operating on its own.

These are tasks to which I will turn in the next chapter. Then, in the chapter after that (chapter 6), I will take up the issue of whether the difference principle, in its normal operation, gives rise to basic rights.

# • 5 •

# THE DIFFERENCE PRINCIPLE

In the previous chapter the difference principle was introduced as the second step (the linked idea of fair equality of opportunity being the first) that society can take in dealing with the problem of undeserved differences in the basic starting points of people. We could, however, think of the difference principle, not as completing the idea of fair equality of opportunity, but simply as a general guide for redistributing, under conditions of inequality, the income and wealth that are attached to offices. Indeed, this is the way in which it is normally thought of. It is the province of the difference principle here (once we assume satisfaction of equal basic liberties and fair equality of opportunity) to be concerned with differences in income, wealth, and offices (i.e., positions and responsibilities); for we assume that differences can be tolerated in such matters (hence the name *difference principle*) so long as basic justice is maintained in the idea that everyone's situation—in particular, the situation of those who are least well-off—can continue to be improved, or even maximized, in a carefully structured scheme of discounts and transfers within a system of such inequalities.

The present chapter concerns the difference principle in its latter, or redistributive, role.[1] Thinking of it in this way does not, however, break its essential link with fair equality. For given the argument (of section one) in the previous chapter, fair equality of opportunity must be presupposed in any just

This chapter is a longer version of sections 2–5 of the paper ''Two Interpretations of the Difference Principle in Rawls's Theory of Justice,'' which Prakash Shenoy and I published in *Theoria*. I am very grateful to Shenoy for consenting to the publication of our joint paper in expanded form in the present book.

distribution of unequal positions. The difference principle, arguably, affords a just distribution or at least is one feature of such a distribution. Therefore, it would presuppose—and in that sense require—the operation of fair equality of opportunity. Even here, in its redistributive role, the operation of the difference principle is subject to the prior condition that a conscientious effort towards fair equality of opportunity has been made.[2]

Thus, fair equality requires the difference principle to supplement it, and the difference principle, in its distributive office, requires fair equality in order to yield just results. There is a mutually supportive relationship between these two elements of the second principle of justice. Neither fair equality nor the difference principle shifts meaning as we move from one relationship to the other, and in each relationship the element of fair equality of opportunity has the priority.

Now, the hypothesis of the present chapter is that if the same distinctive argument that supports fair equality of opportunity (with the difference principle as complementary) can be shown both to lead to an elaboration of the difference principle in its characteristic form and to support that principle in its redistributive role, then the philosophical account of the second principle of justice will be complete. That principle will be seen to be a coherent and unified one.

In the present chapter, accordingly, the difference principle is examined in detail, and alternate formulations of it are provided. Thus, in the first section, the difference principle is discussed as a "maximin principle"—the usual characterization of it in Rawls's own discussions.[3] This also is the way in which many scholars have viewed the principle and on the basis of which it has been criticized and even rejected.[4] In the second section, we present another way of formulating the difference principle, using the concepts of pareto efficiency and egalitarianism. However, this formulation of the difference principle is shown to be equivalent to Rawls's statement of the difference principle. More precisely, in the case in which society can be classified into two economic classes, our suggested version of the difference principle is shown to be exactly equivalent to Rawls's standard version of the difference principle. In the general case where society can be classified into $n$ economic classes (where $n > 2$), the equivalence of the two versions of the difference principle is shown assuming that a regularity condition called "chain connection" holds. (The formal algebraic proofs of all the assertions made in the second section are relegated to the Appendix.) The arguments, in the original position, for the pareto efficient–egalitarian version of the difference principle will be taken up in the third section. Finally, the many advantages of our restatement of the difference principle are discussed in the fourth section.

## 1. *The Maximin Interpretation of the Difference Principle*

As formulated by Rawls, the difference principle states that social and economic inequalities are to be arranged so that they are to the greatest benefit to the least advantaged. To illustrate this principle, let us consider a society that can be classified into two groups of individuals, a more-favored group and a less-advantaged group. Consider two individuals: the first, a representative of the more-favored group; the second, a representative of the less-advantaged group. We can represent their possible expectations under various basic structure alternatives by means of an attainable set A in a two-dimensional space. That is, the *attainable set* A consists of all possible (practicable, feasible) pairs of expectations $x = (x_1, x_2)$ where $x_1$ is a real-valued aggregated index of social primary goods of the more-favored representative and $x_2$ is the corresponding index of the less-advantaged representative. Such an index, then, indicates the distribution of income, wealth, and position that the representative person would receive, or could reasonably be expected to receive, over his lifetime under some feasible basic structure arrangement. But to avoid clumsy language we will normally refer to $(x_1, x_2)$ simply as a distribution of income, wealth, and so on. Since we are concerned with the Rawlsian difference principle, we, of course, exclude from the distribution space all pairs of expectations, arising from basic structure alternatives, that fail to satisfy the prior demands in justice for equal basic liberties and for fair equality of opportunity. In this two-dimensional space, we can draw indifference curves, each one of which is a locus of distributions of income, wealth, and position $(x_1, x_2)$ that satisfy the relevant criterion of justice (the difference principle in the case at hand) to the same extent; the distributions on any one indifference curve satisfy the governing principle of justice to a lesser extent than the distributions on all the *higher* indifference curves. We realize, of course, that different criteria of justice would give different indifference curves. Under the difference principle, the indifference curves are as shown on page 90 in figure 1 corresponding to the criterion of justice $\max_x \{\min \{x_1, x_2\}\}$ with higher indifference curves in the direction of the arrow. Note that two distributions would satisfy the above criterion to the same extent when the minimum expectation in each distribution is the same.

Now, given the attainable set A and confining it to the distribution space marked out by the satisfaction of prior demands of justice, we can pick the distribution favored by this particular criterion of justice by selecting a distribution in the attainable set that lies on the highest indifference curve. For example, if the attainable set is as shown in figure 2 (the region on or below the curve *oc*), the difference principle would favor the distribution *a*. The point *o* (the origin) represents the hypothetical state in which all primary goods are distributed equally, and the point *a* is the distribution in which the expectation

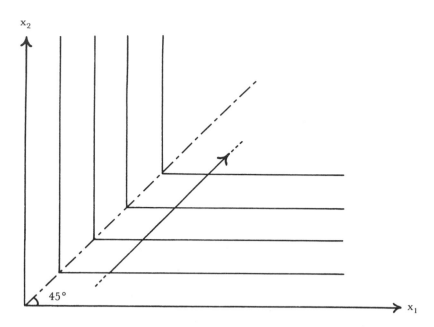

$x_2$

$x_1$

45°

FIGURE 1

Indifference curves under the difference principle, using $\max_{x}\{\min\{x_1, x_2\}\}$ as a criterion of justice.

of the least-advantaged representative (min $\{x_1, x_2\} = x_2$) is maximized. Hence the difference principle is often referred to as a maximin principle.[5]

One final point. Justice is, or should be, a virtue of society, specifically of its "basic structure." The problem for Rawls, then, is to choose a basic structure and not simply a favored distribution to individuals. Each basic structure alternative (among the set of all feasible basic structures that satisfy principles 1—equal basic liberties—and 2a—fair equality of opportunity) gives rise to a particular distribution of income, wealth, and social position. Any one such arrangement of the basic structure can thus be mapped onto a single point in the distribution space; this point represents the distribution of economic and social primary goods to representative individuals in a society that has a particular basic structure. Point *a*, then, represents a distribution of income, wealth, and so on, to such representative individuals under a basic structure arrangement that is just by Rawlsian principles (in particular, the difference principle—principle 2b).[6]

It should be especially noted that throughout this account of the difference principle, we treat it, following Rawls, as applied to the basic structure and not to any particular set of distributions to individuals on a

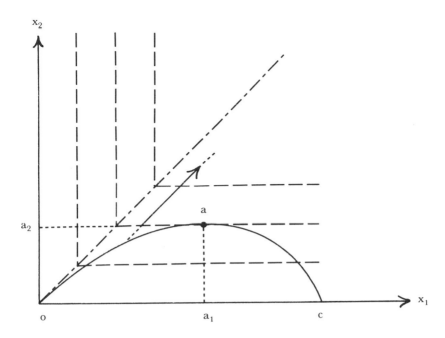

FIGURE 2
The attainable set and the difference principle.

given occasion. Thus, in our own interpretation of the difference principle, we conceive the criterion of pareto efficiency (when constrained by egalitarianism) to be applied to the basic structure of a society. We are concerned to see, under the conditions specified, what the difference principle would require in regard to the distribution of income and wealth as attached to unequal offices. Accordingly, we assume no prior maldistribution that might have to be corrected. This approach conforms to the procedure of the earlier chapters in which our object was merely to determine the *normal* operation of the principle that was under review.

## 2. *Pareto Efficiency and Egalitarianism*

We will now attempt to provide an alternate characterization of the difference principle in terms of pareto efficiency (or optimality) and egalitarianism. Let us start by defining the concept of a pareto efficient arrangement of the basic structure. We say that a distribution of social primary goods (specifically, income, wealth, and social position) is *pareto efficient* relative to a set of distributions if and only if there does not exist another distribution in this set that would make some (at least one) representative person better off without at the same time making some (at least one) other representative person worse off.[7] Also we shall say that a basic structure arrangement is pareto efficient if it gives rise to a pareto efficient distribution.[8] For a two-group society, if the attainable set is the region on or below the curve *oc* (as indicated in fig. 2 and also in fig. 3), a pareto efficient arrangement of the basic structure would lead to a distribution which lies on the northeastern boundary of the attainable set, indicated by the curve *ac* in figure 3.

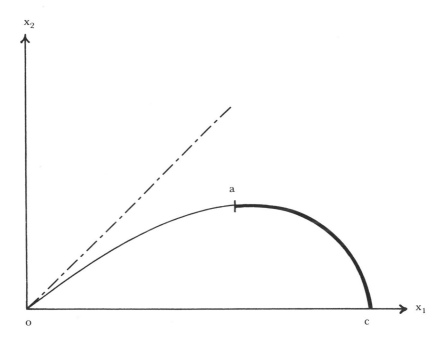

FIGURE 3
The pareto efficient distributions are indicated by the curve *ac*.

It is interesting to note that Rawls's difference principle (in its maximin version) also leads to a pareto efficient outcome, a result that is formally proved in the Appendix. This result requires that Rawls's second priority rule, which states that the second principle of justice is lexically prior to the principle of (pareto) efficiency, be interpreted in a special way: the difference principle is lexically prior to pareto efficiency, taken generally, in that some points selected as pareto efficient would be ruled out by the difference principle; but that principle does not exclude pareto efficiency per se. Indeed, at least one pareto efficient point would be selected by the difference principle. By the same token, Rawls's claim that justice as fairness is lexically prior to efficiency would have to be interpreted in this same special way.[9] The point is that there are several arrangements of the basic structure that are pareto efficient. Pareto efficiency by itself is not enough to single out one of these distributions as *the* just distribution.

In defining justice as fairness, it seems natural to appeal to egalitarianism to supplement the principle of efficiency. The principle of egalitarianism would pick a distribution that is the more nearly equal or the "least unequal." For example, in our two-group society, the principle of egalitarianism would favor the distribution $(x_1, x_2)$ that minimizes the difference between the expectation of the most-favored representative and the expectation of the least-advantaged representative—that is, minimize $\{x_1 - x_2\}$. The indifference curves under this criterion are shown in figure 4 on page 94, where the arrow indicates the direction of the higher indifference curves. The indifference curve through the origin $o$ is of course the highest indifference curve, for it is the line that marks out a strictly equal distribution between the two representative persons.

If the attainable set is the region on or below the curve $oc$ (as indicated in fig. 2 and again in fig. 4), then the principle of strict egalitarianism would pick the distribution $o$. However, if we make the principle of pareto efficiency lexically prior to the principle of egalitarianism, this combination of the principles would result in the distribution $a$ (from among the points on the pareto curve $ac$) because picking a distribution less unequal than $a$ would violate the priority of the principle of pareto efficiency (see fig. 4).

Thus, at least in the two-group society, pareto efficiency and egalitarianism (with the former lexically prior to the latter) would result in the same distribution as the one that would result by maximizing the expectation of the least advantaged. This is not a coincidence and can be proven always to be true, as we show in the Appendix.

Rawls himself has noted that, where there are only two relevant classes, the difference principle (or "maximin," as he calls it there) "selects the (Pareto) efficient point closest to equality."[10] He continues, "Thus, in this instance at least, [the difference principle] has another interpretation"; but he adds, "I do not know, however, whether the focal point can be defined sufficiently clearly to sustain the second interpretation . . . when there are three or more relevant classes."[11] It is to this particular problem that we now turn.

In the general case in which society is classified into $n$ groups, where $n > 2$, the situation naturally becomes a bit more complicated. For there are correspondingly many ways in which one can define egalitarianism. We will

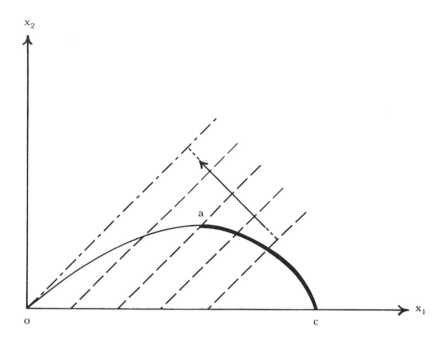

FIGURE 4
The most egalitarian pareto efficient distribution in the attainable set.

define egalitarianism here as minimizing the difference between the expectations of the most-favored representative and the least-advantaged representative, that is, as minimizing the difference $x_1 - x_n$ where $x_1$ is an expectation of the most-favored representative, $x_2$ is the corresponding expectation of the next-most-favored representative, and so on until $x_n$ is the corresponding expectation of the least-advantaged representative.[12]

We can simplify the matter further by saying that if the distributions in the attainable set exhibit a condition that Rawls calls "chain connection," then, again, pareto efficiency and egalitarianism (as just defined) will lead to the same result as that obtained under the maximin version (see the Appendix for a mathematical proof of this assertion).

According to Rawls, chain connection means that whenever the expectation of the least-advantaged group is increasing (as a result of increasing the expectation of the most-favored group), the expectations of all the other intermediate groups are also increasing.[13]

Interestingly, the coincidence of results which we have established as holding between the maximin criterion and that of pareto efficiency and egalitarianism, under the condition of chain connection, is not duplicated for the difference principle and utilitarian principles under that same condition. In figure 5, although chain connection holds, the difference principle, in its maximin version, selects distribution *a,* whereas the principle of average utility and that of the sum of utilities would both select distribution *b.*

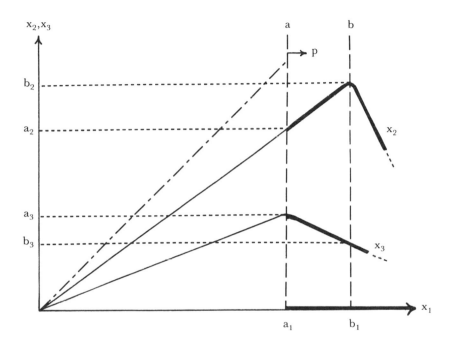

FIGURE 5

An attainable set that exhibits chain connection but in which the maximin principle differs from utilitarianism.[14]

It should be noted that Rawls claims[15] that the difference principle is not contingent on the chain connection condition being valid. So where chain connection does not hold, it is then possible that pareto efficiency and egalitarianism could lead to an outcome that is different from the outcome preferred by the maximin version of the difference principle. For example, in figure 6 on page 96, where chain connection does not hold, pareto efficiency and egalitarianism would select distribution *b,* whereas the maximin version of the difference principle would select distribution *a.*

Clearly, however, Rawls also believes that the normal situation in which the difference principle is to be applied is one in which chain connection does hold. In particular, chain connection can be expected when the other

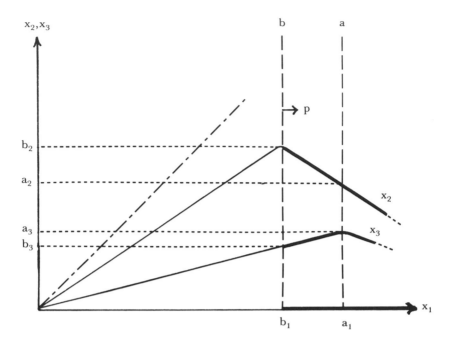

FIGURE 6

An attainable set that does not exhibit chain connection and in which the maximin principle differs from pareto efficiency and egalitarianism.

principles of justice—namely, equal basic liberties and fair equality of opportunity—are fulfilled.[16] Now, it should be noted that there is no necessary connection here and, hence, that chain connection could fail even where the prior demands of justice are satisfied. There is nothing automatic about it: for it is always possible, say, for the top and bottom classes to improve their situations without its also being true that all the intermediate groups improve theirs. Nonetheless, we can say that for Rawls, the cases in which chain connection does not hold are assumed to be unusual ones, and the application of the difference principle in such cases is problematic. We believe that Rawls would be reluctant to see the difference principle applied in precisely those situations.

Indeed, he stresses that a well-ordered society should "operate only on the upward rising part of the contribution curve (including of course the maximum)."[17] Or as he puts the same point later, it is "desirable when the justice of the basic structure is involved" that "we should stay in the region of positive contributions."[18] This particular emphasis is wholly in line with

Rawls's representation of the difference principle as being one of "reciprocal advantage."[19]

In short, chain connection holds, or at least tends to hold, in Rawls's view, in a *just* basic structure. It is plausible there. And where chain connection fails to hold, transfer payments to the adversely affected intermediate group(s) could be employed—precisely as they are now in the case of the least-well-off group. For Rawls is committed to chain connection in a well-ordered society, and this would constrain his maximin version of the difference principle. Hence, our use of chain connection in a reformulation of that principle is wholly legitimate insofar as we are attempting to explicate the Rawlsian difference principle.[20]

We now propose (and shall argue in the next section) that the combination of pareto efficiency and egalitarianism is more plausible than the maximin version of the difference principle and that the second principle of justice should be reformulated thus:

*Second Principle:* Social and economic institutions in the basic structure are to be arranged so that

(a) the offices and positions are open to all under conditions of fair equality of opportunity,

(b) the resulting distribution of economic primary goods is pareto efficient, and

(c) the inequality between the most favored and the least advantaged is minimized.

(Regarding priorities, fair equality of opportunity is lexically prior to pareto efficiency which in turn is lexically prior to egalitarianism.)[21]

## 3. Pareto Efficiency, Egalitarianism, and Justice

In this analysis we have assumed that there will be several pareto efficient (or optimal) points on the boundary of the attainable set A. But only one of these points can qualify as being more nearly equal (i.e., as minimizing the difference $x_1 - x_n$). This unique pareto efficient–egalitarian point marks the criterion for distribution under the difference principle in the version that we have been developing. In the present section we will attempt to show the peculiar relevance of the pareto efficient–egalitarian criterion to Rawls's theory of justice. We will begin by indicating how the considerations developed in the previous chapter, in particular the collective asset idea, provide an argument for the difference principle—that is, an argument for the version we have identified, in which the criterion for the distribution of income, wealth, and social position to representative individuals from various groups is marked out by (1) that pareto optimal point which is (2) the most egalitarian one. We shall take up these two points in turn.

We will assume from the beginning that the persons in the deliberative group have already accepted the principle of equal basic liberties and the principle of fair equality of opportunity (with the lexical priority of the former over the latter). In short, we have an attainable set A in which distributions are constrained by the acceptance of these prior demands of justice.

Now consider a simple problem in which an individual—it could be any individual—in the original position is asked to choose between exactly two basic structure alternatives labeled $c$ and $d$, such that $d$ is not efficient relative to $c$; that is, alternative $c$ results in a distribution that is at least as good as the distribution resulting from alternative $d$ for each and every economic group, and $c$ results in a strictly better outcome for at least one economic group as compared to $d$. Assume that both $c$ and $d$ satisfy the principle of equal basic liberties and the principle of fair equality of opportunity. We shall assert that regardless of the other attributes of alternatives $c$ and $d$, a person in the original position will prefer $c$ to $d$. The reasoning is quite obvious. Alternative $c$ results in an outcome that is at least as good for each and every segment of society as the outcome resulting from alternative $d$. Furthermore, $c$ is actually better than $d$ for at least one economic group. Then, clearly, one should not choose alternative $d$ but, rather, alternative $c$.[22]

This argument for preferring $c$ to $d$ is quite strong and holds even if more alternatives are available. Thus, we can assert that an individual in the original position will never choose a basic structure alternative that results in a distribution of economic primary goods that is *not* pareto efficient relative to other feasible basic structure alternatives. The reason for this is given in the set of considerations which led up to the adoption of the collective asset idea in the original position. The idea is that inequalities are justified only if certain conditions are met, among them the condition of mutual benefit. This condition can be met in the case of choosing between a pareto efficient outcome and one that is not (but it cannot be met in moving from one pareto efficient point to another). It follows, then, that the perpetuation or increase of inequality can be justified only in the former sort of case, where we choose between an efficient outcome and one that is not. Thus, we restrict ourselves to such cases.

Nonetheless, there may well be several arrangements of the basic structure that are pareto efficient, each representable as a point (on the efficiency frontier) to which it is possible to move. But clearly, it would not be reasonable, from the perspective of the original position, in which all participants have an equal status, to prefer a pareto efficient outcome that allowed for greater inequality than did another eligible pareto efficient outcome.[23] Therefore, that pareto optimal outcome which minimizes inequality (i.e., minimizes $x_1 - x_n$) is selected. To do otherwise would be to opt for a surplus of inequality, that is, an inequality without compensating benefit(s). Such a choice would unnecessarily perpetuate or increase inequality. Any such choice would be unreasonable and unjustifiable. Thus, individuals in the original position settle on the most nearly egalitarian pareto efficient basic structure alternative.

One problem remains however. For it is not clear how the principle that we have identified would govern the choice between nonpareto outcomes—the choice of options that stayed strictly within the nonpareto zone. It seems to us, though, that the argument already developed would cover these cases. Accordingly, the principle that we have formulated could be extended to them with only a slight change in wording.

Consider, first, the choice between two points as given in figure 7.

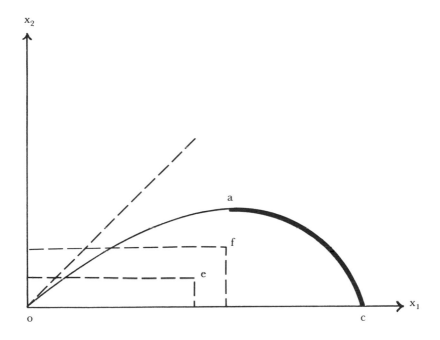

FIGURE 7
A choice in the nonpareto zone between two points *e* and *f*, where *e*'s "box" is wholly contained within *f*'s.

In such a case, *f* would be selected over *e* on the grounds that it would increase the total amount of socially available goods and services and that it would serve to improve the life situation (at least as regards income and wealth) of the various constituent groups, thus satisfying the conditions imposed by the idea of collective asset.

Our version of the difference principle, then, could be reworded to require, as here, that the resulting distribution of economic goods is relatively pareto efficient (relative, that is, to the alternatives under consideration). The change in language is marked by the introduction of the concept of relative pareto efficiency.[24] But the underlying rationale for this revised wording is unchanged from the argument that supported the original version. And since the underlying argument remains wholly unchanged, the reformulation seems to be fully justified.

Consider, next, the choice between two points $g$ and $f$, as given in figure 8.

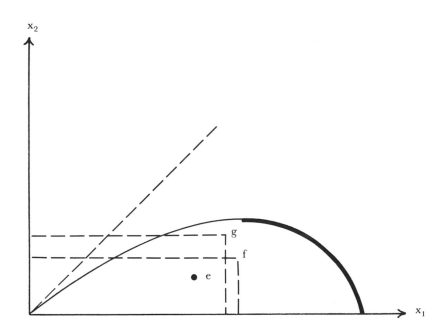

FIGURE 8

A choice in the nonpareto zone (of the attainable set A) between two points $f$ and $g$, where $g$'s "box" overlaps $f$'s but is not wholly contained within it and where $e$ is contained in both "boxes."

In such a case, $g$ and $f$ would both be regarded as relatively pareto efficient. Accordingly, when each point is relatively pareto efficient with respect to some third point *e,* then the more egalitarian of the two points is preferred. It is the point that minimizes $x_1 - x_n$ (in the above example, that minimizes the difference $x_1 - x_2$). There is only one such point in any given set. In the example in figure 8 it is the point *g.*

Accordingly, the version of the difference principle that we have formulated can be extended, with the addition of the concept of relative pareto efficiency, to cover cases in the nonpareto zone. The choice problem that we faced earlier can be generalized. Initially it was the problem of moving from some nonpareto-efficient point to any of several pareto efficient points; the choice problem in that case was solved by selecting that one pareto efficient point which is most egalitarian. By the same token, when one moves from some nonpareto-efficient point, the preferred choice between two *relatively* pareto efficient points (where yet further improvement, beyond them, is still possible) is that one which is more egalitarian. The number of relatively pareto efficient points could be increased, but so long as the choice in the nonpareto zone assumes—with respect to some fixed point (e.g., point *e*)—a finite set of discrete options, all of which are relatively pareto efficient, then one and only one of these points can be selected as the most egalitarian one.[25] Thus, the principle that we have formulated can be extended to choices within the nonpareto zone, with only a slight change in wording.

The choice problem that we have confronted (regarding the nonpareto zone) is one that Rawls himself is characteristically concerned with. It is the problem of specifying "a fair social process" for distributing the primary goods of income and wealth in the case where "the fruitfulness of social cooperation allows for a general improvement."[26] The solution that we have hit upon, while verbally different from his maximin criterion, is one that Rawls could accept. In the next section we will examine the advantages of our formulation over the maximin version of the difference principle that Rawls has provided.

### 4. *Pareto Efficiency and Egalitarianism versus the Maximin Interpretation of the Difference Principle*

One way of viewing our reformulation is to regard it as *another* characterization of the difference principle. Our reformulation (in terms of pareto efficiency and egalitarianism) can hardly be considered a radical departure from Rawls's usual version. The operational equivalence of these two formulations is demonstrated in the Appendix (subject to the chain connection condition in the general case of *n* groups in society). The main difference between them, then, must come at another point.

To bring this out, let us distinguish a *criterion* for distribution (e.g., Rawls's maximin version of the difference principle) from an *argument* for that criterion.[27] Many people have objected to Rawls's characterization of the difference principle because it appears to rest on a particular argument, specifically, that a rational individual in the original position would use the maximin rule for decision making under uncertainty. "The maximin rule tells us," Rawls says, "to rank alternatives by their worst possible outcomes: we are to adopt the alternative the worst outcome of which is superior to the worst outcomes of the others." In the course of conducting his maximin argument Rawls rules out the use of objective probability values in the original position, decrees that it would be unreasonable to arbitrarily assign *equal* probability values to each possible life situation under the indeterminate conditions prevailing behind the veil of ignorance, assumes (implicitly) that individuals in the original position are extremely risk-averse, and so on.[28] This argument is perhaps the weakest link in his chain of reasoning, and utilitarians such as Arrow and Harsanyi have attacked it in defending their own doctrine.[29]

In sum, these critics have reasoned that since the maximin argument was inherently suspect or since it did not apply under the conditions envisioned, or was not uniquely applicable, the criterion supported by that argument was itself defective or precarious. Thus, doubts about the maximin *argument* tended to translate into doubts about the maximin *criterion;* that is, into doubts about Rawls's favored way of characterizing the difference principle.

We will not say that Rawls's preferred criterion for distribution—his favored version of the difference principle—*requires* the support of the maximin argument. We say only that it is difficult to see how this particular formulation of the criterion of distribution would have been chosen *except* in the context of the maximin argument.[30] The formulation that we have hit upon sets a different criterion for distribution (that of pareto efficiency constrained by egalitarianism). More important, a different argument—that of mutual benefit as implicated in the idea of collective asset—is used to support this criterion; and this argument, while in itself Rawlsian, does not draw, directly or indirectly, on the maximin *argument.*

We would stress, parenthetically, that the main use of the maximin argument in Rawls's hands is to rule out or to constrain utilitarian alternatives to his preferred two principles of justice. It is important in this regard to note that Rawls intends for the maximin strategy to support the *two* principles per se against utilitarianism; the strategy is not specifically intended to support the difference principle.[31]

Interestingly, in some of his later writings, Rawls suggests a two-stage argument for the two principles.[32] In the first stage, the two principles, as a set, are contrasted to a utilitarian alternative (say, that of maximizing *average* utility). Here Rawls alleges that the two principles will be preferred because they protect the equal basic liberties and fair equality of opportunity from utilitarian social calculations in which the well-being of some persons, in these respects, might be sacrificed in the interest of maximizing average utility. It is principally this notion—namely, that citizens want to protect liberty and opportunity against risk—that Rawls tries to capture with his maximin strategy. But it is not a first-order strategy or argument, in any case, as the discussion in the two preceeding chapters should make clear. Rather, the point of maximin is to rule out utilitarian alternatives because they threaten or fail to guarantee these particular social primary goods.

Now we move to the second stage. Here principles 1 (equal basic liberties) and 2a (fair equality of opportunity) are taken as accepted across the board. So the competition between the two principles and utilitarianism is reduced to the question of whether the difference principle (2b) is to be accepted for the distribution of the other social primary goods—specifically income, wealth, social and economic position—or whether, alternatively, a principle of maximizing utility (again let us say average utility) is to be chosen. 2b, or not 2b—that is the question.

At this point, Rawls shifts from the maximin strategy (for it has already successfully done its work in seeing to the protection of the equal basic liberties and fair equality of opportunity) to introduce another argument specifically in support of the difference principle—the argument from collective asset.[33] It is this argument that he calls the "compelling" one for the difference princi- ple,[34] and it is this argument that we have been emphasizing throughout the chapter.

Rawls's use of a two-stage argument makes it clear, then, that the maximin strategy does not support the difference principle in particular and that the argument specifically and peculiarly designed for that purpose is the one based on the idea of collective asset; namely, the argument from mutual benefit as it would be developed in the original position.[35]

Once the two-stage argument is in place, it seems clear that the next step should be to replace Rawls's preferred version of the difference principle (with its strong verbal affinities and resonance to the maximin strategy) with a version that is more attuned to the supporting two-stage argument, in particular its second stage. The version that we have been developing in this chapter has precisely this character.

In any event, one signal advantage of our reformulation (in terms of pareto efficiency under the constraint provided by egalitarianism) is that it does away with any need to rely on the maximin principle as the main support for the difference principle. For the criterion of distribution that we have provided is not dependent on the maximin argument and, hence, would not be brought down by its failure. Accordingly, insofar as there are doubts about the efficacy of the maximin argument in the conditions imposed by the original position, our formulation of the difference principle criterion would escape that difficulty.

Another point. The maximin principle is understood, specifically, as a principle for decision making under conditions of uncertainty. Hence its formulation and choice as a decision procedure presuppose a thick veil of ignorance; extreme uncertainty is its home ground. But the real social world, in which such a principle would have effect, probably does not exhibit a correspondingly high level of uncertainty. It seems anomalous, then, actually to employ the maximin *criterion* under conditions in which the degree and range of knowledge are sufficiently great to make the maximin *argument* unnecessary. Under real world conditions the maximin criterion seems not so much artificial as inappropriate.

Our formulation avoids these difficulties. Its principal conditions of support, in the original position, do not require the radical and stringent restrictions on knowledge that the maximin principle does. Accordingly, the conditions for the original formulation and selection of our criterion are much more like the conditions of its actual use in the real social world. This is a virtue in itself, and the anomaly that we have cited would not arise.

There are other signal advantages as well. The formulation that we have provided and the argument that lies behind it—the notion of mutual benefit and the idea of collective asset—are more clearly linked to other important features of Rawls's system than is the maximin criterion. An additional advantage of the criterion of pareto efficiency–egalitarianism is that it serves to integrate the Rawlsian account of justice. Here we suggest consideration, in particular, of two problematic points: (1) the relationship of the difference principle to the principle of equal basic liberties and to fair equality of opportunity and (2) the connection between two versions—or readings—of the difference principle itself: between (a) its maximizing version and (b) its "improving" version. We shall take these up in turn.

Rawls's first principle states that inequalities in the basic liberties will not be tolerated. It would be unreasonable and unjust for the basic liberties to be unequal. In addition, the theory requires "fair equality" of opportunities. Thus, two of the primary goods—liberty and opportunity (at least insofar as we are concerned with basic rights to opportunity)—must be distributed equally to all if the distribution is to be a just one. However, Rawls does not, similarly, require equality in the distribution of goods such as social position and authority or income and wealth. Provided that unequal distribution here allows persons to be better-off than they would have been if some original distribution had been absolutely equal and provided that the constraints of the difference principle are met (as well as the lexically prior demands of justice), unequal distribution of *these* primary goods is just. Now the problem is that if the difference principle is formulated, as Rawls usually puts it, in maximin version, then the deviation from equality which is allowed in the second principle (and duly registered in the so-called general conception) is not seen to serve an underlying equality in any explicit way or to be constrained by it. Thus, the two principles seem to incorporate radically different standards, and the connection between them is obscure. In our formulation, the difference principle is interpreted in such a way that the deviations that are allowed in order to achieve pareto efficiency, either absolute or relative, are constrained by the minimizing of the necessary inequality. Thus equality continues to operate *explicitly* in our version of the second principle, and the connection between the difference principle and the egalitarian first principle is thereby mediated.

There is also, though it has not been much noted, a tension within the difference principle itself. We can bring this out, in an interesting way, by noting Rawls's distinction between a basic structure that is *thoroughly* just and one that is *perfectly* just. He says: ''The basic structure is just throughout when the advantages of the more fortunate promote the well-being of the least fortunate, that is, when a decrease in their advantages would make the least fortunate even worse off than they are. The basic structure is perfectly just when the prospects of the least fortunate are as great as they can be.''[36] In short, we might say the difference principle has two versions, or two variant emphases that can be struck: one emphasizes *maximizing* the prospects for wealth and income of the least-advantaged group; the other emphasizes *improving* the situation, in those respects, of that group. It should not be surprising, then, that Rawls sometimes explicitly incorporates the one emphasis or the other, and sometimes both, in his statements of the difference principle.[37]

The problem is that the maximin formulation (along with the arguments that lie behind it) does not appear amenable to both of these emphases. After all, if what is required is the maximum possible distribution of wealth and income to, let us say, the lowest quartile in income, then we are committed to saying that they are to be about as well off as can be arranged without cutting into the incentive and so on of the more-productive groups, ultimately to the disadvantage of the least-well-off group itself. Now, if what is required by justice is the maximizing of the life situation (as measured in income and wealth) of the least-well-off group, then any arrangement of income and wealth that fell short of that—even one in which their life situation was being improved—would be unjust by that criterion. The maximin criterion is such a criterion, and the argument that supports it forces us to precisely such a maximizing criterion.

However desirable it might be to have it do so, it is not clear how the maximin criterion does or even could justify situations that are less than maximal. Since there does appear, for Rawls, to be a criterion governing such situations—namely, that the prospects of the least advantaged are being improved—there is a tension between this "improving" criterion and the favored maximin one. It is not clear how they are to be brought together and given a unified treatment. In our formulation, however, this difficulty is avoided altogether.

All judgments about distributive justice are made from the perspective of a fixed nonpareto-efficient point (that is, fixed in the given case). All preferred steps away from that point count as improvements for *all* representative persons at the various income levels. Those steps that ended in a pareto efficient distribution would be improvements for all concerned, but they would also be limiting cases (since no further such improvement would be possible). Hence, our analysis draws at every point on a single intuition (mutual benefit—the idea implicated in the notion of a collective asset—as constrained, of course, by egalitarianism). There is no gap, either conceptually or in language, between the two emphases—the maximizing one and the "improving" one—that Rawls characteristically builds into one or another of his various formulations of the difference principle.

In sum, our restatement of the second principle of justice has several virtues. Chief among these is the degree of simplification that it affords Rawls's overall theory of justice, for it integrates main elements of the theory more fully by showing how the two principles follow from features and considerations that are developed in the original position.

A principal feature of the analysis in this chapter has been the deployment of the idea of a collective asset as an argument and the determination of where this argument leads. My object has been to carry to its conclusion this distinctive line of argument (which began in the previous chapter). I also wanted, in the course of the present chapter, to make the difference principle more plausible—to cut it away from certain highly restrictive and unsatisfactory supporting arguments—and to show the nature of the principal reasoning that best supports it—namely, the argument based on the collective asset idea. The function of this chapter, then, has been to bring the collective asset argument to conclusion.

Now, one of Rawls's main complaints against utilitarianism is that it is insensitive to the well-being of particular individuals; something like that could conceivably be said against the collective asset argument and, by extension, the difference principle. Accordingly, there is need to integrate the discussion of the difference principle into the rights analysis. I will turn to that issue in the next chapter, where some further implications for rights are drawn from the collective asset argument. And then, in chapters 8 and 9, I will continue discussion of the bearing of the collective idea on individual well-being.

# • 6 •

# THE PRIORITY OF LIBERTY

Now that the main features of Rawls's two principles of justice have been explored, we are ready to examine the relationship that is said to hold between the first principle (equal basic liberties) and the second (allowed and justifiable inequalities of income or of social and economic position). I turn to that issue in this chapter, where I examine Rawls's doctrine of the priority of liberty. My strategy is to recast the matter somewhat by claiming that it is the system of rights that has the priority. I then go on to examine the grounds that one might have for asserting some such priority. Here I do endorse the contention that a system of rights should stand in an order of preference to aggregative considerations such as the GNP (or social productivity), utilitarian general well-being, what economists call public goods, and even the difference principle itself insofar as it is, quite properly, conceived as an aggregative matter. Despite this, however, I argue that the pareto efficient–egalitarian principle can, with a somewhat different twist, give rise to basic rights. Thus, rights to income supplementation, as generated by the difference principle, have a place within the system of constitutional rights in Rawls's theory of justice.

## 1. *Arguments for the Priority of Liberty*

The presumed solution to the problem of priority, at least insofar as we are concerned with the prevailing interpretation of Rawls's position, has been that liberty itself enjoys some sort of priority over the other primary goods, in particular over income and wealth. The priority is of a very general sort, of one *kind* of primary good over the others. It is alleged that, beyond some minimum point, liberty per se is preferable to income and wealth per se. Liberty has here a sort of generic priority over the other social primary goods.

Let me be more precise. Rawls asserts that income and wealth have priority up to the point at which subsistence levels for all persons are possible; then, after that, liberty takes priority, a priority that is more firmly established the more wealth increases beyond that point.

I do not see, however, that Rawls in his book has provided us with a good argument in favor of the priority of liberty over wealth, let alone its priority over all the other primary goods. The difficulty may be, in part, that his frame of reference at this point has become too broad and too amorphous. After all, the primary good of liberty is simply liberty in the abstract, and this, in turn, refers to liberties in the gross, to all liberties promiscuously and to none of them in particular. It is not likely, whether in the real social world or in the original position, that individuals with the psychology that Rawls assigns to them, with full weight given to their rationality, would prefer for themselves an increase in liberties so conceived over, say, an increase in the available amount of goods and services. Thus, it is not likely that any sort of calculus of ''marginal significance''—whether in the original position or elsewhere— could help us determine that liberty has a generic priority over the other social primary goods.[1] Indeed, almost any conceivable calculus would suggest to us that liberty does not have such a priority.

The argument that Rawls actually presents (a variant on the diminishing marginal utility analysis of economists) is not of the right sort: it rests on a presumed factual assessment of desires that people have, or would have, in the original position. It reaches an unwarranted conclusion by means of the very doubtful claim that, beyond a certain fairly minimal point, the strength of the preference that people have for an increase in liberties diminishes less rapidly than that which they have for an increase in income and wealth. But were we to drop this claim, while still staying within the domain of desires that people actually have, we would almost certainly reach the *opposite* conclusion. Thus, the argument is radically unsuited for the purpose intended.

More to the point, where we take liberty to mean *all* liberties (and not merely the basic liberties) and where we rely on the accounts provided by social science and by common experience for the evidence of what people do prefer (correcting these accounts by reference to the constraints of the original position and eliminating preferences that cannot pass through this filter), then people most likely would prove to be indifferent. For we have no reason to think that they would prefer another liberty—of any description whatsoever— over another good or service—again of any description whatsoever. Nor have we reason for thinking they'd prefer the reverse. So long as the choice is between liberty *as a type* (hence any conceivable liberty) and goods and services *as a type* (hence any conceivable one of those) the results would probably be inconclusive in a run of preference tests. Hence, the argument does not support the priority of liberty.

In any event, the quest for generic priority seems to be off the mark. For justice, in one of its parts, concerns the equal basic liberties and, in another, the provision of income and wealth in an economic system the workings of which satisfy a definite and appropriate principle (such as the difference principle). It is by no means clear that, within this narrower context, we could devise an argument for the priority of certain specific liberties over specific patterns of income and wealth that satisfy the appropriate principle of economic justice. Certainly, the argument that we have been examining is not designed to do this job.

We need not, however, belabor these points; for Rawls has, in "Basic Liberties," repudiated the marginal significance argument of his book.[2] The argument—as an argument for the generic priority of liberties *en bloc*, as one *kind* of primary good among the others—seems doomed to fail.

I have considered the notion of generic priority and the argument for it only because these represent the most accurate interpretation of Rawls's priority doctrine, as expressed in his book, and because, though obviously defective, they continue to dominate the literature. Are there no other interpretations and no other arguments in Rawls's later writings that could take the place of the discredited quest for generic priority and the unsound argument from marginal significance?

The most likely candidate, at least on the rather scattered evidences in Rawls's texts, would be one that draws on the idea of highest-order interests. Thus, we find Rawls saying, "The second principle of justice is subordinated to the first since the first guarantees the basic liberties required for the full and informed exercise of the two moral powers in the two fundamental cases."[3]

What Rawls apparently had in mind, if constructed as an argument, would go as follows. Persons—that is, moral persons—have two fundamental powers: that of advancing a determinate conception of the good (which power includes the capacity to revise and rationally to grasp such conceptions) and that of having a specific and active sense of justice. Moral persons, then, Rawls says, are "moved by two highest-order interests to realize and exercise these powers."[4] Now, as we saw in chapter 3, these two interests pick out the *basic* liberties from among the liberties generally; thus *each* basic liberty is specifically tied in with one or with both of these highest-order interests. Let us grant, at least for the sake of argument, that Rawls has convincingly shown that the liberties and noninjuries in question are necessary means or essential parts of realizing these interests—and grant that they are otherwise practicable. It would seem to follow, then, that the basic liberties and noninjuries, in their association with the two highest-order interests, have a priority. Certainly, they would have priority over those primary goods which are associated with any lesser interest(s). The primary goods of the second principle of justice (opportunities, powers, income, and wealth) are controlled by a master argument (the idea of a collective asset) that makes no essential reference to the highest-order interests of the representative citizen or person. Therefore, the *basic* liberties have priority over the other social primary goods. And this provides the ground for the priority of the first principle over the second.

This argument, though apparently plausible, simply will not work in Rawls's theory of justice, as that theory is developed and amplified in his later writings. For it is one of the central claims in these later writings that the social primary goods are—all of them—to be understood as associated with the model of a moral person—specifically, with the two moral powers and, hence, with the two highest-order interests.[5] In short, it is the highest-order interests that pick out *all* of the abstract social goods and allow them to be designated as *primary* goods. Thus, the notion of highest-order interests establishes no preferential or even special status for the basic liberties, because all of the social primary goods (including as well opportunities, powers, income, and wealth) are on the same footing regarding those interests. And since all of the primary goods, simply in being primary goods, have an equal standing in serving the highest-order interests, there is no reason to single out the basic liberties over, say, income and wealth (in the requisite amounts).

What would follow, then, from the idea of highest-order interests is merely that *all* of the social primary goods have an intrinsic connection with moral personhood. Of course, the formulation of the two principles of justice goes beyond this simple, basic fact. The principles are concerned with the social arrangement of these primary goods in some determinate amount or to some determinate degree. Accordingly, the master arguments are developed to deal with questions of the relative arrangement or distribution of the social primary goods, emphasizing, in particular, the categories of equality and inequality. The fact that the master argument for the second principle makes no mention of the highest-order interests, or of universal interests, is immaterial. The relevant point, rather, is that the second principle necessarily presupposes these highest-order interests simply insofar as it deals with social primary goods, because all of these are, in being primary goods, intrinsically connected with the notion of such interests. This would include positions and income and wealth (as primary goods). The fact that the two principles of justice serve to elicit some specific "amount" as a standard for achievement— for distribution—in the case of each primary good under discussion (as, e.g., the first principle does with *equal* basic liberties and the difference principle does with the pareto efficient–egalitarian point) *builds* on the idea of highest-order interests; it does not set that idea aside. So, neither the connection of basic liberties with the highest-order interests nor the fact that the master argument for the second principle makes no mention of these interests provides a ground for the priority of the first principle over the second, or of the basic liberties over the other social primary goods (as determined in justice).

I see no way in which this argument could be saved for Rawls's theory. We could, of course, sever the connection between social primary goods and the two highest-order interests. Thus, we could say that the denomination of certain things as primary goods is a merely contingent matter, depending on historical and cultural circumstances. This would make it possible to connect the two highest-order interests with the basic liberties but *not* with the other social primary goods (in particular, positions and attendant income and wealth). To do so, however, would work considerable violence on the theory of justice as it has developed under Rawls's hand. For he has made clear that one distinctive thing about the development of his theory, in his later writings, is precisely the doctrinal addition that we are here being asked to jettison.[6] I do not think it is our business to redo Rawls's theory, at least not if our object is to understand that theory and to see how its various parts fit together. So, I suggest that we resist the temptation to chuck out a major part. But if we leave the theory intact, more or less as written, then we have no ground in the idea of highest-order interests for the priority of liberty.

I suspect, by the way, that the radical surgery that we have just been contemplating would not have saved the priority doctrine. Unless the procedure in this case is to be wholly question-begging, we cannot simply assume that the *only* universal interests, with respect to the two moral powers, are those constituted by basic liberties. There likely will be other significant interests, beyond mere wherewithal to survive, that center on other social primary goods: for example, the interest in a commodious life, in an appropriate plenitude of good things. And if this should prove to be so, that would leave us back where we started: the highest-order interests would still support, in some rough way, not only the basic liberties (as determined in the first principle) but also the distribution (as determined in the second principle) of economic and social offices and the income and wealth that derive from them. Thus, in the mere idea of highest-order interests there would still be no priority, as determined in justice, of the basic liberties over the social primary goods of the second principle, and no priority of the first principle over the second.

Is the argument that we have been examining the only argument for priority to be gleaned from the later writings? There is the hint of one more. I will try, in concluding this section, to bring it out.

At one point, Rawls says that "the first principle of justice is to be applied at the stage of the constitutional convention." This means that "the constitution is seen as a just political procedure which incorporates" the equal basic liberties. Thus, to cite one example, "the basic liberties of liberty of conscience and freedom of association are properly protected by explicit constitutional restrictions.'' But ''the second principle of justice . . . is not incorporated into the constitution itself.'' Indeed, Rawls adds significantly, ''the history of successful constitutions suggests that principles to regulate economic and social inequalities, and other distributive principles, are generally not suitable as constitutional restrictions.'' They are left, instead, to be settled at the legislative stage.[7]

This is, admittedly, a sketchy argument; but enough is said to suggest the outlines of a possible grounding for the priority of liberty. The basic liberties are incorporated in the constitution; all the primary goods of the second principle are further specified and settled, in any given basic structure, at the legislative stage. Thus, simply because the constitutional stage has priority over the legislative one, the basic liberties have priority over all the other social primary goods. By the same token, the first principle has priority over the second.

This argument is confined, I would suggest, to a written constitution (note the reference to ''explicit constitutional restrictions''). But there are, as we know, other features in the basic structure of a society than the written constitution. There are, for example, a number of economic institutions, some of which are identified as main institutions (e.g., the supply/demand market) and others as background institutions (e.g., antitrust legislation or full employment policy). These are meant to be excluded. Rawls is talking specifically about the written *political* constitution. His claim is that the basic liberties should be included in the written political constitution (we presume that there is one) but that matters of economic and social policy—in particular, the specific details of such policies—should be left, insofar as these matters are objects of governmental action, entirely to the legislative stage.

What is important here is the reason that Rawls gives for this claim: that the history of successful constitutions indicates the wisdom of this pattern. But the claim is open to doubt, for this history points to no such uniform conclusion. One of the most successful innovations in the last hundred years or so has been the widespread introduction of a policy of free public education. This social policy has often found expression in the written political constitution, usually in the form of a provision that schooling is to be required for all (up to a certain age) coupled with the mandate that the government is to provide for schools, open to all, at public expense. In the United States such a provision is not to be found in the national constitution but, instead, in the constitutions of many of the states of the union (e.g., the state in which I reside, Kansas). One would be hard pressed to say that public schooling was not one of the institutions of the basic structure in this country today and hard pressed to deny, once the federal character of American government was understood, that this policy was specified in the written political constitution (for it is a feature of *state* constitutions). Thus, we have a significant exception to the uniform pattern that Rawls endorses; here the history of successful constitutions allows for the incorporation of a specific piece of social policy into the written political constitution.

What history has shown is not, however, the basic issue; for one could be interested in *explaining* the success of such constitutions. Here one would ask: Why should the basic liberties (including the political-process or political-participation liberties) be incorporated into the written political constitution? An appropriate answer would be that this should be done because the constitution directs the behavior of legislators and administrators and judges. The citizens in a well-ordered society want these governmental agents to promote the basic liberties; they want to put action that would be inimical to these liberties beyond legislative or judicial reach, as far a possible. So these citizens incorporate the basic liberties and noninjuries into the written political constitution, or at least include them in the laws that are taken to be fundamental in that society. This approach to the basic liberties is the one that has proven to be the best. Here we have defended the incorporation, not by citing the bare history of successful constitutions, but by finding a main reason for this success.

This very reason would, then, dictate a similar policy toward public education. If there is a basic structure right to public schooling (as determined in accordance with the second principle of justice, under the category of fair equality of opportunity), then it is a constitutional right, and there could be no objection in principle to including it in the written political constitution.[8] Indeed, *whatever* is a basic structure right, as determined in justice, could be specified as a right in the written political constitution and probably should be, given the reason for incorporating therein the basic liberties. Hence, I would presume that a roughly similar argument could be made for incorporating the basic structure right to free choice of occupation.

The argument that Rawls has presented has things backward. We do not say that the basic liberties and noninjuries have priority because they are incorporated into the written political constitution; rather, we say that they should be so incorporated because they have a certain priority. They cannot have *this* priority, the requisite priority, simply by being incorporated into the written political constitution, or into the set of fundamental laws. To put the same point differently, the issue in normative theory is what things *should* have the kind of priority that the history of successful constitutions says is afforded by incorporation into the written political constitution. This is an issue that must, necessarily, be determined on grounds other than the history.

Rawls thinks that the first principle emerges from the original position with a settled priority over the second, that the basic liberties emerge with a priority over the other social primary goods. This is the priority that Rawls is intent upon establishing, and this priority cannot be determined by the history of successful constitutions.

Thus, to assign priority to the basic liberties solely on the basis of their being given a favored place in the written political constitution, or solely on the basis of the history of successful political constitutions, is to beg the question. And this is what Rawls's argument does. His argument from the nature of the policy process fails, then, for two reasons: because it begs the fundamental question and because the history that is cited does not uniformly support his favored pattern.[9]

We seem, then, to have reached an impasse. We have examined, albeit briefly, all the arguments for the priority of liberty that could plausibly be said to be found in Rawls's book or in his later writings, and we have found all of them wanting. None of them points to the required priority, for none of them supports the doctrine that the first principle of justice has priority *en bloc* over the second, or that the basic liberties, as determined in justice, have priority over all measures or all patterns, as determined in justice, for arranging and distributing the other social primary goods.

Nonetheless, I think there is a kind of priority in Rawls's theory of justice. It is not the priority of basic liberties per se but, rather, the priority of basic rights. I have used the idea of some such priority in my discussion of the argument from the nature of the policy process. In the next section, then, I want to see what can be said for the priority of constitutional rights within the confines of the argument that I have been making in the earlier chapters of the present book.

### 2. *An Argument for the Priority of Rights*

Rawls seems to be preoccupied with one issue of priority in particular: that involving the relation of liberty to wealth (or sometimes liberty to efficiency). There are two quite distinct perspectives that one can take on this relationship. Wealth can be the wealth of various individuals taken singly, or it can be, as Adam Smith would have it, the wealth of a nation (or of some other collective entity). Similarly, liberty could be the liberties of various individuals severally, or it could be the liberties that are found in a whole system of rights. We have, in short, an individuals focus and a systems focus. I would suggest that for Rawls the main priority concern is whether a system of rights (i.e., of equal basic liberties and noninjuries and of basic rights under fair equality of opportunity) has priority over aggregative goods or collective goals (such as efficiency or the wealth of a nation).

This is an especially interesting question because there are, in fact, a good many aggregative concerns with respect to which the issue of the priority of a system of rights could be raised. Several are worth singling out for special mention. Besides the two already named (efficiency, wealth or GNP) there is the famous utilitarian principle of general welfare ("the greatest happiness of the greatest number") or, alternatively, the utilitarian principle of the greatest *average* welfare. There are, as well, such further aggregate goods as (a) the self-determination of a nation or a people—a goal that is much favored in Third World rhetoric; (b) national defense—a value that is much favored in the rhetoric of the other two worlds; and (c) what economists call public goods or services (things such as roads; urban transportation; clean air and water; measures for public health, public safety, or police protection; provisions for retirement or for disability benefits).[10]

Finally, we could include, as yet another competing aggregative scheme, the operation of the Rawlsian principle of economic justice itself, or at least of that part called the difference principle. For the most straightforward reading of that principle would require that the income and wealth of the different economic classes conform to the standard set by the pareto efficient–egalitarian point (as developed in chapter 5) and thus that, in a well-ordered society, the relevant prospects of the class that is least-well-off in terms of income and wealth (say the bottom quartile) are to be improved or maximized as the income and wealth of the other classes increases. Here the difference principle, like the things mentioned in the previous paragraph, operates at the aggregative level—determining how the GNP is to be divided among various income levels or classes over a finite period of time (a year, say, or a decade). The principle does not require an increase of a certain level (or percentage) or of any determinate amount. The principle does not specify any particular distribution of income/wealth to given individuals within the targeted class. It talks, rather, of average sums accruing to "representative individuals" of the various income-level classes. Its focus throughout is the entire economic system and, within it, the changes in income amount or level of the various constituent classes. The point of the principle is to require that the income and wealth of a certain class (the least-well-off) rise so long as other classes were experiencing a rise.

So, the question of whether a system of rights has priority over aggregative schemes can be posed against a large number of eligible candidates, the operation of the difference principle among them. Some of these confrontations are given copious treatment in Rawls's book (e.g., justice over efficiency; liberty over wealth; the two principles over the utilitarian principle, in either of its varieties; the Rawlsian first principle of justice over the second). But I do not want to be side-tracked into considering a single one of these specific confrontations, just on its own. In the present section, rather, I want to treat the problem in its most general terms and to ask why one scheme—a system of rights—might be preferred or given precedence over aggregative schemes of the sort that we have identified.

The main reasons, I think, can be found in the following set of considerations. A system of rights has distributive features which aggregative schemes—or many of them—lack. First of all, not every aggregative scheme can be "individuated," that is, set up to allow for the parceling out of the good in question to individual persons. For instance, there is no clear sense in which GNP—or, perhaps, market efficiency—could be individuated. We might describe those schemes which in principle lack individuation as *essentially* aggregative ones; they can provide only aggregative goods, goods that can (under the characterization that they have) be enjoyed only collectively.

Other of the aggregative schemes, however, can result in or have effect for various people on an individual basis. This can be granted, even though they have these effects in a somewhat random way. Thus, the achievement of the greatest happiness for the greatest number will have distributive effects— for some, good; for some, ill—for a whole variety of individuals; but it is never clear in advance, from the relevant principle itself, what the particular effect will be for any given individual or, for that matter, whether there would even be an effect for every individual.[11] Nonetheless, what is distinctive about the aggregative schemes in this second grouping is that they can distribute goods directly to all or most individuals, for it is part of their character, unlike the nonindividuated schemes, to have distributive effects.

Now, what differentiates a system of rights from aggregative schemes, even from those that have intended distributive results, is that a system of rights will have distributive results for *all* individuals; these results will be of a determinate sort, in a definite amount or at a definite level; and these determinate distributive effects on each individual will be predetermined and on strict principle. These results will be the same for each and every one.

A system of rights includes the equal basic liberties. By hypothesis these liberties are as extensive as can be justified. The basic liberties and noninjuries, each of them representing an accepted fundamental interest, are distributed to each and every individual (with a few well-accredited exceptions such as children or prisoners); they are distributed on a principle of strict equality under the defining rule. This wholly determinate distribution (of the same good to everyone) is also reproduced for those opportunities, under the heading of fair equality, that count as basic rights.

If we were to consider a system of rights, then, in competition with aggregative schemes, we would find that it would be preferred, within the context of the original position, to any aggregative scheme for the design of the basic structure of a society. It would be preferred over those schemes which were essentially aggregative (e.g., GNP or, perhaps, market efficiency), and it would be also preferred over those schemes which were distributive but without determinate and acceptable results for each and every individual (e.g., utilitarianism or the theory of public goods in economics).[12]

A system of rights commends itself to the parties not only because it distributes basic liberties and opportunities on a principle (of universality and equality) that would have been selected in the original position but also because it has predictable and desirable distributive effects for given individuals in accordance with that principle—effects that could then be guaranteed by the operations of the basic structure. Accordingly, it would be given a certain priority: it would be singled out, selected first, sought for consistently, and given a standing exemption from the sacrifices of individual interests that aggregative concerns might impose on equal basic liberties or opportunities. These concerns would yield to rights, not rights to them, because the *distributive* results of a system of rights can be counted on—and affirmed—by one and all. The priority of basic liberties and opportunities—that is, of a system of rights—holds over aggregative considerations insofar as we are concerned with the distribution of the basic liberties (and noninjuries), and so on, or are concerned with the basic liberties and opportunities in relation to the *other* primary goods (specifically, income and wealth).

The argument here, some parts of which are already familiar to us, would go roughly along the following lines. (I will confine it, for simplicity, to the basic liberties.) It would begin with the recognition that basic liberties, like all of the other social primary goods, are very important, and it would include the acknowledgment that no individual in the original position or at the constitutional stage would be willing to tolerate, and therefore would not risk, either the entire loss of a single basic liberty or the unequal distribution of any one of them. Any scheme that would allow such risks, where the risk could be avoided, should be either ruled out as inferior (e.g., utilitarianism or the various forms of perfectionism) or set aside and constrained (e.g., the so-called general conception, were one to consider it a substantive conception of justice). The posture is defensive. Because we know what we want with basic liberties—that they be assured and equal to all—and because we want what we know, we disallow risky alternatives or impinging side considerations. We strictly prefer equal basic liberties, and their assurance, over any of the aggregative schemes, which presume—at least in effect—to distribute liberties or to distribute them along with other primary goods.

Perhaps distribution principles could be worked out for the *other* social primary goods (or for utilitarianism as a theory of all such goods), but each such principle would have to be as precise as the scheme for distributing basic liberties equally in order to attain the same standing, in the original position or in the constitutional stage, as is accorded to a system of basic liberties as rights. Attaining this would eliminate the priority of a system of rights in one respect (the priority of determinateness over indeterminateness); it would not, however, eliminate it in the other respect (the priority of a system of rights as the preferred scheme for the distribution of basic liberties), and any alternative would have to be wholly compatible with a system of rights (in the results that such an alternative gives) with respect to the basic liberties.

We can take it as a benchmark that no principle for the *other* social primary goods would be acceptable in an "ideal" or standard-setting theory of justice if it required the sacrifice or the significant alteration of the distributive principle of equal basic liberties.[13] Suppose, for example, that an acceptable theory of distributing income, wealth, and offices (i.e., of distributing social and economic positions together with their reasonable lifetime expectations) could be devised. We presume the difference principle to be such a principle. But we necessarily assume, in admitting the difference principle as a part of the ideal theory of justice, the *compatibility* of that principle with an extensive system of equal basic rights. Now, if compatibility is assumed, it could mean little or nothing to say that the distributive scheme of the one sort (equal basic liberties) had priority over that of the other sort (in which shares of income were justifiably distributed to members of the least-well-off quartile). If we are within the confines of ideal theory and thereby assume compatibility, there seems to be no place for priority.

Priority might exist pretheoretically and in the abstract (as between a determinate and a relatively less determinate principle), a point that I have been at some pains to make, but no significant priority could exist between principles *within* a theory of justice, once we had assumed, or required, their compatibility. Thus, if we had acknowledged the *abstract* priority of liberty by saying that the operation of the difference principle would be constrained so as not to interfere with the equal basic liberties, then there would be no further sense in which a system of such rights would have priority over a difference principle so constrained. When the main parts had been put together—that is, once compatibility had been engineered in—it would seem that the parties in the original position or in the constitutional stage would be equally concerned to specify *both* principles and to institutionalize both so as to achieve their appropriate results. So, there is no clear way, within an ideal theory, that one principle could be said to retain precedence or lexical ordering over the other, because each must be compatible with the other. This is the point of ideal theory.

Indeed, on any strict reading, the notion of the lexical priority of the first principle over the second makes no sense *within* the theory of justice, as Rawls has structured it. For his theory requires the simultaneous satisfaction of both principles, and this, of course, requires their compatibility at the same time that it rules out the adequate satisfaction of either one in the absence of the other. Thus, we cannot fully satisfy the first principle *before* we go on to the second. And if we have regard to the "worth" of liberty, this cannot be adequately achieved in Rawls's theory without the full satisfaction of the second principle.

A significant question of priority between the equal basic liberties and the difference principle could arise for practical purposes, then, only when we could achieve one but not both of these ideal goals. Here one might claim— presumably Rawls would—that from the perspective of the original position an equal distribution of basic liberties is preferred to an unequal one (or to a lesser extent of basic liberties), even if that inequality (or that diminution) is paired with the full satisfaction of the difference principle. The main alternative to this claim would be to prefer the full satisfaction of the difference principle (even with diminished or unequal basic liberties) over an extensive system of equal basic liberties but without that satisfaction.

The principal argument that exists for Rawls's claim is simply an adaptation, to the special case of the difference principle, of the general argument that has already been advanced. The parties have a preference for a system of rights insofar as it guarantees to each of them a definite good in satisfactory amounts (in the case at hand, the basic liberties equally). Now, where we regard the difference principle as *primarily* an aggregative considera- tion that has an uncertain distributive impact for any given individual, this general argument can be used to good effect.

By hypothesis, then, person $A$ will receive the result of the operation of the difference principle differently depending on whether he is in fact a member of the lowest income group or, alternatively, of one of the other income groups. In this sense there is no *guaranteed* result to $A$, let alone a guaranteed *particular* result. And since $A$ could be anyone, there is no guaranteed result to any individual, hence to *all* individuals. Accordingly, each individual, hence all individuals, would opt for the result that is in everybody's interest; they would prefer that program which in fact guarantees determinate results in accordance with universal fundamental interests to one which gives results that favor only some persons (in this case the bottom quartile, otherwise undetermined) and which, in any event, does not give guaranteed determinate results even for members of that class.[14]

If this argument is sound, then we have an argument for the priority of basic liberties over the difference principle. But the character of this priority is quite distinctive. It rests, first, on considering the difference principle in but one of its aspects, the aggregative. And it rests, second, on contrasting the difference principle, under that aspect, with certain features that basic liberties and noninjuries have: namely, that they also are primary goods (and, hence, desirable), that they can be given a fairly determinate specification in the original position or at the point of the setting up of the basic structure, and that they can be distributed in a predefined and acceptable amount and on a guaranteed basis—the same thing in the same amount—to all members of the relevant class (i.e., persons, citizens). These are the features, precisely, that make for basic rights. Thus, any *particular* primary good that has these rights-making features will have a similar priority over aggregate or collective goods. The basic liberties, then, are said to have a priority, not because they are liberties per se, but because they are *equal basic rights*. Accordingly, the basic rights that are specified under the heading of fair equality of opportunity (e.g., the right to schooling or to a free choice of occupation) will have a similar priority. For the argument establishes that basic rights have a priority over aggregate goods—over public benefit or the general welfare (as defined in utilitarianism) or, in the case at hand, over the difference principle in its primary aspect as aggregative principle.

This is an interesting argument if for no other reason than that it does not depend on any belief about the alleged generic priority of one kind of primary good (liberty) over another (income and wealth). Let me also add that the argument is, in my view, sound, as an adaptation of the general argument that has already been considered. That is, it is sound insofar as we regard the difference principle as being *primarily* aggregative and, hence, as being uncertain in its impact across the board for given individuals in the various income classes.

We must, of course, recognize, however, that the difference principle, unlike some aggregative principles, has definitely intended distributive effects. I have argued throughout that the difference principle can be viewed as having two aspects: an aggregative one (in which the concern is income relationships or transfers between classes) and a distributive one (in which the concern is income results or transfers to actual individuals). So the priority issue ultimately must hinge on whether the difference principle in its *secondary* (i.e., distributive) role can guarantee an acceptable result, in a more or less determinate amount, to *each* individual. We will consider this precise issue in the next section.

### 3. *Basic Rights under the Difference Principle*

Here I want to argue against Rawls. Let us start with a point that is not in dispute. The difference principle does guarantee to each individual that if he or she is in the bottom economic class (say, the bottom quartile), then that person has an acceptable expectation (either of a minimum level of income or, alternatively, of an absolute amount of income supplementation).

One might retort, however, and I believe Rawls would, that this guarantee is not to everyone but only to those in the bottom quartile. In turn, one could say against this retort that, equally, the guarantee of a fair trial (which Rawls includes among the basic liberties and noninjuries) is not a guarantee to everyone but only to those who have been indicted. Clearly, this latter way of putting the right to a fair trial will not do if such a right is to be included in a system of *basic* rights. It will not do because all such rights are universal. So, the defender of Rawls must say that the right to a fair trial is one that everybody has (insofar as it is a basic right) and has equally, even though it is a right that comes into play only under certain circumstances (that is, when one has been charged with a crime).

By the same token, then, it is open to critics of Rawls's initial response to say that the guarantee to a distributive share, of the sort that is enjoined by the operation of the difference principle, is a guarantee that everyone has, even though it is one that comes into play only under certain circumstances (i.e., when one is in the most-deprived income group).

The right to a fair trial, it should be noted in passing, does not designate a liberty in the strict or proper sense. It is not something that the rightholder does or can do; rather, its object is to prevent others from doing an injury to the rightholder. Thus, its status is that of a basic noninjury (though, for reasons that have already been discussed in an earlier chapter, Rawls tends to count these, without distinction, among the basic liberties). The function of the basic right to a fair trial is to provide a fundamental protection. Likewise, the provision of a guaranteed share of income to members of the most-deprived income group could be viewed as a form of protection. It is more than that, however; it is the provision of a service or a benefit (specifically, the provision of funds, through transfer of income or negative taxation, to members of the least-well-off group). In this respect it is more like the basic right to public schooling, which is also a right to a specific service or benefit as determined under the second principle of justice.

The points made so far have merit, as well as persuasive appeal, but they do not reach one of the fundamental challenges: that the distributive effects enjoined by the operation of the difference principle do not constitute a definite, determinate result to individuals in the target class. There is no way, in short, that an abstract settlement could be hit upon for specific goods and services, or for income, at any specific level for such persons. This is so, in part, because any viable, good faith settlement must presuppose a complex reticulation of particular facts: the structure of incentives, of taxes, of restrictions on inheritance, and so on. There is, accordingly, too much uncertainty and dispute as to what a good faith settlement would be in the absence of these facts. So we would be, Rawls suggests, unable to determine any required specific content for such a settlement in advance of these facts (in the original position, for example, or even in the basic structure). Hence, without knowing the relevant parameters of a going economic and social system, we would be unable to specify the amount or level to be distributed to the relevant individuals. Matters are simply too indeterminate for rights to be constituted prior to this point. We conclude, then, that there can be no basic structure right under the difference principle.

The points cited here are true, but they are not dispositive. We can grant that the difference principle on its own, unlike the principle of equal basic liberties, gives no determinate results. But the difference principle, when imposed on the actual operations of a given economic system, would yield such results. Once we knew the actual income levels at some original point of comparison and their current values, we could determine not only whether the redistributive features of the difference principle came into play but also what determinate amount (or level) was being enjoined. We presume, of course, a good faith effort here. So there is no failure of certainty or determinateness once we allow for the actual operations of the relevant economic systems.[15]

Let me put this contention somewhat differently now. If there is for each and every citizen a basic right to income supplementation (a right that comes into play when one is in the bottom income group), then we must be able to state the rule that *defines* this right—for each and every one—in the original position. Or failing that, we must be able to state it in the basic structure, at the point of designing the political and economic constitution of a particular society. But the *rule* that defines the right in question can be stated in the original position; it is the difference principle, and that principle is quite precise. It enjoins a pareto efficient solution (either absolute or relative) as constrained by egalitarianism—by the minimizing of the necessary inequality in income between the highest-level income group and the lowest—under conditions of chain connection. There is only one such point, in a given basic structure at any given time, that gives this result. It is the same result for any citizen: the protection provided, the service rendered, is the same for each and every one and could affect any one of them (through discounts on income or through transfers). Receiving that service requires only that the citizen be in the target class in a particular well-ordered society.

We cannot tell, for a given individual picked at random, whether he will be in that target group. Nor can we tell the actual amount of transfer payment that he would receive. This is not unusual, for often we cannot know in advance how the possession of basic rights will affect given individuals. The right to a fair trial is held by all, but it applies only to some at a given time. Even the ''worth'' to an actual individual of a basic liberty right is not laid down by its defining rule but, rather, by the actual circumstances in his life, including such things as his actual goals and plan of life, his vocation, his income, and so on. Similarly, the application of the basic right to income supplementation (like the basic right to a fair trial) cannot be determined by its defining rule. The application requires a context: it requires results that can only be given by the actual operation of the economic system and the actual place of a given individual in it.

Thus, once we make the crucial distinction between the formulation of the rights-defining rule and the conditions required to apply the rule in good faith in a given case, we have reason to believe that the results given by the characteristic operation of the difference principle—in its redistributive role— are sufficiently determinate to figure in basic rights. Specifically, they are determinate enough to guide the application of the basic right to income supplementation, a right that is formulated in the original position as holding for each and every citizen.

There is an exact parallel between the basic rights that we discussed earlier (the basic liberties and noninjuries under the first principle and the basic rights, such as schooling, under fair equality of opportunity) and the basic right to income supplementation under the difference principle. All require appropriate institutions at the constitutional (or basic structure) stage to achieve an adequate degree of determinateness.

A difference, though, seems to remain. The difference principle still appears to be indeterminate at points where the other principles are not. The basic rights that were discussed earlier could be established at the point of *setting up* the basic structure; whereas the basic right to income can be so established only through the *operation* of the relevant basic structure institution(s).

I do not regard the distinction here as hard and fast. For example, schooling was not a basic structure right when the United States was founded (at the time of the adoption of its Constitution); it became such a right sometime during the nineteenth century, arguably, or during the present one. And if we were to go back to an even earlier time in American history, to the colonial period, we would find that liberty of conscience itself was not a basic structure right. Rather, it arose at some point in American history and can be dated, for constitutional purposes, somewhere between 1791 (the adoption of the Bill of Rights amendments to the U.S. Constitution) and 1833 (the demise of the last established church in any state in the United States). Accordingly, I am not inclined to give great weight to this distinction but will instead emphasize the parallel between the basic rights discussed earlier and the basic right to income supplementation.

We have, then, in the text of the present section, two important counterarguments to the contention that there is not a basic right to income supplementation under the difference principle. One is based on the claim that the same thing—a redistributive transfer of income—can be guaranteed to *everyone* equally (under the defining rule); the other is based on the claim that what is guaranteed is relatively *determinate* in amount, at least at the point of application. With these counterarguments in hand and relying on selective analogies with already-established basic rights, we find that the argument, in nonideal circumstances, for the priority of liberty over the difference principle is less convincing, and even substantially undercut. The counterarguments force us to consider the distributional effects of the difference principle in the light of a theory of basic rights.

Here one could say that a system of rights takes precedence over aggregative schemes because of the distributional principle that it enshrines: equal basic rights to each and all. This principle takes precedence over the distributional effects of the other schemes insofar as these effects are indeterminate or unequal for each and all. Now, for Rawls, rights include both liberties and noninjuries and certain opportunities as well. There is, indeed, no limit to the *kinds* of things that one can have a right to. It all depends on whether the distributional principle for that kind of thing enjoins a particular share (or level) of some primary good which can be guaranteed equally to each and all. If it does, then such a share arguably constitutes a basic right and is eligible for membership in the Rawlsian system of basic rights.

I have contended that the distributional results of the difference principle meet this test: these mandated effects for the bottom group, at least as regards the primary good(s) of income and wealth, constitute basic rights to that good for each and every person and, hence, come *within* the system of rights. There is a right of every person in a Rawlsian well-ordered society to a minimum level of income or, if not to that, to a particular share of income supplementation if he happens to be in the least-well-off income group. It is an equal right (the legitimate expectation of a guaranteed equal share) the reason for which could be developed and appreciated by persons in the original position (or in a constitutional convention).

The economic matter in question constitutes a basic equal right; accordingly, it cannot be significantly distinguished in that respect from other equal basic rights. Each belongs to the system of rights. And since what gives priority to basic rights is, precisely, their rights-making features, there can be no such priority between basic rights. Thus, there can be no priority of basic rights over this aspect of the difference principle; for difference principle-determined income supplementation is itself a basic right.

## 4. *Equal Basic Rights: A Summing Up*

Now that I have completed the line of argument, we must at this point begin to gather the various conclusions of our inquiry into a single, coherent intuition. In this chapter, I have argued that the difference principle has two aspects and thus can be viewed from two perspectives: the aggregative (e.g., income transfers between classes) and the distributive (e.g., income transfers

124

to actual individuals). The discussion under these two headings has wound its way through the previous two sections.

In the first of these (section 2) I took things up from an aggregative perspective. There I argued (a) that there is a *pretheoretical* priority, or a preference, for a distribution that is determinate and acceptable in amount, one that can be guaranteed. Next I argued (b) that in a context of compliance or pure theory this priority gives way to the much simpler and more relaxed notion of mutual compatibility, (c) but that in less than ideal contexts, the sort of priority that has already been identified in (a) is reasserted.

What guided our deliberations here was a principle of priority of a quite distinctive sort: that of the priority of rights (equal basic rights) over aggregative considerations which either are nonindividuative altogether or are distributive on an uncertain principle. It was determined on that basis, then, that a system of rights has priority over the difference principle. But the asserted priority has to be confined to the context of the relevant argument; thus, the priority of rights over the difference principle holds only when the difference principle is viewed simply as an aggregative notion, or primarily as that. Accordingly, we could assert the priority of basic rights over, say, tax policies and other measures for raising revenue that are connected with the difference principle. And we could, on the same basis, assert that priority over several of the opportunities that are gathered under the heading of fair equality (as was shown in chapter 4).

At this point I shifted to the other main perspective. In the immediately preceding section (3), then, I argued that the operation of the difference principle can also be viewed as distributive and determinate (to a degree) and that when it is so regarded, it can generate rights (specifically, rights to income supplementation).

Thus, we find in Rawls's account a number of basic rights arising under the various main headings of his theory of justice:

(1) Rights to basic liberties and noninjuries under the first principle,
(2) rights to certain economic liberties (e.g., free choice of occupation) under the fair equality of opportunity part of the second principle,
(3) rights to certain other opportunities (e.g., to public schooling) under that same part, and
(4) a right to transfer of income under the distributive aspect of the difference principle.

All these are basic rights. They can all be identified in the original position (as supported by one or the other of the master arguments there) and spelled out in the constitutional stage. Thus, each right pertains to a particular primary good (e.g., liberty of speech, which is a kind of liberty), and each must specify, with respect to that good, a central content which can be *individuated* (parceled out, equally, to the individuals within a certain class) in some *determinate* amount or to some determinate degree, under publicly recognized rules, such that the distribution of that good can be *guaranteed* to each and every member of that class.

All of the rights in the above list have qualified because they fulfill the basic rights-making conditions, in particular, because they can be individuated and guaranteed. These are the very features that serve not only to distinguish Rawls's account of justice from the utilitarian one, as we saw earlier, but also to establish the priority of rights over aggregative considerations. Thus, all the rights on this list have the same preferred status, and all will be constitutional rights in a Rawlsian just society. They are the rights (or kind of rights) that one finds in a well-ordered system of rights.

Toward the difference principle–generated rights in this system there is no priority, no superordinate category in Rawls's theory of justice. For Rawls's theory, I have argued, has as its first claim the priority of *basic rights*.

And it remains true in justice, then, that basic rights have priority over either essentially aggregative considerations (such as the GNP or market efficiency) or over distributive results (such as, quite possibly, the ownership of productive property) which do not establish and guarantee the same social stake—an acceptable one—for each and all. It is this insight that our analysis has been designed to capture.

The crucial insight here is not well put in saying that liberties per se have priority over economic matters. For not all liberties are rights (but only the basic ones), whereas some economic matters are rights. Since economic matters are not excluded from the class of rights, there is no restriction in principle which would give rights priority over economic matters as such. Rawls's famous discussion of the priority of liberty over wealth and economic position suggests the opposite;[16] this is a good reason for amending, if not discarding, it.

From the perspective of the original position, a system of basic rights has priority over all aggregative schemes with respect to both liberty and the other social primary goods. This is, I believe, the correct way to characterize, in general terms, Rawls's conception of the priority of liberty.

In this chapter, I have attempted to provide an outline for a new doctrine of priority, by indicating what is at stake in Rawls's discussion of liberties and the priority of liberties. I have done so by advancing the idea of a system of basic rights and by posing the problem of priority against that. I have argued that we should take Rawls's dictum about the priority of liberties to refer in fact to the priority of equal basic rights as a set. No single liberty or freedom from injury or economic distribution within this set is primary; rather, it is this whole system of basic constitutional rights that has the priority.

But I have not actually shown that basic rights can form a system, or "family," as Rawls came to call it.[17] Nor have I shown how such a system is to be formed. These topics will be addressed by examining the problem posed by the conflict of rights. I will take them up in the next chapter, chapter 7.

After that I want to turn again to the vexing set of concerns that surround the redistributive workings of the difference principle. My present analysis has not plumbed the matter in its depth; in particular, it has not penetrated to the question of whether, under the difference principle, there are other basic rights than the right to income supplementation (through transfer payments).

My analysis in the present chapter has covered only this one feature of the difference principle. As we know, however, the difference principle distributes social and economic "offices" (roles and vocations) as well as income and wealth. It is important to remember that these offices could be regarded not merely from the perspective of the income expectations of the officeholder but also from the perspective of *other* intrinsic features that offices might have. We cannot, except at the cost of oversimplification, reduce an "office" merely to its income dimension. For example, the quality of life, the habits involved, and the relevant skills (not to mention prestige) are considerably different in the case of a Supreme Court justice from those same things in the case of a successful retailer of dresses, even though their incomes may be the same. It may well be, then, that the income-distributing feature of the difference principle reaches only one important detail of an economic or social office and cannot capture other crucial dimensions. Thus offices, on these other points, may not meet the rights-making test that I have outlined; and thus the difference principle here, like all other schemes that are not inherently rights-productive, would not come within the orbit of rights at these particular points and would, in fact, be subordinated to a system of basic rights.

Which economic matters come within the province of basic rights and which do not is a topic that I have left largely undetermined. I have argued only that one of the cases that Rawls cites (the redistribution of income under the difference principle) is in fact a matter of rights—despite Rawls's apparent leaning to the opposite conclusion. I have not, however, examined a number of further issues in which Rawls also seems to deny rights status to an economic matter. I have not considered whether the ownership of productive property is a right, or whether worker participation in the management of firms is, or whether important needs of individual persons constitute claims that, where practicable, individuals have a right to have satisfied. These are important issues, and I will turn to them in the final chapters of the book (chapters 8 and 9).

# • 7 •

# ON THE CONFLICT OF RIGHTS

This and the next two chapters represent attempts to apply Rawls's theory—as simplified, reformulated, and focused on rights—to certain problem areas. This chapter concerns the conflict of rights.

The issue addressed here is crucial to an overall assessment of Rawls's theory of justice. The analysis in the previous chapter suggested that it was basic rights as a set that had the priority in Rawls's system. But if a conflict of rights is possible, then that very possibility would threaten the favored characterization of basic rights as forming a stable system made up of mutually compatible elements. And if basic rights cannot be so characterized, if they cannot in fact be gathered into a systematic or coherent set, then the solution proposed in the last chapter will have to be disowned; and the place of a basic right to income supplementation, in relation to other basic rights within the putative system, would again become controversial. Thus, as long as the issue of conflict of rights is left unresolved, the status of the Rawlsian "family" of basic rights—and within it, the place of those basic rights that arise under the difference principle—is uncertain.

In this chapter I attempt to deal with that problem. I do so by first presenting a Rawlsian (or Rawls-like) theory of how the conflict of rights might be avoided by a careful drafting of the scope of potentially competing rights. For its argument motif the analysis here draws on the idea of the universal fundamental interests of the representative citizen. After that, I attempt to show, with an example, that this strategy will not work to prevent conflicts that arise *within* the central core of any given right. There are, then, special and intractable difficulties posed for judges who must decide, in Dworkinian fashion, between conflicting instances of the same right, using the principles that Rawls has provided. At this point I go beyond Rawls's account to indicate how, nonetheless, judges can properly be regarded as resolving this conflict of rights in a principled way. I then assess their adjudicative procedure in the light of Rawls's overall theory and conclude that the described method does restore, in a way compatible with Rawls's theory, the systematic character of rights and, with it, the priority of rights as a set.

## 1. *The Scope and Weight of a Right*

Rights can conflict. I do not mean to suggest here that such conflict is inevitable (for that is the very point that needs resolving). Rather, I want simply to say that such conflicts are very common. Thus, we find frequent conflicts between, say, the right to a free press and the right to a fair trial (as in the current issue of the De Lorean tapes) or between either of these rights and the right to privacy. And because specific rights do tend to conflict, we are prepared to say, in a more general way, that rights can conflict. Usually the conflict is not wholesale but, instead, is limited to an incompatibility between an instance of exercising or enjoying right A, by one person, and an instance of exercising or enjoying right B, by another. But the possibility of conflict seems to cut across the various main categories and to arise not only for garden-variety legal rights but also for constitutional rights, for human or natural rights, for the class of moral rights as a whole. There is nothing in the concept of rights that would rule out conflicts—or, at least, potential conflicts. We should not expect Rawlsian basic rights, then, to be exempt.

Every right has conditions of possession, a scope, and weight. The conditions of possession specify who has the right and how, indicate when it is said to be suspended or forfeited, and so on. The scope of a right specifies what the right is to (be it a liberty of conduct or an avoidance of injury at the hands of others or the provision of a service of some sort) and includes any limitations that are built into or decided upon for this right. The weight of a right is a determination, sometimes explicit and sometimes not, sometimes quite exact and sometimes rather imprecise, of how it stands with respect to other normative considerations and whether it would give way to them, or they to it, in cases of conflict. The question that we want to address is how these notions (of possession, scope, and weight) could be used to reduce or eliminate entirely the conflict of rights, in particular, conflict within the class of basic rights.[1]

One gambit would be to say that when right A and right B appear to conflict, we will eliminate the potential for conflict by saying that one of the rights is not possessed at the time, or not possessed at all, by the person who wants to exercise or enjoy it. This expedient is frequently resorted to as part of justifying punishment for lawbreakers. Thus, we might believe that strong measures are required as a response to a violation of person C's right by person D; we might also believe that these measures are likely to infringe D's rights (though they ought not do so insofar as these rights of D are equally stringent with those of C). The potential conflict here between the vindication of the rights of C and the rights of D is short-circuited by saying that D, in his violation of C's rights, had forfeited his own rights—or at least had forfeited those of his rights which would be invaded by the punitive countermeasures.[2]

The expedient of denying possession is not available to Rawls as a *general* solution to the problem of conflict between basic rights. Rawls argues, as we saw in chapter 3, that such rights are possessed fully and equally (except for a few accredited exceptions—such as children or aliens) by all citizens within a given well-ordered society. Citizens have the basic rights in virtue of the significant contributions that such rights make to the exercise of the two moral powers. Or they have them in virtue of the significant role that such rights play in realizing and maintaining the idea of a collective asset. Such rights are rights of (moral) persons, of lifelong agents within the social union. Thus, if persons have basic rights for the reasons indicated, they will continue to have them when there is a conflict of basic rights. And if persons or citizens have them on this basis, it is by no means clear that they would lose some or all of their basic rights when they act badly, even when they go so far as to commit violations of rights rules. For they remain persons and are still parts of the scheme of mutuality (though perhaps less worthy ones than they were previously). Basic rights are thus said by Rawls to be inalienable or, in an older language, "imprescriptible."[3] This means that they cannot be forfeited, given up, taken away, or annulled.

Thus, to eliminate conflict between basic rights, we must look elsewhere than to restrictions on possession. The likeliest solution would come, then, in limitations on scope or in the fine tuning of weight. We can see this most clearly by examining one right in particular, taking as our specimen the basic right to freedom of political speech and of the press. This is the right that is given the most extended treatment in Rawls's essay on the "Basic Liberties."

For convenience we can visualize a basic right as a sort of "space" marked off by a rectangle. The content of that space is given by the liberty (or the avoidance of injury or the provision of a service, as the case may be) named in the basic right. Thus, we can initially envision liberty of speech and press as simply covering all that is spoken and all that is printed. This is its operating "space"; we reach the basic liberty through successive partitionings of that space. What we would be left with after all the partitioning was completed is the central core of the right. This would be the indisputably protected or guaranteed part of the basic right in question.

The first boundary drawing, the one that defines the original space, is the distinction of speech from action. Thus, a distinction is made between advocacy and incitement. Crying "Fire!" in a crowded theater, to adapt Justice Holmes's famous example, is not speech but action—direct incitement to direct action. And again, so-called fighting words, as direct incitements, are not considered to be speech.

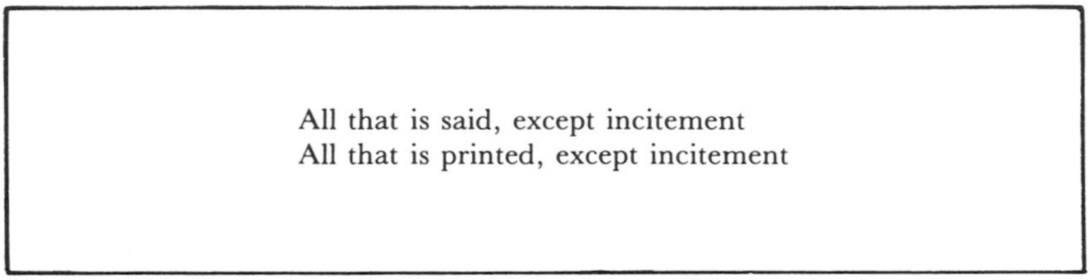

All that is said, except incitement
All that is printed, except incitement

FIGURE 9
Unpartitioned liberty of speech and the press.

Of course, persons in the original position or in the constitutional stage (or even at some lower stage in the policy process) could introduce further partitionings, this time *within* the domain of speech and press. Thus, obscene speech or libelous speech might be partitioned off. Although these things count as speech, such speech is not within the protected area of liberty of speech and press. It is not part of the basic liberty—the basic right—in question.

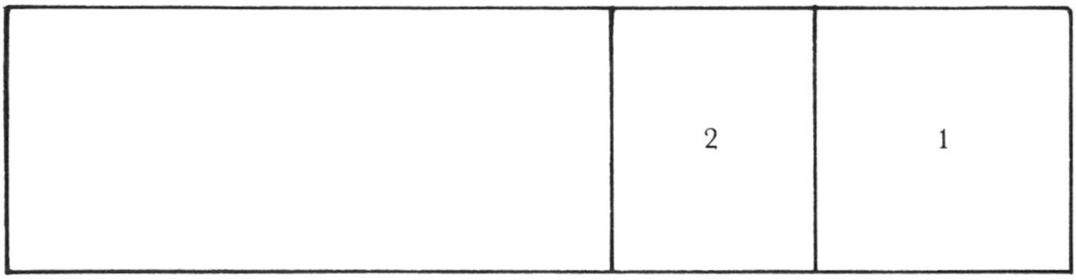

|  | 2 | 1 |
|--|---|---|

FIGURE 10
The original space now partitioned so as to exclude (1) obscenity and (2) libel.

There is another kind of constraint on the protected area which is not reached through partitionings. We should note it briefly. Speech often occurs—political speech, in particular—in a parliamentary setting or in some other relatively orderly give-and-take situation. Rules of procedure (such as General H. M. Robert's *Rules of Order*) are thus required in order to allow everyone to be heard and to assure that interested persons do not fail to speak, or fail to speak effectively, through misunderstanding of the process.[4] Often these rules of procedure are spontaneously arrived at, on the spot, as representing a consensus about what is fair. I would suppose, even, that rules for sporadic heckling and harassing of speakers by members of the audience could be codified in some such rules of fair procedure. Also, courts and administrators often undertake to regulate permissible speech, not in content, but in regard to its time, place, or manner (e.g., through permits to hold a large rally at a certain time and place and under conditions that ensure sanitary facilities, crowd safety, etc.).

These belong—in particular, the rules of orderly procedure—to what Rawls calls the "self-limiting" character of a basic liberty. Thus, he distinguishes between the *regulation* of a basic liberty (which has to do with acceptable limitations within its protected area) and its *restriction* (i.e., by partitioning). Restriction simply removes an activity from the protected area altogether; the thing that is partitioned off no longer lies within the scope of the right in question (as, for example, libelous speech is said to fall outside the protected area of the right of free speech). Regulation, however, does not remove an activity from the protected area of a right; rather, its function is to restrict or qualify a permitted action (as, for example, parliamentary speech is qualified in being subject to procedural rules). Partitioning *defines* the protected area by leaving some activities out; whereas regulation *modifies* those activities that remain within. Thus, regulation is part of the correct understanding of the activities (including ways of being treated) that come within the area protected by a right; hence, the regulation is part of the proper characterization of the activities within the central core of any given basic right.[5]

The point remains that without restriction, without partitioning, the basic right in question (as defined by this central core) will conflict with other accredited basic rights. For simplicity, I will emphasize in this section conflicts that could arise between one basic liberty (or noninjury) and another. Thus, for example, we must engage in further partitioning to mark the limits at which the basic right of speech and press is allowed to impinge on the basic right to a fair trial. There will, of course, be areas of overlap where the two rights can normally coexist; but there will have to be some ultimate line drawings—for there must be some restrictions, at the margin, on what is to count as within and what is to count as outside the area protected. And a similar partitioning would probably occur between the basic right of free speech and press and, say, a right to privacy.

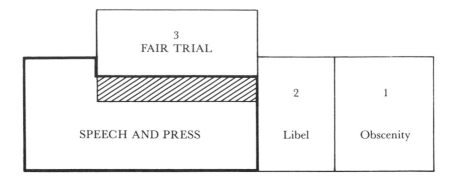

FIGURE 11

The protected space of the basic liberty of speech and press is indicated by the darkened border. This space is the result of a further limitation on scope so as not to impinge on activities within the central core of the right to a fair trial. The shaded area represents a zone of permissible overlap between the two rights. Thus, activities in that area fall within the scope of *each* of the basic rights in question, liberty of speech and of fair trial.

Not all of the restrictions introduced after this point, however, will concern the conflict between rights, because it is possible for a given right to conflict with other kinds of normative values. Thus, for example, the liberty of speech and of the press could conceivably conflict in time of war with a society's interest in national security. Rawls argues that a justifiable restriction on speech and press could occur only in a "constitutional crisis of the requisite kind," which means that "free political institutions cannot effectively operate or take the required measures to protect themselves" and that, without some such measures, those institutions cannot survive.[6]

It is unlikely such a crisis would ever occur, Rawls believes. So we need not partition liberty of speech against that unlikely event. More important, we may not be inclined to limit the exercise of the national security interest in advance by saying that where it conflicts with free speech, it has gone beyond its scope and, hence, is simply not permissible. It is very hard to draw such lines, especially in the abstract, and we realize that sometimes the interest in national security will involve great efforts and many sacrifices (including voluntary and self-imposed restrictions on speech and press). We might prefer, then, to let the right and the interest coexist, albeit uneasily. (Just as we prefer a similar coexistence between the basic rights to free speech and to a fair trial.)

We do not try, then, to limit conflict through redrafting of scope. That would often prove unnecessary and would probably prove to be too restrictive, of the interest or of the right or both. For, after all, there is nothing out of bounds about the speech in question except for its conflict with the national security interest. It is only because of such conflict, with another value or another right, that the speech might fail of protection *on a given occasion.* Thus, we do not treat it like libel, as being intrinsically outside the area of protection.

What we do instead is to identify an area of concern, in which national security interests and liberty of speech could conflict in a significant way, and then specify a test (rather like the "clear and present danger" test) that would determine when liberty of speech was to give way to the interest in national security. The test would be stronger than the one invoked by the U.S. Supreme Court, for it would link the "clear and present danger test" specifically to the imminent and unavoidable danger of a "constitutional crisis of the requisite kind."[7]

Thus, we resolve the problem of conflict here by specifying the *weight* of the liberty of speech against that of national security (an aggregate good): the weights are such that liberty of speech is given precedence as a consideration, in cases of conflict, except when that one very stringent test is satisfied. Indeed, we can generalize from the present case and say that whenever there is an area of overlap and hence of possible conflict, between two rights or between a right and another value, then the respective weights should be specified—at the points where significant and otherwise intractable conflict could arise—by reference to appropriate tests.

We have here a rough sketch of the basic liberty of speech and of the press. We have identified the area in which speech and press are protected (i.e., A + x + y in fig. 12 on page 135) and, within that area, the central core (i.e., A) of the right in question. The space outlined by the darkened border (in fig. 12) gives us the scope of the basic liberty; that space, as modified by "self-limiting" regulations and by the notion of competitive weight (which operates in the shaded areas), gives us a graphic representation of the proper understanding of significant features of that basic liberty.

At the beginning of the present section we said that we were concerned specifically with liberty of *political* speech and press. (This is also the way in which we described that basic liberty in chapter 3.) Accordingly, in order to reach this exact basic liberty, under this rather precise description, we need not consider commercial speech (e.g., advertising). This can be bracketed off, not because it is somehow ineligible for protection (because it is eligible, under the heading of fair equality of opportunity as discussed in chapter 4), but because it is not *political* speech. It does not come primarily under the basic liberties and noninjuries, as grounded in the universal fundamental interests of citizens, which we are here investigating. I will not bother to draw this particular functional partitioning into the figure, but we can presume its presence from this point on.

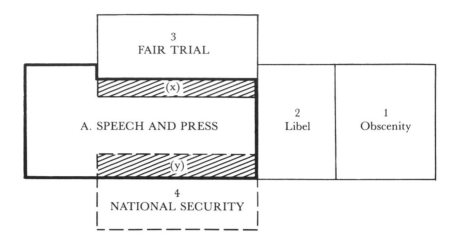

FIGURE 12
The space occupied by the basic liberty of speech and of the press, once delimitation is completed, is indicated by the darkened border. The shaded areas represent zones of overlap and possible conflict between that right and other normative considerations.

We have now reached, by a rather elaborate process, the main scope and the central core of the basic liberty of *political* speech and press. Once there, we can spotlight those "fixed points" which the "history of constitutional doctrine shows to be . . . within the central range of the freedom of political speech." Rawls names three points in particular: (1) that there be no such thing as the crime of sedition, the crime of libeling the government; (2) that there be, in the usual case, no prior restraints on the freedom of the press; and (3) that the advocacy of revolutionary or of subversive doctrines be fully protected.[8] These three points deepen our understanding of the scope and of the central core of the basic right to free *political* speech and press.[9]

Repeated applications of this same procedure—introducing limitations on scope through partitionings, identifying the main internal regulations, and establishing competitive weights in the zones of overlap—would allow us to achieve a similarly deep understanding of the other basic liberty rights. There is, moreover, nothing in principle that would prevent the employment of this same procedure to work up the profile of those basic rights that come under the second principle of justice: (a) liberty rights under the heading of fair equality, such as that to free choice of occupation; (b) rights to opportunities—for example, to schooling—as given in the basic right to education under that same heading; and (c) the basic right to income supplementation, under the difference principle.

136

More important, such repeated applications of the procedure would be, precisely, the way in which to reduce or even to eliminate conflict between basic rights. Thus, the possibility of a system of such rights is strongly supported by the analysis, in the present section, of the scope and weight of a right.

There are, however, problems with this analysis which were not addressed in the present section. Specifically, we need to determine where in the policy process these limitations on scope (and establishments of competitive weight) are to occur, and on what principle(s). These are matters to which we turn in the next sections.

## 2. Stages of the Policy Process

There is some difference of opinion regarding the proper stage, in Rawls's theory, at which the boundaries between rights are to be drawn. I mean the stage at which the basic liberties and noninjuries are balanced against one another and at which their main scopes and internal modifications are blocked out to form a single system of rights. The principal options suggested have been that this is to occur either at the constitutional stage (Bowie) or at that stage as supplemented by the legislative one, with particular emphasis on the latter (Fuchs).[10]

What seems to be at stake in this dispute? We can begin with the most obvious point: that the main stages in the policy process differ in the constraints that are imposed on relevant admissible knowledge. Thus, the constitutional stage is said to differ from the original position in this very respect. But the relevant difference, as we saw in chapter 3, is not great; it is merely that general facts about the society in which the constitution is being designed are allowed to penetrate the metaphorical veil of ignorance in the deliberations of the constitutional stage. But the corresponding differences in knowledge between the constitutional stage and the legislative one are not made clear in Rawls's book. He says merely that legislators are not to consult or favor their own particular interests (but this, of course, does not allow us to distinguish between the stages, since constitutional delegates would be subject to that same restriction). One expects there to be *some* difference between these two stages, however, if only because the very last stage named (the judicial/administrative) allows full knowledge at the point of decision, and that would make for an awfully big jump from the knowledge constraints imposed in the constitutional stage, were there nothing in between.[11]

I puzzled over this problem for some time, until I chanced to read a brief essay by Rawls, written shortly after his book was published. There he made clear that legislators, in drafting a law, could take into account the particular interests and needs of constituents.[12] But by that time I had already decided that what is central in the distinction of the constitutional from the legislative stage is not the differing constraints on knowledge but, rather, that each stage is marked by a difference in its governing task.[13]

Now, it is very common to divide the main tasks (constitutional, legislative, and judicial or administrative) among more or less distinct bodies, sometimes even wholly separate bodies (with no overlap in membership at all). But I will leave this fact aside, as being interesting but not essential. What is absolutely fundamental to the policy process, as we have described it, is that the priorities be observed by the bodies that carry out these tasks. Thus, work at the constitutional stage presupposes as settled the decision about principles of justice. Work at the legislative stage takes the established constitution as its framework. Likewise, adjudication and adminstration occur in a framework of formulated law, which in turn is compatible with the constitution, and so on.

It does not follow from any of this, however, that the same body cannot perform tasks at both levels, the constitutional and the legislative. Thus, the House of Commons, functioning as the British sovereign and without a written document called the constitution, notoriously wears two hats—the constitutional and the legislative—sometimes donning the one, and sometimes the other. It's merely that when it engages in legislative tasks, it must do so in conformity with the received constitution. And at either stage, that body—any such body—will perform its assigned task most effectively by observing the appropriate constraints on knowledge.

In sum, the main distinction between stages is drawn by functional differences in the main tasks (constitutional work, legislative work, etc.). Between these stages runs a line of priority. And at each stage a difference in the relevant constraints on the knowledge involved is properly invoked.

It is obvious, then, that a legislative body can engage in constitutional activity. Thus, a legislative body—to avoid confusion, we shall call it a parliamentary body—can formulate constitutional rights. It can draw and redraw the boundaries between basic rights. It can establish the competitive weight of a right in the zones of overlap between one such right and another (or between a basic right and a wholly different kind of normative consideration). But where it does engage in constitutional work, the parliamentary body takes the point of view appropriate to that task or purpose.

It does not, accordingly, consult the particular interests of citizens, those interests that can divide some citizens from others; rather, it considers only the universal interests of the representative citizen. And in its constitutional role, the parliamentary body presupposes the established theory of justice. Thus, the rights that it fixes on and elaborates in this role are those which are identified (e.g., under the heading of basic liberties and noninjuries) in the two principles of justice—that is, where these principles constitute the public sense of institutional justice in the well-ordered society in question. By the same token, decisions about weight (between, say, the right to free speech and the interest in national security) would necessarily take as settled the priority of basic rights, hence that particular right, over aggregative concerns. And when the issue was constitutional amendment, the parliamentary body, in its constitutional role, would accept as given the existing political and economic constitution that surrounds the part to be amended—while taking care that the priority of basic rights over aggregative matters is respected throughout the process.

Sometimes, of course, a parliamentary body merely extends a basic right—or strengthens one or adjusts a balance—through legislative enactment. This work is properly described as legislative rather than as constitutional (the passage of the U.S. Voting Rights Act of 1965 would be an example). The determining consideration here, in our decision to call it legislative, is not the body that does the work but, instead, the nature of the task performed—whether it presupposes an already-existing constitutional right, the nature and degree of modification it involves for that right, the character of the knowledge restraints that are properly invoked in the task, and so on.

All establishing of basic rights—where their main scopes and principal internal modifications are set forth against the backdrop provided by a theory of justice—and all balancing of basic rights against one another and against other normative considerations compose work that occurs at the constitutional stage. It is a constitutional task. My point is simply that parliamentary bodies can reach this stage and do this work.[14]

We need, in sum, to keep two issues distinct: the *stages* of the policy process and the political *bodies* that are in on the work at each stage. Constitutional work can only be done at the constitutional stage, but it can be done by both constitutional assemblies and parliamentary bodies. Thus, Bowie is right in suggesting that the specification and adjustment of basic liberty rights is done at the constitutional stage but wrong in suggesting that it is work that can only be done by a constituent assembly; Fuchs is right in suggesting that it can also be done by parliamentary bodies but wrong in suggesting that this takes us to the legislative stage.

Of course, Rawls is aware that sometimes courts also engage in constitutional work. Thus, we find him criticizing the U.S. Supreme Court for its decision in the *Buckley* v. *Valeo* case.[15] In this decision the Court considered two parts of the Federal Election Campaign Act of 1971, as amended in 1974; it sustained those parts of the act which limited eligible *contributions* to a candidate for federal office but declared invalid those parts which put a *ceiling* on the *amount* of personal or group expenditures that could be made in support

139

of individual candidates. The Court argued, in the latter instance, that the act substantially burdened the First Amendment liberties of free political speech and association.

The point of Rawls's criticism is not to object to judicial scrutiny of acts of Congress (with the power to invalidate them); rather, Rawls objects to the view which the Court apparently had taken, namely, that the basic right of political speech could not be limited by the political-participation rights (one person/one vote, etc.), as defined in the notion of "fair value." In short, Congress had attempted to adjust the scope of these two rights and to strike a balance between them. This was, Rawls suggests, a correct move to make in principle—the principle being that the boundaries of rights can be drawn and redrawn to avoid potential conflicts between rights and to realize as fully as possible the interests that are being served in the central cores of adjoining rights. But the Court had denied the principle itself—or at least had denied that it holds between liberty of political speech and the "fair value" of the political-participation liberties.[16] This, then, is the gravamen of Rawls's objection.

Matters of rather general import emerge in this brief discussion of the *Buckley* decision. First, the law under consideration is an example of constitutional work by a parliamentary body. Rawls endorses this work—in principle. Second, it affords a further example of the drawing, by a competent body, of a particular boundary between two adjoining rights, thereby affecting the scope of each. (Hence it could have been used as an illustration in the first section of this chapter.) Finally, it reveals that Rawls does not object in principle to judicial review, that is, to court annulment or invalidation of acts of Congress (or of state legislatures).[17]

Thus, we would have to add that courts too, and not merely parliamentary bodies, can engage in constitutional work. Courts can be involved in the business of establishing the main scope and internal modifications of particular basic rights and of balancing basic liberties and noninjuries against one another.

It follows, accordingly, that courts, in their role as constitutional interpreters, should adopt the appropriate perspective. Here they must repair to the standard of the universal interests of the representative citizen and must observe the priorities between stages and respect the relevant constraints on applicable knowledge which operate within that perspective. Hence, courts in this role do not utilize their capacity for "full knowledge"; it is suitably restrained at the constitutional stage. Similarly, when courts engage in statutory construction, they must adopt the perspective appropriate to that activity: the same perspective that the legislature occupies when, by taking into account the needs and interests of those who are subject to the law, it sets policy and enacts law under the constraints provided by the established constitution itself.[18]

The capacity of courts to exercise full knowledge of particulars in their decisions takes hold, then, at the point of performing a single one of the judicial tasks: that of applying valid law on given occasions to individual cases. In this respect the work of courts is like that of administrators. Indeed, courts sometimes themselves engage in administrative work—when, for example, they oversee the desegregation of a school district or supervise the carrying out of the terms of a will. Hence, in their work at this level, both courts and administrators (and individual citizens in obeying a given law) come under the same knowledge conditions.

The upshot of the discussion in this section can be put succinctly, then. Parliamentary bodies operate at different levels in the policy process; sometimes they operate at the constitutional stage, and sometimes at the legislative. At each stage there is an appropriate perspective to occupy and attendant constraints on knowledge which should be invoked in order to do well the work at that particular stage. Likewise, courts operate at these two levels, and the point about perspectives and knowledge constraints holds for them at these levels just as it holds for parliamentary bodies.[19]

In the constitutional work of establishing and balancing basic rights, both parliamentary bodies and the courts are concerned to restrict the main scope and to devise internal modifications for particular rights so as to prevent conflict between those rights and to preserve intact the central core of each. We would expect them, then, to have due regard for each of the basic rights that are listed in the first principle of justice. But the constitutional work of these bodies, as I have described it, also results, in effect, in a system of rights. Thus, we would want the bodies to be guided not merely by a list but, more particularly, by consideration of what would make for an optimal arrangement of the basic liberties and noninjuries mutually. We must look to some conception, available to the bodies, of how such a system is to be made coherent.

### 3. A Criterion of Coherence

One guideline that might be cited here is that legislators and judges, in their constitutional work on basic rights, are to follow the maxim that one is to achieve "the most extensive total system of equal basic liberties compatible with a similar system of liberty" for each and all. This maxim apparently represents the explicit emphasis of Rawls's first principle of justice. It has been subject to much criticism, most notably by Hart.[20]

141

The simple fact, though, is that Rawls does not advocate any such criterion. Rather, he argues that we are to prefer that array of mutually adjusted basic liberties which would be selected in the original position (or at the point of constitutional action) for the design of the basic structure of a society. One might be tempted to say that the choice between two arrays which differed qualitatively (where the one was more extensive, in that it included more diversity in the content of liberties or extended over more persons than the other) should be governed by the mere extent of the basic liberties. This would not be correct, however. Rather, if the more extensive set was in fact the *rational* choice under the relevant constraints, then it should be chosen. It would then be the choice that best meets the relevant normative consideration: the consideration that it would be preferred in the original position over the alternative option. But if the array that has the lesser extent of basic liberties was in fact the rational choice under these same constraints, then it should be chosen.

What governs all such choices is not the greater extent of liberty but, rather, the satisfaction of the relevant normative standard. Thus, we might note, in passing, that Rawls's preferred scheme of basic liberties is not as extensive as are conceivable alternatives. It is less extensive on the issue of voting, for example, than a scheme of liberties which would allow the vote to all persons above the age of five or which would make *all* political offices elective. And it is less extensive than a scheme which would include not only the basic liberties that Rawls lists but also the liberty of individual persons to own productive property or to make unequal economic contracts. So we could not say that Rawls has attempted to achieve "the most extensive total system of equal basic liberties."[21]

We should not conclude, however, that he thereby leaves out altogether a consideration of the extent of liberties. For the parties in the original position are concerned to identify, and would prefer, as extensive a set of equal basic liberties as it would be reasonable to select under the constraints given there. Thus, the correct way to read Rawls's well-known first principle of justice is to say that it recommends the selection of a more-extensive *justified* set, or list, of basic liberties over a less-extensive one, because it enjoins the selection of the most-extensive *justified* array. If we remove the italicized words, we get the usual way in which Rawls states his first principle—the way in which it is normally understood. However, as we saw in our discussion on chapter 2, Rawls characteristically puts the first principle in the form of one grand, architectonic moral right: "Each person is to have an equal right. . . ." Here the force of calling the set of liberties *justified* is captured in describing the whole set as something that one has a right to. This I take to be the point of Rawls's rather eccentric use of the term 'right' in this regard.

In his later writings, Rawls, realizing that his initial statement was neither clear nor to the point and that it had been subject to misunderstanding, attempts to put things in a substantially different way. Thus we find him saying, in "Basic Liberties," that the scheme of basic liberties and noninjuries is not drawn up to maximize anything.[22] He even goes so far as to offer a reformulation of the first principle of justice so as to remove misleading language: the principle now is to be taken as requiring, not "the most extensive total system," but, instead, a "fully adequate scheme of equal basic liberties," so long, that is, as it was "compatible with a similar scheme of liberties for all."[23]

In this article, Rawls emphasizes that the coherence criterion for the basic liberties should tie in closely with the "master argument" (as I have called it) for the first principle and that, accordingly, we should adjust the scheme of liberties "so as to allow the adequate development and the full and informed exercise of both moral powers in the social circumstances [which] arise in the well-ordered society in question."[24] Rawls brings this normative perspective to the fore in his reformulation of the coherence criterion. Thus, it is with this result in view (i.e., to allow for the adequate development, etc.) that the basic liberties are to be specified and adjusted "in accordance with the rational interests of the representative equal citizen" as determined from the perspective of the original position and from "the point of view of the appropriate later stage" (i.e., the constitutional).[25]

We can take this version as Rawls's latest and best attempt to provide the relevant political agencies with a guiding principle for blocking out the main scopes and internal modifications for particular basic liberties and noninjuries and for balancing them against one another (and against other normative considerations) so as to form a single coherent, nonconflicting system of rights.

This principle, it should be noted, is restricted to basic liberties and noninjuries. That is not surprising, since the principle was extracted from an essay devoted to the basic liberties. But it will not do in the context of the system of rights we have been developing in the present book, out of the entire corpus of Rawls's writings. For that system includes basic rights that come under the second principle of justice, and not merely the first. I refer here to rights such as those to economic opportunity (as found in the free choice of employment and occupation), to social services (e.g., free public schooling, under the principle of fair equality), and to income supplementation (under the operation of the difference principle). Accordingly, we should open up the formulation of the coherence criterion to include these rights—the basic rights of the second principle—as well as the more familiar rights to the basic liberties and noninjuries.

This much would seem to follow from points made in the previous chapter: that diverse elements in a theory of justice must be made compatible with one another in the theory and in a well-ordered society and that basic rights have priority, as basic rights, over aggregative concerns. It is a priority that has accrued to them simply insofar as certain conditions were met.

Thus, they must be distributions of something desirable or beneficial to all persons in a society; the distribution must be specifiable under public rules that could be devised in the original position or in the constitutional stage; the distribution, in equal determinate amounts or at equal determinate levels, must be guaranteed to every citizen by the arrangement of the basic structure. All basic rights meet these conditions. There can be no such thing, accordingly, as the priority of one basic right over another. It is necessary, then, to adjust them to one another in a single system of rights.

I grant, of course, that the determination of basic rights here has been arrived at via two quite different routes. Arguments on the one path draw directly on the idea of fundamental interests in reaching the conclusion that certain liberties and noninjuries, as significant means to or as essential parts of realizing the two moral powers, should be distributed *equally* to all citizens. These are the basic rights to liberty and noninjury, which are specified in the first principle of justice. Arguments on the second path—in particular, the one from collective asset—start from a radically different point (that of differences in natural endowment and initial social circumstances) and, assuming a resultant inequality in economic roles and positions and in attendant income and wealth, conclude that there are certain opportunities and levels of material well-being which must be assured equally to all. These are the basic rights of the second principle of justice.

Thus, there are two distinct master arguments involved here, each of which ranges over discrete sets of primary goods; but this fact in no way detracts from the claim that there are basic rights (in one and the same sense of *basic rights*) generated under each argument. At the core of all basic rights, in virtue of their character as basic rights, are interests which it would be rational to identify and protect, for each and every person, when viewed from the perspective of the original position or of the constitutional stage. All basic rights, then, are rational interests of the representative citizen. Hence, all basic rights fall within the general scope of the Rawlsian criterion for coherence and should all be mutually adjusted to one another under that criterion.

My argument should not be taken as requiring that the criterion be reworded (as regards its general scope, that is, as regards the harmonizing of the rational interests of citizens). The wording is fine as it stands. What *is* required is that in reading it, we understand the criterion to range over all of the basic rights. They are all to be molded under it, despite their source in different master arguments. The coherence sought is the coherence of all of the basic rights toward one another.

Thus, delegates and legislators and judges, in doing their work of constitutional adjustment (through partitionings and limitations of scope and through the assignment of weight at points of overlap), cannot assign a greater weight to a basic liberty right than to a basic right to opportunity (where these overlap and hence potentially conflict) on the ground that the former is a right to a liberty. Such a move is ruled out by the Rawlsian criterion of coherence, understood in the way that I have specified. The priority of any basic right over another is simply not a relevant concern.

This, of course, does not inhibit legislators and judges from drawing boundary lines between basic rights. They draw them all the time between one basic *liberty* right and another in situations in which no such notion of priority could be said to operate. Hence, there is no problem, in principle, in their drawing boundary lines, again without resort to notions of priority, between basic liberty rights and basic rights to opportunity or to income supplementation—or between rights of the two latter sorts.

Nor does the coherence criterion rule out all assignments of weight, for properly designed assignments can satisfy it. To show this, let me draw on my experience in New Zealand for an example. During several months of 1981 that country was agitated by controversy and torn by strife over a series of rugby matches which were to be played, at various sites in New Zealand, between a select team from South Africa (called the Springboks) and a select team from New Zealand. Although there was one black player on the Springboks, his selection was widely regarded as a token, and the South African team was perceived to be constituted on racially invidious grounds and to be representative of a country whose official policy was one of apartheid. In their justification for allowing the Springboks in for these matches, the New Zealand government cited the overriding importance of one consideration in particular—namely, the policy of allowing all sports events as being attached to the right of free association. In my judgment, since the issue involved gainful employment *in New Zealand,* the government would have done better to cite as overriding a different consideration—namely the policy of not allowing matters of race to interfere with the right to free choice of occupation and employment—and to have disallowed, on that ground, the immigration of the Springboks to play in the matches.

I have suggested, in sum, that it might be rational for a parliamentary body to assign more weight to a policy that is attached to one basic right (e.g., a policy of not allowing discrimination to burden the free choice of occupation and employment) as opposed to another policy that is attached to a different basic right (e.g., a policy of allowing *all* sports events, as attached to the basic right of free association, even where one or both teams were constituted on invidious racial grounds). It would be rational, that is, if the former policy were judged, after due consideration and careful argument, to be closer to the central core of the one right than the latter is to the core of its right, or even if the former policy were judged to be more tightly associated with its core, in historical or popular experience, than the latter is with its core.

These are difficult judgments to make. Nevertheless, one could say that a policy is close to the central core of a right if, when that policy is discontinued or disallowed, other policies under that same right are weakened. Or again, it is close if there was thought to be a gap in the area protected by the right when the policy was absent. Now, all such judgments require that we have a proper understanding of the rights involved. Thus, if the *political* character of the right of free personal association were emphasized, as it would be with freedom of speech or of peaceable assembly, we would probably conclude that a policy of allowing sports events is less closely associated with that right, properly understood, than the policy of not burdening the marketplace with racial discrimination is with the right to free choice of occupation and employment. Or if the commercial nature of sports events (and their corresponding character as a "public accommodation") were emphasized, then we would probably reach the same conclusion. Or again, that same conclusion might well be drawn in cases where we associated the sports event policy, as we properly should, with a person's moral power to have and to advance a determinate conception of the good and where we associated the antidiscrimination policy with fair equality of opportunity.

It follows, by the same token, that it would be rational for a judge or an administrator to give greater weight to the exercise of one basic right (by person A) than to the exercise of a different basic right (by person B), if the former was close to the central core of the right or was done regularly (by everyone) and if the latter was remote from its core or done infrequently (by anyone). Of course, the fact that the Springboks would be coming into New Zealand "just this one time" might influence the determination somewhat, but I doubt that it could make a decisive difference. In any event, we can leave the matter and its details here, for my concern is principally to exhibit the kind of reasoning that goes into the determination of the weight of policies under respective basic rights and to show that such a determination can be fully compatible with the Rawlsian criterion of coherence.[26]

From the argument conducted in this section, it should be obvious that the Rawlsian criterion for coherence is only a schema. It requires factual filling in order to operate. It merely guides decisions; it does not make them. The policy makers—the delegates and the legislators and the judges who adjust the basic rights—must identify the relevant facts and take them into account. They have the coherence criterion, understood by reference to its philosophical background (the three "model" conceptions—of the original position, the person, and the well-ordered society—and as well the priority of basic rights; the reliance on the two master arguments to help specify the central core of the various rights; the stages of the policy process; and so on). The coherence criterion in effect summarizes and encapsulates to this point the theory of justice (as found, for example, in the sections of the present book preceding this one). It is this criterion—when combined with the facts, the relevance of which is, in part at least, determined by the criterion—that allows the political agencies to accomplish the actual balancing of basic rights.

The political agencies start from the idea of the rational interests of the representative citizen, as determined by the two master arguments in the original position. This is the point of orientation that anyone has in occupying the perspective of the constitutional stage. Delegates to a constitutional convention may find this idea adequate to their task, but only when they combine it with the relevant institutional history of the society whose basic structure they are designing. Legislators may have to go beyond it, but only in an acceptable way. They can never use the information available to them, of the sort found at the subsequent legislative stage, to override any of these rational interests of the representative citizen. Thus, they cannot elevate the needs and interests of actual constituents over any such rational interest. But they can—when the perspective of rational interest proves inconclusive regarding a particular boundary making between rights, or regarding a particular assignment of competitive weight to them—draw on their knowledge of the needs and interests of actual constitutents to help determine the decision they are making. They can, that is, if the decision reached is consistent with the idea of rational interests, with the coherence criterion and its philosophical background, from which they started.

Accordingly, judges, too, in their constitutional work should not override any one of these rational interests, as determined in the original position and in previous constitutional work. Full knowledge of particulars, excluding only that which is illegitimately prejudicial in the case at bar or is narrowly self-interested respecting their own lives, can be utilized here. Such knowledge, together with the relevant traditions and existing rules of law that are appropriate to the bench they occupy, can help to guide judges in their drawing of boundaries and in their assignments of weight. Again, however, we must limit the acceptable intrusion of this kind of knowledge to those instances in which the notion of rational interests, as properly defined in existing law, proves inconclusive for resolving the issue under consideration and in which the resulting judicial decision about rights is consistent with the notion of the coherence of the rational interests of the representative citizen from which we started.

Thus, the Rawlsian criterion of coherence, understood in the way I have specified, and the decision procedure that it enjoins seem to be workable enough. The political agencies ought, in principle, then, to be able—through judicious partitioning, limitation of scope, and assignment of competitive weight in zones of overlap—to adjust the basic rights to one another and to eliminate conflict of rights.

Once these rights have been satisfactorily balanced definitionally, they cannot conflict with one another. Or in the rare but foreseeable case in which one right and another might conflict, the drafting bodies could add a determinate weight to policies under each, such that the possibility of real conflict would be wholly forestalled.[27] Within its assigned scope and given its determinate weight, a well-defined right simply governs all applicable situations that arise in the domain of rights.

If the relation between a well-defined right (e.g., the right to free political speech) and other normative considerations (e.g., the interest in national security) is set up in the same way, then that right would literally govern all applicable situations. Thus, there would be no true conflict (conflict outside of the rights-defining rules) even here.

It might happen perchance that a "constitutional crisis of the requisite kind" would never arise and, hence, that the right to free political speech would never, justifiably, be outweighed by the national security interest—that is, never outweighed as long as such "reasonably favorable conditions" prevailed. This is not to say that the right to free political speech would be absolute in any stronger sense over against any such aggregate good. It is merely to say that no proper exercise of the right could ever be outweighed, on occasions when the right was applicable, if the tests for justifiable overriding were never triggered—thanks to favorable conditions—in the zone of overlap between that right and these other normative considerations.

This is not a feature simply of that one right within the system, however; it is a feature of every one of them. All incumbent basic rights in a constitutional system are absolute in this same, quite restricted way—as never being justifiably outweighed by an aggregate good under favorable conditions.[28]

## 4. *The Problem of Internal Conflict*

Rawls and his interpreters correctly claim that boundaries of rights *could* be drawn so as to prevent any conflict between rights. I think, however, that they have exaggerated the degree to which this can actually be done, especially *in advance* of situations in which conflict could occur. Accordingly, there will probably always be a need for courts to balance and weigh competing rights on the spot, even within the situation that Rawls and his interpreters have described.

I would be willing to concede, however—if only for the sake of argument—that rights could have a sufficiently well drawn scope. I would also concede, though more reluctantly, that rights could be assigned a tolerably determinate comparative weight by the drafting body. I am willing to concede these points because it is at least *theoretically* possible that scopes and weights could be competently drafted into the rules defining rights, by constitutional conventions or by legislators and judges in their constitutional work. Let us suppose, then, that this drafting has been done expertly—to the point where conflict between rights (and between rights and other values) could be eliminated.

Even so, a problem with conflict of rights remains. It is unlikely that, even with a well-defined scope and a clear central or "core" content, a right could be so formulated that conflicting claims within that selfsame right could never arise.[29] I would suppose, for instance, that conflicting claims could arise under the right to freedom of conscience (a constitutional right).

Consider the case of two persons, married to each other, who belong to quite different religions: the husband is of the Mormon faith; the wife, of the Jewish. Each feels a special religious obligation—that is, it is a significant internal feature of the religion that each faithfully adheres to—to include their son (aged about eleven) in the religious beliefs and practices appropriate to that parent's respective religion. Each parent is devout and dedicated to the religion in question; neither wishes to coerce the other parent or the son; but neither is willing to let the matter ride—to leave it to the son to decide, for example, after he has come of age—and neither thinks that a nuisance, or anything offensive, is created by the practice of the other's religion (nor could anyone reasonably allege so). Clearly, if these people stick to their convictions and exercise their religions freely, there will be a conflict between them: for each in exercising the right of freedom of religion will run athwart the allowed exercise of the other's selfsame right.

This conflict is between instances of one and the same right and would, although it is technically a conflict within a single right, be described as a conflict of rights. Even if one were to set this description aside, as being somehow peculiar, the fact remains that such a conflict would challenge the coherence of a system of rights and might disqualify Rawls's characterization of such rights as absolute (even in the restricted sense that he had in mind).

For the important point is that we are here dealing with the "core," or essential liberty, of the free exercise of religion. The right has been carefully defined, and the exercises under consideration are uncontroversially within its scope, well away from the boundary (and well away from any zone of overlap).

Now, it might appear that the son has a right not to be indoctrinated—that is, a right to freedom of conscience on his own part. Suppose that he does. The fact remains that this right could conflict with the right of the parents at some point. It might even be that at some point continued activity by the parents would be regarded as coercive of the son and as impermissible under the right to free exercise of religion. In the present example, however, I have supposed that such points have not yet been reached.

I would not claim, by the way, that every well-ordered society will have a religious dimension (and, hence, that religion will inevitably be included in the notion of liberty of conscience). Nor would I claim that it is necessarily true that a religion would always have the character here described: that of being exclusive and requiring the indoctrination of minor children and their incorporation into the religion of the parent(s). But if a society has a notion of religion of this sort, then the right to liberty of conscience, as incorporated into the constitution of that society, would cover religion so understood. I do not, then, rule out such religion from a well-ordered society.

Hence, conflict of the sort that I have described could arise. And insofar as we restrict the matter to the right of each parent to free exercise of religion, the conflict here is between two equally eligible and equally central instances of the same right. Although the envisioned conflict would not be easily resolvable, it is possible that strategies could be devised that both maintained the full exercise of the right and avoided the specific conflict. There is no built-in guarantee of such a resolution, however. The parents might even feel the need to go to some impartial third party to help mediate their dispute. In the unhappy event that the matter did pass into the hands of a court—perhaps when one of the parents had yielded to the urgings of relatives or of coreligionists—then the court, in choosing between them (and such choice might prove unavoidable), would override the one exercise of the right in the interest of the other. So long as conflict *within* rights is possible, a problem remains, then, for Rawls's theory.

It might be replied, on behalf of Rawls, that I have missed a significant aspect of judicial reasoning. The rights under adjudication in a given case may only appear to conflict; for a proper account would stress that in actuality the court is trying to determine what these rights really are, when precisely considered, and to bring the case at bar under the one that, after refinement, correctly applies. (Or perhaps the court is trying to determine what such a right really is, when precisely considered, and to bring the case at bar under the one version that, after refinement, correctly applies.) In order to accomplish such a program, the courts may engage in a bit of theorizing. Here the relevant precedents to the case are considered, as well as the constitutional principles involved, should there be any, and even the governing moral norms; and these things are then brought together into a single coherent theory. From this theory emerges a principled drawing of the rights boundaries in question. Thus, on this model it is part of the job of courts to determine, in Dworkinian fashion, what our rights actually are (definitionally) and to affirm that one right, or that one exercise of a right, which properly holds in the circumstances of a given piece of adjudication. Judges aim at finding, applying, and, if need be, enforcing the right right.[30]

I would suggest, however, that this account is itself in need of refinement. The defender has failed to see that the very judicial procedure which he has endorsed violates the hypothesis from which we started. For initially we assumed that, in principle at least, problems of scope and weight could be competently dealt with. And the supposition at the start of this section was that they had been. Thus, the hypothesis we began with is that the criterion of rational interests—as determined from the standpoint of the representative citizen—had fully done its work *before* we reached the courts this time. We assumed that the scope had already been formulated and that the weight of the various rights had already been determined competently and expertly from that perspective.

Thus, it is precisely this standpoint that is no longer available to the judge, not because the judge, unlike the ideal legislator behind the veil of ignorance, has full knowledge of the relevant facts, but because the standpoint in question—that of rational interests—has already been exhausted. That perspective was used up when we formulated the scope and weight of the various rights—by hypothesis—competently and expertly.

The point is that the conflicting exercises that we are contemplating are equally eligible instances of the same right, as competently determined from the perspective of rational interests; hence, it would not be useful to employ that perspective in deciding between them. Nor would it be useful to revert to the grounds for determining weight in making such a decision, for these are already incorporated in the weight actually—and expertly—assigned to that right. Rawls's theory of rights, then, fails to give us guidance in resolving the conflict between exercises of the same right, exercises that come equally under the core or central content of the right, under the very same clause, so to speak.

The court, of course, need not be doing constitutional work here. It might decide, rather, merely to select one exercise of the right over the other and to give it judicial protection. That, and nothing more. And in so doing, it might draw on technical procedural points or on rules of precedent that did not touch the essential matter, as determined by the principle of rational interests; or it might even draw on peculiar historical and constitutional facts of the polity in question. Here the court would resolve a particular conflict of rights but would do so in such a way as to acknowledge the possibility of conflict of rights, then and in the future.

I conclude, then, that conflict of the sort that I have described is possible, even in cases where, as in Rawls's theory, stringent measures have been taken (under carefully specified conditions) to prevent conflict of rights. Accordingly, any theory of rights must recognize the possibility of such conflict and take it into account. We cannot assume that principles which are appropriate to the original formulation of rights, even when the principles are expertly applied, can be used to resolve all conflict of rights disputes. The dispute I have characterized is peculiarly immune to the sorts of considerations one brings to bear in such matters: that is, in the determination of the core content, the precise scope, and the weight of various rights. As we saw, the criterion Rawls relied on—that of rational interests—was effectively out of commission at the point where conflict arose *within* a given right. Thus, any theory which asserts or implies that individual rights can never conflict, simply by virtue of being well-defined rights, must founder on this point.[31]

### 5. *A Family of Rights*

The failure of Rawls's claim that well-drafted rights can never conflict does not, however, jeopardize the central features of his account of constitutional rights. The point on which the claim foundered—namely, that *internal* conflict within given incumbent rights is still possible—does not touch his more basic contention that conflict *between* rights can be avoided, or at least appreciably reduced, through judicious drafting of the scope of potentially conflicting rights. Such drafting allows identification of the central core and protected area of each right, and it includes assignment of determinate weights to govern the conflict of rights, in cases of overlap between adjoining rights, and to govern the conflict between rights and other normative considerations. Thus, this important idea in his account of a system of rights remains substantially intact.

Although we cannot say that every eligible exercise of a well-drafted right has priority (for this is precisely what the possibility of internal conflict would preclude), we can still say that, under "favorable conditions," constitutional rights will not be outweighed by other sorts of normative considerations (such as the interest in national security). Thus, it continues to be true that, in the normal course of things, an exercise of a constitutional right should always be given judicial preference and protection when competing with an aggregate concern.

The utilitarian might intervene at this juncture to note that after all is said on this point, Rawls's theory does in fact allow a basic right to be overridden, on a given occasion at least, by an aggregate concern. However, the very permissibility of such an overriding appeared initially (in chapter 1, for example) to be the main ground of Rawls's criticism of the utilitarian theory of justice. What becomes, then, of Rawls's notion of a guarantee? And what in the end, the utilitarian might ask, is the difference between Rawls's theory and his own?

The main contrast, in my view, is that in the Rawlsian theory, basic rights can be overridden by nonrights (e.g., the utilitarian considerations of general welfare, public safety, etc.) only when such an overriding is required in order to preserve a system of rights in existence. This, of course, is in sharp contrast to utilitarian theory, which would allow an overriding, all things considered, on the simple ground that it would increase the general well-being (where that increase could amount to nothing more than the increased well-being of *other* individuals). It is at this point that the Rawlsian guarantee comes into play: for the individual is assured that his basic rights will not be sacrificed simply to promote the general well-being. This is a pledge that the utilitarian cannot make.

In sum, then, the Rawlsian approach to the overriding of rights is geared to considerations that are internal to rights (as a set); the other approach is geared to utilitarian considerations (i.e., to increasing the *total* net benefit or, alternatively, the *average* net benefit). Not only are overridings justified differently in these two approaches but also, it is likely, different overridings would be allowed by them.

In this way, then, the leading idea in Rawls's theory—the doctrine of the priority of basic rights—is preserved. Their priority is over other normative considerations (over rights that are not basic and over goods, such as economic efficiency or national security, that are not rights). It is the priority of each basic right over any normative consideration which is not itself a basic right. And under circumstances that were less than favorable, a basic right would yield to one of these considerations only when doing so was necessary to preserve the system of rights itself.

In order to have these features—of coherence and priority—within a political setting (within the basic structure), basic rights must be made incumbent; they must come to have well-defined scopes, with identified core contents and assigned weights. Care must also be taken to reduce and, as much as possible, to eliminate conflict of rights.[32] They thus become in intention, in prospect, a family of rights.

The ideal of harmonization of rights—the creation of a system or family of rights—is served not only by the work of constitutional drafting but also by the low-level work of judges and administrators who, relying on established institutional processes and on standards and rules that are internal to these processes, resolve conflicts *within* given constitutional rights. The sort of work that is done in the latter case is different from what is done by the constitutional drafters (be they delegates or legislators or judges), and it cannot be done on principles that are appropriate to the constitutional stage.

In this work of systematization, the principles at one level are thus not available at the other. The work at the lower level—the level of judges and administrators—supplements the work at the constitutional level. The closure of the system of rights is thus completed.

To my mind, the single most important point that emerges in the analysis set out in this chapter is the indispensable role of political agencies and of institutional processes in the development of a family of rights. Such agencies are required in order to formulate basic rights, to promote and maintain them (as is necessary, if they are to be more than merely nominal rights), and to harmonize them through judicious drafting. The bodies here rely primarily on principles for rights formation that could be determined in the original position (or in the constitutional stage); I have in mind, of course, the two master arguments that underlie the two principles of justice. And the work of harmonization is conducted throughout by following a rather abstract criterion of coherence.

Even in constitutional work, though, the principles and the criterion must be supplemented: their use requires facts, and sometimes the facts that are brought in are more like those typical of legislative work or even low-level judicial work than they are like those available to delegates at a constitutional convention. The use of such facts in constitutional work is necessary, if basic rights are not to remain unduly abstract and irresolute; and it is permitted if the facts that are admitted are not antithetical to the perspective and to the principles of constitutional work. Even in constitutional work, then, the institutional processes of parliamentary bodies and courts are required and will be utilized, but only when they are compatible with the project of making basic rights incumbent.

In resolving conflicts *within* a given right, these facts and these institutional processes become the principal recourse. They are the main devices available for achieving a principled resolution that is consistent with the establishing and harmonizing of basic rights on grounds determined in the original position or in the constitutional stage. Thus, the use of facts and the deployment of institutional processes that are appropriate to each level—the level of constitutional work and the level of judges and administrators—work together to help create and preserve a family of rights.

In the end, the principal concern in a Rawlsian well-ordered society is not with specific rights so much as it is with a total *system* of basic rights; for any given right within such a system can be delimited.[33] There is no priority of one basic right over another within a family of rights. Rather, it is the system of rights itself, the family of rights embedded in the basic structure of a specific well-ordered society, that has the preferred status in Rawls's theory of justice.

Having an operative system of constitutional rights could plausibly be said, then, to outweigh all other moral or legal considerations. And no exercise of a well-drafted basic right would ever be outweighed by one of these nonrights considerations in the normal course of things.[34] In this very restricted sense—which assumes the existence of reasonably favorable conditions—a *system* of rights could be called absolute.[35]

The analysis in this chapter, together with the argument of previous chapters (in particular, the argument in chapter 6 favoring the priority of the distributive and determinate over the primarily aggregative, with its inbuilt indeterminate distributions), seems to have yielded a comprehensive endorsement of the primacy and coherence of the Rawlsian basic rights as a set. Now that this coherence has been affirmed through the workings of the institutional processes of a well-ordered society, and the problem of conflict of rights resolved, we are in a position to return to the issues about social and economic rights which I raised at the end of the previous chapter. For the way is open to consider expanding the notion of basic rights under the difference principle, to include things other than the basic right to income supplementation, without disrupting the idea of a system of rights or the priority of that system in Rawls's theory of justice. I turn my hand to that task (the determination of basic rights in the general domain of economic distribution) in the final two chapters.

# • 8 •

# RAWLSIAN ECONOMIC JUSTICE

This chapter and the next one explore the application of Rawlsian justice, not in the political or legal arena, but in the area of economic life.

In the first section of this chapter, I trace the main features in the application of Rawls's two principles, in particular the second (which we might call, for shorthand purposes, Rawls's principle of economic justice), to the basic economic structure of a society. For Rawls, the principal economic institution is a supply/demand market system. That is, he wants a more or less open and competitive market to provide the basis for allocating resources, for pricing, for setting levels of demand and consumption, for wage income levels, for many important investment decisions (where the system is one of private ownership), and so on. Markets, though, pose problems for Rawls's theory; they do not, while staying more or less in character, lead to results that will satisfy Rawls's principles of justice, especially the second. Accordingly, background institutions have to be installed, and I try to indicate roughly what these would be.

In the next two sections, I attempt to bring out more clearly the exact bearing of the principle of economic justice and its application by considering Rawls's account of the contribution of individuals to the economy and of the share that each could expect to receive in return. I then attempt to use this account to tackle the difficult issue of the ownership of productive property, an issue that Rawls tends to side-step in much of his discussion.

## 1. *The Market*

We could never know in advance (in the original position, for example) the relevant parameters of a going economic and social system and, hence,

157

would be unable to specify in the abstract the amount or level of income or wealth that any individual should have, given his contribution. This is why we have the market, to yield such determinate results: for that reason, of course, and also to provide for coordination of effort, for efficient use of resources,[1] and for fair returns.

Are we, then, to presume that market results are, over time, just? I think Rawls believes they are, but in a special sense of 'just.' A market is a procedurally fair way of determining what is produced, and so on, and of determining "legitimate claims, the honoring of which yields the resulting distribution."[2] What Rawls contends, then, is that since there is no independent or self-standing criterion for *the* correct outcome in the distribution of goods (wealth and income), we should institute instead a procedure that is fair in itself and let the fairness of the procedure translate to the results. The outcome (a particular distribution of goods ) is fair if the procedure by which it was reached (an open and competitive market) was itself fair. It is in this sense that a market can be said to be inherently just: it is a procedurally fair way in which to make allocations in the absence of an independent standard of what a *just* outcome would be at all the different points.[3]

In short, the operation of the market gives us determinate results (e.g., a particular price for a given commodity; a particular income or wage for a given kind of job). If we have an open and competitive market—that is, a market which is *open* in the sense given by the idea of equality of opportunity and *competitive* in the sense given by the economist's model of "perfect competition"—then we can assume that these determinate results are appropriate ones. We can assume that they reflect, as both Karl Marx and Adam Smith would put it, "natural prices" and the natural returns to the factors of production.[4] More important, we can assume that these determinate results are procedurally fair ones, undistorted by special transactional advantages (such as monopoly control of production) that some might have over others.

The picture that we have sketched is much too simple, however. Certain relevant complications have to be introduced immediately, for actual markets pose three distinct sorts of problems in Rawls's view.

First, as we saw in chapter 4, no actual market could ever be "open" in any absolute sense, because no actual market could ever satisfy the entry conditions, of *strict* equality of opportunity between persons, such that it would be in itself a fair procedure for achieving determinate results (including among these results the income shares of contributing individuals). Hence, the Rawlsian idea of fair equality of opportunity emphasizes that measures for such equality, even when conscientiously pursued, will yield only a passable equality of opportunity and will require, as their complement, some non-laissez-faire principle (the operation of the difference principle) which would further sift these results to provide basic fairness. The operation of this

principle further mitigates the effect of initial differences in natural endowment and social circumstance (in cases where measures for equality of
opportunity fall short, as they inevitably do). It would perform this role even
in an acceptably open and perfectly competitive market. So, one notable
complication, which must be introduced, is that the market, even under its
most favorable characterization, is not a scheme of pure procedural justice (as
Rawls says quite explicitly).[5] This complication, which is already present in
Rawls's theory in his discussion of fair equality of opportunity, would inhibit
any straightforward reliance on market results.

This particular complication can be set out in a somewhat different way.
We cannot assume that the results even of an acceptably open and competitive
market will be just ones, as measured by the standard of the difference
principle, for all individuals in a society. The contention here is not that the
open and competitive market does not, in some deductive way, follow from the
two principles. This has never been claimed. The market is proclaimed to be
virtuous in a different sense—that of procedural fairness—and it is enough if
the market, when just in that sense, is compatible with the two principles. But
that's just the point: it is not. The market, even if it were procedurally fair,
would violate the difference principle. For a market system, even when it stays
reasonably open and competitive, does not in any consistent or automatic way
serve the betterment of the prospects of the least-advantaged group. A
competitive market will not guarantee the compensating benefits for the less-
well-off that are required where differences in wealth and income are working
to the advantage of the better-off. So we conclude that, even in a reasonably
open and competitive market, difference principle–determined redistributions
of income and wealth are still required in order to achieve economic justice.

This brings us to the second complication. We should not assume that the
market will stay open and competitive (even it if was originally that way),
because it could be argued that actual markets tend over time, if left to their
own devices, to become less open and less competitive. This means that,
under modern conditions of production (in the factory system as described by
Marx, together with such subsequent facts as corporate ownership, finance
capital, the multinational firm, automation, and computerization), actual
markets tend to depart from the very features that would allow us to describe
them as open and competitive in the first place. Their long-term tendency,
then, is away from fair outcomes as defined in the notion of procedural
fairness. Thus, even if we had started with a fair system, we would have to
modify our appraisal of the determinate outcomes (in income shares, for
example) as the market "procedure" itself became less fair.

The second main complication, then, is that the market system is
unstable; the "invisible hand" moves us (and here I paraphrase Rawls) in the
direction of oligopoly, of imperfect competition.[6] So we must make do with

many market imperfections. These, however, tell against the very points that were originally cited as virtues of the market: that it was efficient and that its results were fair. Market imperfections undermine the claim that the market is open and competitive (in the economist's sense of perfectly competitive) and hence that market results are efficient or that they are procedurally fair. Here we have an additional reason for wanting to mitigate unfair and undeserved starting points. It's not merely that nature and initial social circumstance deal undeserved hands; the market does too.

Unstable and imperfect markets, as they tend away from those features that make them procedurally fair (in being open and competitive), tend to create larger and larger concentrations of both productive and personal wealth. And these concentrations progressively threaten the higher-order principles of justice (equal basic liberties and fair equality of opportunity). This is the third complication that markets pose for the Rawlsian theory of justice.

In sum, the market, although it has to some degree the virtues initially mentioned (practical coordination of efforts, determinate results, efficiency, and procedural fairness), also has serious defects. Even at its best—as a reasonably open and competitive supply/demand system—the market will not conform to the requirements of the Rawlsian principle of economic justice. Thus, even under optimal circumstances, the operation of the difference principle will be required to supplement fair equality of opportunity and to redistribute shares of income up to the minimum level set by the standard of collective asset (i.e., the pareto efficient–egalitarian point, as developed in chapter 5). Nor can we expect optimal circumstances to prevail. The market is unstable; it does not stay open and competitive; it tends to become imperfect. There are, thus, further or continued inequalities in the life prospects of people which are engendered by market imperfection. And these market imperfections (especially the growing concentrations of wealth and power) have an adverse effect on the "value" of the equal basic liberties for representative citizens in the various walks of life. In particular, such imperfections undercut the fair value of the political-participation liberties.

This general picture can be further amplified. Economists have long recognized certain inherent market "failures": the tendency to imperfect competition is, of course, one of them. The supply/demand market can also fail to provide desirable public goods or fail to deal with so-called externalities (i.e., the unwanted side effects of a specific production process).[7] Thus, Rawls's theory builds on conventional political economy; the theory recognizes not only the standard market failures, as sketched by economists (in particular, in its emphasis on the tendency to imperfect competition), but also certain market failures in matters of justice.

Rawls does not require, however, that the market be junked; for this would make its virtues—even in the attenuated form that they have—unavailable as well. Rather, what he requires is that we not rely simply on market results, that we take the market in hand and not let it run off on its own.

Thus, market results would continually have to be adjusted by the redistributive operation of the difference principle; and measures for shoring up fair equality of opportunity and for controlling the degenerative tendencies of the market would have to be put in place and maintained. There would also have to be devices for reducing or counteracting the growth of economic privilege, with its distorting effect on the equal basic liberties.

The solution that Rawls hits upon is to make the market the main economic institution and to include certain other features as additional background institutions that can be coordinated with the market. Among these he includes institutions that are designed to fulfill such diverse goals as full employment, transfer or side payments for welfare purposes (payments to bring the income level of workers up to some social minimum), antitrust regulation, and the redistribution of corporate and personal income and family wealth through taxation.[8]

We would simply build certain institutions into the market or into its immediate context, set certain goals down alongside market goals (namely, the market goals of efficiency, practicality of coordination, determinate results, fair outcomes), and then try to do justice by the whole mix. There are, of course, nonmarket costs that the market will have to bear—because there are goals and benefits which it cannot supply on its own.

We can look at these background institutions from two distinct perspectives. They are, in the first view, devices that are designed to alleviate the problems, or some of them, which arise when we consider the market and its tendencies in actual operation. The various devices used have as their object the maintenance of a competitive market—or more generally, the remedying of market "failures." Here, policy aims such as antitrust regulation would clearly fit. And since the notion of a competitive market as a fair procedure requires, as a precondition, that positions be open to all on a principle of fair equality of opportunity, there would also have to be other devices, such as universal public education and programs against discrimination, in place and operating.[9] The second perspective is, of course, the one afforded by the two principles of justice. Under this heading, the background institutions are regarded as fulfilling policy aims which themselves follow from the two principles. For example, transfer payments can be regarded as that part of the unskilled worker's total income which is required by the difference principle. And some devices, such as full employment or public schooling or redistributive taxation, would likely come under *both* headings, that of maintaining an open and competitive market (and hence the market values of efficiency, practicality of coordination, etc.) and that of maintaining the two principles of justice.

The crucial point is that the basic institution (the market) and the surrounding or background institutions must, as a set, be compatible with the two principles and must, in their collective tendency, satisfy those principles. In this way they can, as a set, be described, loosely, as compatible with the two principles and, hence, as just.

In our simple model, then, we are conceiving the background institutions as superimposed on the operations of an open and competitive, but unstable, market. There are two analytic stages here. First, there is the result given by the market: that is, the procedurally fair or appropriate arrangement (in market terms). Then, second, there is the background institution-determined adjustment, or set of adjustments, to that result.


## 2. *Just Returns*


Now, the Rawlsian account of the returns earned by individual economic contribution—and the related idea of desert—is mapped directly onto this two-stage analysis. In the first stage we consider individual persons as making their economic contribution in a particular institutional context, specifically through a reasonably open and competitive market. We can take this stage in abstraction and determine what the character of earned returns (shares of income, say) in it would be. Then we move to the second stage, to identify the differences that background-institution adjustments would make in these results. We must recognize, however, that this abstraction is something of a fiction—in most or in many cases. So we adopt a simple expedient: we pay attention to the income that is actually earned in an actual market. Then, after that, we take up the adjustments.

From the point of view of governmental agencies, these adjustments represent measures that are dictated by accredited general policies (antitrust regulation, full employment, taxation of inherited wealth and other devices designed to secure fair equality of opportunity, etc.). From the perspective of individual persons in the economic system, these measures often take the form of discounts on market-determined income—that is, on income actually earned (with the preferred case, the benchmark, being the income that each would earn in a reasonably open and competitive market). We know, of course, that the income actually received by some people is greater than it would have been in such a market. So, these discounts do not seem to be unjust. The crucial point is that even in an open and competitive market, justifiable discounts would still be taken. Such discounts might be taken directly (through taxation, for example) or indirectly (e.g., through increased product costs that were required so as to impound the cost of reducing pollution or of making a certain item safer for use by children).

The rationale for these adjustments follows the lines that have already been laid down in section 1: (a) that the market is to be made or kept reasonably open and competitive and that agreed-upon "failures" are to be dealt with; (b) that the first-order concerns of justice (the equal basic liberties and fair equality of opportunity) are to be served; (c) that even where a policy of fair equality is conscientiously implemented, undeserved circumstances are not nullified or discounted altogether but are merely mitigated, so that further adjustments at the point of distributing income and wealth are required; and (d) that in a well-ordered society, justice requires further adjustment, as determined by the pareto efficient–egalitarian principle, at that same point— that is, at the point where market-determined shares are actually received. So the adjustments are made at that point—not continuously, but regularly— through discounts on the income of those who are better-off (e.g., through annual tax payments). Likewise, at other appropriate points, other discounts on income, as required by the theory of justice, would be made. Thus, justice requires that a part of what individuals have earned in the marketplace be discounted or removed.

These discounts are taken in accordance with public rules or in accordance with well-accredited features of the economic system. In this way they are known by the citizens in advance, or could be. Thus, the citizens understand that their earnings are subject to such discounts and therefore adjust their expectations and make their vocational plans accordingly. The specified discounts and the adjustments that are required are simply part of the ongoing economic life, as determined by the institutions of the basic structure, of that particular well-ordered society.

Once individuals have passed the point of justifiable discounts, however, then the returns that they have remaining are returns they have justly earned. For these adjusted earnings (or income shares) are things that individuals can be said to be entitled to in the well-ordered society in question.

The idea that I have just sketched could be developed quite straightforwardly except for one thing. It is not clear how the Rawlsian idea of a collective asset, as set out in chapter 4 of the present book, would affect this theory of fair earnings (as adjusted returns on contributions).

For example, Rawls says at one point that "one might assume that the parties [in the original position] hold the principle that no one should be advantaged by unmerited assets and contingencies."[10] It follows from this assumption that *all* returns earned by economic contributions, based as they are on such assets and contingencies, would be morally suspect. I hasten to add that Rawls does not regard the parties as reasoning from any such initial assumption; hence, the inference need not be drawn. Nonetheless, there is much uncertainty and even confusion about the exact point of the collective asset idea and its implications. So, some attention must be paid to this point in any account of a Rawlsian theory of earnings.

Perhaps the simplest way to make a beginning here would be to mark a distinction between *having* a talent and *using* it. Rawls, given his market orientation, thinks that a contribution is made only through *using* a talent. The market does not reward the mere having of talents or abilities, just as it does not reward virtue per se;[11] rather, it is the use of ability, or the performance of the actions which are appropriate to good character, that earns returns—if, that is, these activities find suitable employment in the marketplace. Hence, a market return is earned only through the use of talents.

There is a more subtle point at issue here, however. Some might agree with Rawls on the use of talents and then argue that individuals do contribute to the *development* of their own talents. Persons do not merely have their talents; they also develop and use them. Thus, the argument continues, where the individual has contributed to the development of his own talents and abilities, he has earned or is owed, as his just desert, a determinate share of what he produces (contributes) through the employment of these talents.

It is this claim that Rawls is particularly concerned to discredit. For it is not clear how desert, in this peculiar moral sense, could enter the reasoning of the parties in the original position. Presumably, its advocates would think that one deserves the return, in some specific amount, because one had used a talent or employed a trait of character the having of which one could be said to deserve, or to have earned, in some precise degree in the first place. Thus, a sort of quid pro quo, a natural right of compensation, is propounded in which an exact share or return is matched with some precisely calibrated level of personal desert as a feature of one's contribution.

Talents, even developed ones, and the traits of character necessary to develop talents (such as perseverance and initial motivation) have a foundation. They are grounded, Rawls believes, by long lines or short ones, by complex connections or simple ones, in a person's natural endowment or in his initial social circumstances. And these no one can be responsible for in his own case; thus, one cannot ever be said to deserve them.

Even if it were universally agreed that natural endowment and parental nurture had together contributed, say, 83% to the development of an individual's talent, the proponents could not go on to conclude that the individual had contributed the remainder. Existing social science gives us no idea of what an individual would be like without these particular starting points and no idea of what he would be, or be able to contribute, in the absence of his actual social setting—for example, the particular well-ordered society in which he lives. Moreover, there is now no viable research program which, so far as we know, could lead to such an idea.

More important, the use of talents (including any use that is made to develop one's own talents) occurs in an institutional framework—in particular, in a market setting. Hence, the return (as measured in income shares, for example) to developed talent is determined in a complex interaction in which the contributions of others through the market (and through the maintenance of that and other basic structure institutions) always constitute a relevant factor. So, even if careful research could reveal the exact role and proportion played by (a) natural endowment and initial social circumstances, on the one hand, and (b) individual effort and initiative, on the other, there would still be need to take into account (c) the contributions of others. And since we could determine the actual economic value of individual initiative and effort only in a context in which (c) was considered, it follows both that we should not ignore (c) altogether and that (b) can never be specified, for purposes of determining economic returns or shares, in the absence of (c).

Accordingly, the notion of desert that we have been examining cannot be simply imported into the original position (for doing so would violate the constraint that we cannot presume moral norms there) and the idea of such desert cannot be generated there (for it runs up against the fact that was just pointed out—as well as the fact that no one is responsible for his own talents, in any complete or absolute way, to any reliably measurable degree). Therefore, we conclude, there can be no *moral* notion of desert available in the original position as a ground for the kind of claim that Rawls is here denying.[12]

It does not follow from this, however, that no idea of personal contribution or of desert is possible. It follows only that whatever idea one ends up with must be compatible with the collective asset idea and with its foundation in the notion that no one deserves his natural endowment or his starting place in society.

It is important to see here that the idea that the talents and abilities of individuals are a collective asset is itself a moral ideal, an ideal of justice, and is meant to operate despite the actual distribution of natural and social endowment in a society and despite the actual contributions that individuals make to improve this endowment in their own case.

Indeed, the peculiar point of the ideal is that one should (*morally* should) put the resources he is able to deploy toward benefiting all persons in a society, and not just himself. Hence, the claim that some person has contributed to the development of his own stock of natural talents is not incompatible with the idea of a collective asset. In fact, there would be no point to this ideal unless one believed that individuals do so contribute. Thus, Rawls's theory gives us no reason at all to deny that an actual individual has contributed to the development of his own talents.

We are not able, then, to say that people deserve nothing because they have, personally, done nothing (which is what the idea amounts to, that all contribution to the development of an individual's talent is to be put entirely on the natural and social endowment side of the ledger). But neither are we in a position to say that when the individual has contributed to the development of his own natural talents, a presumption is created that he deserves a *determinate* share of what has consequently been produced, a share that is exactly proportionate to the contribution made by his self-developed talents.

The notion that an individual deserves something, as based simply on talents that he has or on talents that he has developed, plays no role in Rawls's theory. It could not, because such an idea could gain no purchase in the original position. At the same time, we cannot repudiate the individual's possession of developed talents, or of the endowment on which all developed talents and their use rest, on the grounds that such possession was contrary to desert. This notion, equally, could gain no standing in the original position. Persons are what they are, even in the original position. Take away natural endowment and initial social circumstance, and they are nothing. Accordingly, a person's gaining possession of his talents in such a context is not a matter for redress.

The resolution to this deep problem, it seems to me, is to use another term than *desert* as the first-order term in which to develop the ideas that we are trying to express. The term that comes naturally to mind is *entitlement.* The two terms, though often confused, are not synonymous. For example, Prince Charles is *entitled* to be Prince of Wales and heir apparent to the British throne; but he does not *deserve* these things, because they are his birthright, and he is in no way responsible for them. *Desert,* contrary to *entitlement,* always connotes that the person involved has actually done something. By the same token, individuals are *entitled* to their natural endowments and their initial social circumstances, even though these persons cannot be said to be responsible for them and, hence, to *deserve* them. We can also say that individuals are entitled to their *developed* talents, even though, insofar as their talents have foundation in these same endowments and circumstances, individual persons cannot be responsible for their developed talents and hence cannot deserve them, "all the way down"—or for that matter, cannot deserve them to any determinate degree whatsoever.

The idea of a collective asset is consistent with this notion of entitlement and would make little sense (as a moral ideal) without it. We are in position, then, to fill in the notion of fair earnings, as adjusted returns on contributions, which I sketched at the beginning of the present section.

166

I will do so by drawing on a central argument that Robert Nozick makes, an argument to which Rawls would agree, step by step, once mutually acceptable qualifications had been added. Both Nozick and Rawls agree that (1) "people are entitled to their natural assets."[13] Nozick then argues that (2) "if people are entitled to something, they are entitled to what flows from it (via specified types of processes)." Rawls would need add only that the specified types include, as a feature, an open and competitive market as constrained by the requirements of justice; Nozick would, of course, concur in this. Nozick next asserts that (3) "people's holdings [income and wealth] flow from their natural assets." Rawls would dispute this, insisting that they flow from their *use* of natural assets, through the contributions of individual persons in a market context in which others are using *their* natural assets; Nozick would, of course, accept this amendment. For Nozick, then, and for Rawls too, the conclusion is that "people are entitled to their holdings" when they have used their developed talents in a fair market process, subject only to the constraints set by justice.[14]

Thus, the Rawlsian conception of just earnings is that they are the adjusted return on contributions that one is entitled to in a reasonably open and competitive market (or, if you will, in an actual market) within a well-ordered society—that is, a society ordered by principles of justice, preferably the two principles. We do not say that there is here an antecedently identifiable *deserved* return which adjustments then seek to approximate, as if the market and the other institutions of the basic structure were contriving to pin a medal on the individual as a reward for his talent or his use of it. Desert is a moral notion, but it is not a first-order one in this theory. It is subordinated, in the case at hand, to the principles of justice and to the institutions of the basic structure of a particular well-ordered society. Thus, we should not say that individuals have the returns that they are entitled to *because* they deserve them but, rather, that whatever the returns are, under the conditions specified, they could be said to be deserved in the relevant sense. (Whether the return received is a good or successful one is, of course, an entirely different matter.)

In the Rawlsian account of just returns, the individual contributes to the production of goods and services and receives back a distributive share (of income, let us say). There is no one-to-one relationship mandated here, nor are background institutions installed so as to accomplish such a result. Thus, if we suppose an individual's contribution to production—by way of the market—to be greater than average (in that he works more hours than average or even manages to build a better mousetrap), it does not necessarily follow that his received share will also be greater than average.[15]

But it does follow that in cases where greater-than-average returns are generally matched with greater-than-average contributions to production, there will be an incentive for individuals to develop the relevant talents and abilities. The individual here is not directly rewarded for the talent that he is able to achieve; rather, he develops the talent in order to make a productive contribution, with the prospect that this contribution will be matched by a greater-than-average share. Not every participating individual will receive such a share; some will actually lose. And the amount of the gain (or loss) is not set exactly (as a precise ratio, for example, of effort to return). For we cannot in justice gauge the fortunes of this person or that one (each known to us by a proper name).

Thus, no given individual, as described simply by his talents or his contribution, has a legitimate expectation of receiving any particular distributive share in a just institutional distribution of income or wealth or position. Hence, no one can rightly believe that he is due, or entitled to, some exact or precise share as the just return on his economic contribution.[16]

Indeed, there is no rule that could be formulated in the original position, or in the constitution of a well-ordered society, that would specify the determinate share of earned income that any particular individual, taken at random, could expect at the various levels (either of talent or of contribution). Now, of course, a general rule of sorts could be invoked. It would simply reproduce the Rawlsian idea of just returns (as adjusted returns on contributions) that I have been developing. However, this rule would not specify an exact or determinate amount, nor would it, of course, require the *same* share of earnings for everybody, for each and all of the citizens.

Let me put my contention more precisely now. There is one rule that could be formulated in the original position respecting a basic right to income (technically, to income *supplementation*). Thus, I argued (in chapter 6) that in Rawls's theory there is a basic right to just returns or shares, at some minimum guaranteed level in any well-ordered society, as given by the operation of the difference principle in that society. It will be the *same* level for each and every person there. Hence I called it a basic right. This point is compatible with what I have been arguing in the present chapter: namely, that there is no rule specifying a comparable basic right to just returns at *all* the relevant levels of income.

Thus, for Rawls, except for the minimum level of income required by the operation of the difference principle, there is no guaranteed provision of determinate and particular shares of wealth or of income or of a given economic position attaching to assignable individuals (and certainly not to *all* individuals) in the basic structure of a society. Hence, there is beyond that minimum no *basic* right to a particular income share in Rawls's theory of justice.

Of course, I would add, there is a place in Rawls's theory for rights to earnings of a sort: that is, rights to determinate and particular shares of wealth or of income or to a given economic position on the part of assignable individuals. For example, workers in a certain industry, such as steel or automobiles, might have a contract with firms there concerning such things as hourly wage rates, pension funds, and recognition of their union as sole bargaining agent, with the requirement that all of the factory workers belong to the union. Indeed, for most people (in our society at least), earnings are not directly in the market but are mediated through firms, usually through wage contracts or agreements. It is at this point, and not in the basic structure, that earnings do become determinate for given individuals and that one could be said to have a legitimate expectation concerning them. In the great preponderance of cases, then, rights to particular shares of income are going to be subsidiary rights. For we can speak of subsidiary rights, as distinct from basic structure rights, to particular earned shares under this contract or that, and so on.

We should not assume, though, that these contracts are insensitive to market forces. In a rough way, they do register them over time. Accordingly, the analysis that I have given above of market-determined income (and adjustments to it) can accommodate the fact of contract-determined earnings. And although we have noted the important role played by such contracts, we cannot regard them—at least with respect to lifetime expectations—as significantly altering the fundamental picture that I have sketched of just returns.

### 3. Contribution and Ownership

Rawls's treatment of the economic contribution of individual persons, as we find it embedded in the notion of just returns, is distinctive and completes the pattern of his basic economic analysis. Indeed, this emphasis on individual contribution has been with us from the beginning; for as we saw again in the previous section, there is an intimate connection between the notion of contribution and the dominant idea of a collective asset.

This connection can be set out simply enough. The idea of a collective asset, even when benefit to the least advantaged is being emphasized, does allow greater-than-average shares of income or wealth to be received by individuals. The availability of such shares can encourage greater-than-average contributions to the stock of goods and services that are socially available. And when, in a rough way, greater shares do encourage greater contributions to production, then the ensuing inequality is justified—the scheme of adjusted returns is just—as long as things are so arranged that nobody's profit comes at the expense, the real loss in lifetime expectations, of anyone else.[17]

Some of the main themes that we have identified here are not explicitly found in the usual statement of the difference principle. They are there nonetheless—submerged, one might say—and the principle should be taken as including them. For the idea of a collective asset, with the role that it gives to individual contribution, forms the theoretical backdrop of this principle. Accordingly, a properly augmented version of the difference principle would read something like this: Inequalities—that is, special offices (or greater-than-average returns in income, or greater wealth)—are justified in a given system only if they (1) encourage contributions that (2) result in increased productivity in goods and services; and only if the resultant increase in goods and services is distributed so as (3) continually to improve—ideally, to maximize—the life situation, as measured in income and wealth, of the least-advantaged group.[18]

The usual version of the difference principle, which gives us essentially only point (3), is a truncated one. For it would seem, in the normal course of things, that the life situation both of the least-advantaged group and of the advantaged groups could not be improved unless there was an increase through productivity of the available supply of goods and services. And since Rawls regards the development and *use* of talents and abilities as the peculiar and indispensable contribution that individual persons make to economic production, such contributions must relevantly attach to the difference principle in any complete version.

It is important to see that the difference principle does not merely start with an existing stock of goods and services. It does not presume that any such stock is simply *there*, like manna from heaven or a windfall of apples. Rather, the conception is that the stock has been produced by persons, through their contributions, in a particular scheme of social interaction. Accordingly, the principle attempts to do justice to the whole process of production and distribution. It can do so only by taking adequate account of individual contributions to productivity as well as the constraints of the pareto efficient-egalitarian point. The expanded version of the difference principle we are here considering has precisely the character, then, that is required by these twin emphases.

Now that we have this expanded version available, let us use it to probe one of the most problematic issues that Rawls raises: namely, the ownership of the means of production. Rawls is conspicuous in defending a market system, consumer preference, free choice of occupation, and so on,[19] without a corresponding commitment to the private ownership of the means of production.

To put this key point differently, Rawls defends a type of economic system as being just, in principle. This system has historically included as an element, perhaps the basic element, the institution of private property. But

170

Rawls is diffident about this institution. We have in his theory, then, capitalism without private ownership—the question of ownership is deliberately left open. Rawls seems to be as willing to allow social ownership as he is to allow private ownership of the means of production.[20]

The ownership of productive property is, I would suggest, an economic "office" and as such comes under the difference principle. Accordingly, we would have to turn to that principle, in its augmented form, to determine specifically how such offices, once they have been attained under conditions of fair equality of opportunity, are to be governed. Rawls's answer is that the institution of ownership within a particular industry, and presumably the size or amount of what can be so owned, is to be determined by what encourages contributions through management, investment decisions, innovation, and so on. We are speaking here, not of ownership in any narrow technical sense (with the clipping of coupons and taking of profits), but of contributions, through entrepreneurial and other skills, which result in increased social productivity in goods and services—subject, of course, to the usual proviso that the life situation of the least-advantaged class is thereby also improved.

Since either private ownership or public ownership, or some mix of the two, could satisfy this criterion within a given industry, or even within the economy overall, Rawls is agnostic on the question of private versus public, or of individual versus collective, ownership. What is important for him is the principle for determining which form of ownership is justified and the satisfaction of the relevant criteria by existing forms of ownership.

This matter is not treated abstractly in Rawls's theory. We start from the fact that the institution of ownership for productive purposes (whatever further detail such ownership might have) cannot be the basic economic institution. That status is reserved, in Rawls's account, for the open and competitive market. Ownership, then, is one of the economic background institutions within the basic structure of a society.[21] The various elements in the institution of ownership (of the means of production) would be determined, then, not only by constraints imposed by the difference principle but also by the ability of ownership institutions to mesh with proper market goals (i.e., goals of efficiency, practicality of coordination, fair outcomes) and with the operation of other economic background institutions, which have such diverse goals as full employment, antitrust regulation, and transfer payments to raise low-level incomes.

Now, as we have seen, Rawls does not distinguish sharply between ownership and management. As regards their acceptable economic functions they are essentially alike. In affirming this, Rawls reverts to an older tradition in economic thought—that of Adam Smith—and to a view of both management and ownership that is in line with his strong emphasis on measurable contributions to increased productivity. Accordingly, decisions about management would be made from the same perspective as ownership.[22]

Whether management is to be largely in the hands of government agencies, or of the representatives of private stockholders and financiers, or of the workers themselves (in a given firm or industry) would come down to whether management in that form—or in some mix of those forms—encouraged the development and use of appropriate managerial skills, with the result that productivity in goods and services was increased. It would come down to that, as well as the ability of a particular form of management to mesh with proper market goals, with the operation of other background institutions, and with the demands of justice as given in the two principles—that is, in the augmented difference principle and in the higher-order considerations of fair equality of opportunity and equal basic liberties.

I realize, of course, that once the initial and inevitable decision has been made to have private, say, or public or mixed ownership—or any of the various forms of management—the institution that is chosen will have its effects on the subsequent operation of the economy, including effects on the returns in income to individual persons. So, no evaluation of the economic results can be wholly free of such effects, of the shadow cast by the institution of ownership and its more immediate implications (for investment, public goods, etc.).

The point is that we cannot have an operating economy without first settling the question of property. So, we cannot begin by evaluating property-free economic results and then go on to install a system of property; rather, we must decide about the institution of ownership in flow—by evaluating results that already reflect a certain pattern of property holding. Indeed, there is no way to subject ownership institutions to evaluation, by reference to their contributory effects, without collecting data that has been "colored" historically by property arrangements that are already in place and by the legal support that has already been given to those arrangements. In any event, the factor of "coloring" or bias will operate to the same degree between public and private and mixed forms of ownership or of management and is not, therefore, a ground for choosing between them.

Thus, private ownership or public ownership, like greater-than-average income, would be justified only if it encouraged the development and use of talents and abilities, with the result that productivity in goods and services was increased. Institutions of ownership define ways of contributing to increased productivity, and details of just ownership are to be determined, as any other economic contribution would be, primarily by reference to the difference principle (in its augmented form).[23]

The picture that emerges is not simple. Ultimately, the economic institutions of the basic structure of a society are a complex set which, together with relevant political institutions in the basic structure, must give results that satisfy the two principles of justice. Nonetheless the normative rationale for these economic institutions and for governmental economic activity has been sketched along fairly straightforward lines.

In this account the justification of the ownership of productive property occurs, not at the very beginning, on the barren wastes of the state of nature, but on a well-populated stage, with a history of results in hand. Ownership is the last brick to be put in place in the basic structure of a well-ordered society. Not because ownership is last on the scene but because the institution is always subject, from the perspective of normative evaluation, to revision—given the results of its actual contributions, as measured by the augmented difference principle as well as by the constraints afforded by the other institutions in the basic structure of that particular society.

Accordingly, legislative and judicial action can always be taken to install or to change an existing settlement of productive property. For there is no natural right, in the traditional sense or in Rawls's sense, to any particular form of holding such property. Thus, what had been a scheme of private property in the means of production could be changed, by justifiable action of parliament or the courts, to one of complete public ownership or to something in between. And vice versa. And what had been a scheme in which the ownership of productive property was largely separated from management or from labor in it could be changed, by justifiable action on the part of parliament or the courts, to one in which these various functions were entirely merged in the same body or to some other arrangement. And vice versa.

Ownership (economically conceived) is a basic structure—or constitutional—institution. There will always be some form of ownership, some form of management, of productive property. But the determination of what form in particular, as given in the legal authorization for the holding of such property and in the support provided by legal and political agencies, is properly left to the action of parliament and the courts.[24]

Thus, in Rawls's theory there is no basic structure right to any determinate form of the ownership of *productive* property.[25] There is no basic right of private ownership and management, but equally there is no such right of public ownership or of workers to participate in ownership and management. And Rawls's stance on this point contrasts, in an important way, I think, with what he is willing to say about the ownership of *personal* property (which was included—as a protected basic liberty, hence as a basic right—under the first principle of justice).[26]

In this section, I have examined a feature of Rawls's theory which has not been widely understood, either in its main conclusions regarding the holding of productive property or in the reasoning that is used in order to support these conclusions. In the next chapter, I will turn to a feature of his theory that has been taken as settled in the scholarly and in the popular understanding of Rawls's theory. There is a considerable consensus that the difference principle does address the *needs* of those who are least-well-off in a society. I want to suggest that things are not so firm and clear-cut here as they have seemed. After that, I want to show that roughly the same kind of analysis which afforded a principled resolution of the property question—that is, one with a heavy reliance on institutional processes—can be used to resolve the problem posed by needs.

# • 9 •

# JUSTICE AND WELFARE

This chapter continues the discussion of Rawlsian economic justice. In the first two sections, I follow out the theme of distributive shares received by individuals by considering the special case of those who are not able to work, for reasons of age or physical or mental disability. It might seem that such persons are provided for under the difference principle. But this is by no means clear, since that principle has been presumed throughout to cover, perhaps only to cover, those who work. These two sections, then, concern the proper response in a Rawlsian well-ordered society to those unable to work. Here I attempt to address the thorny question of rights to welfare.

Then, in the postscript, I briefly turn to consider the bearing of the analysis in this chapter (and in the book as a whole) on the Rawlsian notion of self-respect. This leads to some concluding observations about the proper relationship of justice to human well-being.

## 1. *The Problem of Needs*

Insofar as individuals can be said to *need* justice—and in a well-ordered society they will need it in order to assure social cooperation along lines of fair and public principles of interaction—then that need is addressed by the two principles. More specifically, individuals need certain goods as a means to or a part of the actual way of life of each person. People *need* liberties (i.e., basic liberties, such as liberty of conscience, or avoidances of injury, such as freedom from torture), just as they need opportunities, positions, capacities and tasks, income and wealth, and thereby the bases of self-respect. Such social primary goods, as Rawls calls them, are the primary needs.[1] And the

175

principles of justice address each of these needs in turn. It is the province of the difference principle (once we assume satisfaction of equal basic liberties and fair equality of opportunity) to be concerned with offices (i.e., positions and responsibilities) and with attendant income and wealth.

If we simplify this picture somewhat by considering offices or jobs as important because of the income that they yield (and this is a valid perspective to take, as long as it is admitted that jobs have other functions as well), then we can say that the difference principle is concerned specifically with the distribution of income and wealth. By income and wealth we intend those "all-purpose means" (things having an exchange value), and we understand that income or wealth can take, besides its principal form as money, the form of various in-kind services or goods.[2] All people do need income and wealth in this sense. The need that the difference principle addresses, in particular, is the need for income and wealth so understood.

We often identify the needs of persons in a way different from this. We say the ignorant need to learn, the sick to be well, the blind to be able to see or, failing that, able to get about. Talk of needs in this mode can become very specific, for if a lack can be specified and it can justifiably be filled, then we can speak of a need. If a person has a fever and needs a medicine, we can fill that need with aspirin (or an antibiotic) or with money to buy it.

The difference principle, by allowing for the redistribution of money and the provision of in-kind services, can speak to the needs of the poor for particular goods and services (e.g., medicine), where the poor are defined by the substantial lack of those very things (when measured as income and wealth). But the difference principle does not address needs as such (as specific needs); it addresses only the needs of the poor.

Under the difference principle we don't consider *what* people need specifically but only whether they are poor enough to need income supplementation. Even where the difference principle appears to address a need specifically, by providing an in-kind service, it isn't the need per se that is addressed; instead, it is the need of a poor person that is addressed. For if a person had the same need but wasn't poor, then his need would *not* be addressed by the operation of the difference principle.

Moreover, it should be remembered that the bottom group is still the bottom group, even after redistribution. Thus, each of its members will end up with less in total (in dollars or in-kind services) than typical members of the other groups. However, we don't assume that the bottom group *needs* less than the others (in fact, we make the opposite assumption); therefore, it follows that need, as such, is not being addressed. For if it were need as such—specific, identifiable needs—we would see to it that more money went to the poor than does (under the difference principle) and that money (or in-kind services) went to others as well, as long as they had unmet needs.

176

Rawls says that the common-sense "precept of need is left to the transfer branch,"[3] that is, to the governmental branch concerned with redistributions under the difference principle. I have interpreted Rawls's claim here as saying that the difference principle attends only to the needs of the poor for income, and only in a certain amount. Specifically, in that amount which is required in order to bring the income of a given person up to a certain *level* of income, as set by the difference principle–determined income of the representative person in the target class (say, the bottom quartile). In this way, then, the difference principle attends to the needs of the poor.

But who are the poor? The poor, for Rawls, are not simply those who do not have sufficient income. Rather, the poor are normal, able-bodied persons who work, who contribute their efforts and the use of their talents toward the production of goods and services but who do not receive a sufficiently high return in income for their efforts. They receive below-average incomes, indeed so low as to be, let us say, in the bottom quartile. Thus the difference principle addresses the need for income supplementation of those who work but have quite substandard incomes.

There are other kinds of poor people, however. There are those who are not willing to work and those who are not able to work. Let us consider only those unable to work. The difference principle does not address the need for income supplementation (in money or in-kind services) of those *unable* to work; it addresses, rather, the need only of those who work and yet are poor.

It might appear that this problem is easily remedied. We believe that Rawls is as good-hearted and as fair-minded as the next fellow, and we are convinced that the friends of justice would be concerned with the well-being of those unable to work. So, we simply interpret the difference principle to include them, or we put this interpretation in there explicitly. But this ignores the fact that there may be systematic pressures in Rawls's theory which require the very reading of the difference principle that we are here trying to modify.

Consider. When we first encountered the difference principle (in chapter 4), it was as the second stage of an attempt to deal with the undeserved and morally arbitrary possession by individuals—as their endowment, so to speak—of natural assets and social circumstances and thereby to mitigate the effect of this endowment on the lifelong prospects of those who were adversely affected. The argument whereby the difference principle was justified in this context was: Since these starting points are undeserved and since we cannot fully overcome the differences by assuring absolute equality of opportunity, we fall back on an expedient. We regard the distribution of assets to each as a collective or common asset, such that when they *use* that asset, it redounds to the benefit of everyone, not simply to the possessor but to all others as well. We don't require that the effect be equal for all but merely that it be positive for all: so that no one is hurt by his initial endowment and all continue together to improve their lots in life.

We conceive this argument as occurring, of course, in the original position; hence, it is an argument that would be developed by and would appeal to rational persons who, under the rather severe constraints on knowledge which are characteristic of the original position, occupy an equal status there. Thus, the idea of a collective asset is one that would be agreed on in the original position, and arguments from this idea would lead ultimately to the difference principle.

The difference principle in its more developed version, then, is justified by the collective asset idea (as we saw in chapter 5, in particular). Thus, if we regard the collective asset idea as *the* argument for the difference principle and if the difference principle partakes of the main features of the collective asset idea—as any conclusion should reflect the premises on which it is based—then the difference principle is properly interpreted as covering, within its central scope, only those who work but are less fortunate.

The collective asset idea looks at individuals as having *assets*. It contemplates their using those assets and, in so doing, contributing to the good of each. The whole motif, then, is the contribution that each can make to himself and others through the use of his talents and abilities (as mediated through the market and the various background institutions, including ownership, and ultimately the augmented difference principle). Those who receive the redistributive effects of the difference principle are, quite naturally, those who have made their contribution, by using their talents, but who have simply fared, often predictably, much less well than their fellows.

In the collective asset idea, individuals are not contemplated as having defects or extreme liabilities in their natural endowment (or in their social circumstances), as having, not assets, but the privation of assets. For critical defects cannot be pooled for the well-being of all and, in fact, are disabling even to their possessors. Because some people have such defects (e.g., severe mental retardation or drastically disabling lifelong illness or physical handicap), they cannot contribute to the well-being of either themselves or others. In this way they are outside the scope of the collective asset idea. Thus, those who are unable to work are excluded from this scope or are marginal to it. Their position is precarious on the margin—given, that is, the essential character of the difference principle and the chief argument for it.

There is another consideration as well. Rawls makes it clear at a number of points that the parties in the original position are to be conceived as normal adults with the full range of powers, mental and physical, of such persons. The parties—in representing the normal adult citizen—do not have some of the defects that are found among actual people in an ordinary population. Hence, in designing the difference principle, the parties do not consider such defects as severe mental retardation or lifelong physical illness or handicap. As Rawls says pointedly, we should first construct a principle for the normal range of cases; if we cannot accomplish even this, then there is no reason for considering the special cases at all; only if we are successful in dealing with normal cases do we go on to consider special cases after that.[4] Consistent with this general view, the citizens in a well-ordered society are, all of them then, able-bodied workers, each of whom is regarded as a contributor, through his use of natural assets and the exploitation of his social circumstances, to the production of goods and services in that society. Thus, a pervasive heuristic principle—the assumption of normal cases only—attends the development of Rawls's difference principle and must be taken account of in any interpretation of that principle. This heuristic procedure is wholly in accord with the collective asset idea as I have represented it.

Now, the heuristic principle is not decisive by itself. For, we presume, it would always be possible to thicken the veil of ignorance (leaving people unaware, for example, of whether they were physically normal or not) and thus allow considerations of permanent disability to filter through. Thus, we might include the permanently disabled in the definition of the least-well-off group and thereby bring them within the scope of the difference principle.

It is not clear, however, what heuristic principle is to replace the one that we are here being asked to discard. We need, in any case, to keep in mind that there must be a considerable likeness of individuals in the original position in order for an agreement to be struck about the terms of justice. It is difficult to see what likeness there could be among the parties if some were permanently unable to contribute to society. Of course, we are being asked merely to *consider* that some might be. Thus, each must be able to imagine that he or someone is permanently disabled. But people can imagine all sorts of things— that they or others are religious fanatics or scientific geniuses or Nozickian pleasure monsters or platonic dictators or what have you. A line has to be drawn, a thin one really. For the more variety that is introduced, if only in imagination, the more difficult it will be to establish as reasonable a preferred theory of justice—or to put it differently, the more difficult it will be to reach real, rather than verbal, agreement about binding principles of justice, principles that are going to have significant bite.

Even if the heuristic principle were to be relaxed in the way indicated, it is not likely that Rawls's idea of the mutual disinterest of the parties (in the original position) would allow for a principle of justice in which some would be treated specially, in view of their incapacity, because then the distribution of primary goods would be awarded to such persons differently from the way mandated by the principles that governed the normal case. We need not assume hardness of heart here. It might seem to the parties, merely, that such matters were being gathered in under the heading of fundamental justice and that these things might, more appropriately, be dealt with at another point, in the institutional processes of the basic structure or even in another setting altogether (e.g., in morality, where considerations of benevolence and charity might be more at home).

The more significant inhibition, however, occurs in the idea of a collective asset—in the notion that people contribute, through the use of their talents and abilities, to the well-being of each and all. It comes, then, in the very notion of mutual benefit. And behind this lies the whole Rawlsian idea of the basic structure of a society as being a single schema of interaction, of actions by individuals and with reciprocal effects. Thus, to solve the problem of those who are permanently unable to work in the way suggested—through a rewriting of the difference principle in the original position—would require a wholesale rearrangement of fundamental features of the entire decision-procedure apparatus.

We are not, accordingly, contemplating minor changes in argumentation and wording. We are not contemplating a mere tinkering with the difference principle. We are talking about far-reaching changes, from the ground up. Most particularly, a radically different master argument from the one provided by the idea of collective asset would be required. And any resultant principle, on such a new and different foundation, would have a wholly different meaning and characteristic interpretation from what the difference principle currently has in Rawls's theory. For the difference principle to take on the character that we are here considering, it would have to become, quite literally, a different principle.

Rawls's theory of justice is a system of justice. The various pieces fit together because they are all of a piece. The main drawback, then, to making the suggested change is that it doesn't fit into the developed system. The two points we have been reviewing (the collective asset idea, as the main argument for the difference principle, and the heuristic procedure of considering only the case of normal, able-bodied workers) are not isolated, self-standing features in an account of justice. Instead, they have to be taken together as mutually supportive aspects of a single theory.

These two points, then, do count heavily in support of the view I have advanced—namely, that since the difference principle governs the arrangements specifically for those who work and contribute to society through the production of goods and services, the difference principle is not set up to address the needs, even the need for income, of those who are *unable* to work. The revision of the difference principle in the original position having failed as a proposed remedy, what possible remedies for those unable to work might we find in Rawls's system?

## 2. *The Welfare of Those Unable to Work*

It seems to me that many problems can be dissipated here if we consider carefully the various classes or types of those unable to work. The main types seem to be:

1. children who are too young to work,
2. adults who are beyond retirement age and considered too old to work,
3. people who are temporarily unable to work due to a disability (e.g., job-related injury, illness, pregnancy),[5]
4. people who are able to work but who are temporarily out of work for such reasons as seasonal unemployment or a general economic recession,
5. people who are able to work but are unable to work at what they are trained to do because that skill is now obsolete or the demand for it has been radically reduced (e.g., old-style linotype operators in the printing industry),
6. people who are physically or mentally unable to work, either permanently or for very long, indeterminate stretches of time.

Each of these groups represents special problems that call for special remedies. The question is, Where in Rawls's system can we find the appropriate remedies, if at all? One thing noticeable about many of these groups is that, although each person in it is not working *now*, there is a clear sense in which members of that group—for most of their adult, working years—are full contributing members of society. Thus, dependent children (and we here count as such only those who are unable to receive adequate support from their families) cannot work now, but they will be workers during their productive adult years. By the same token, old people beyond retirement age cannot work now (we presume this), but they were workers during their productive adult years. And people who are temporarily disabled cannot work now but can, during almost all their productive adult years, be presumed to be full contributors in the work force. These groups, then, can be regarded as alike in a significant respect: all can be presumed to be full contributors during all or most of their productive adult years. Thus, these groups can be regarded as constituting a single type.

Perhaps the simplest way whereby this composite group could be dealt with, within the Rawlsian system, is to devise an insurance scheme into which all workers would be required to contribute so as to assure funding for (a) dependent children and, perhaps, the parent who is responsible for the care and nurture of such children, (b) retired adults, (c) people who are temporarily disabled. Such a scheme would not burden workers for the benefit of nonworkers but, rather, would be a social security insurance plan in which workers are taxed, so to speak, to provide benefits to workers—possibly themselves—when they were not able to work. In short, I am here regarding the provision of such funds as a public good (in the economist's sense) and providing for a standard mechanism (a compulsory payment scheme) to generate the necessary money. Rawls allows for such a provision of public goods in his discussion of a special "branch" of governmental activity (called the Exchange Branch) which would, with full knowledge of the relevant particulars, devise schemes for some public goods and provide for funding them. (It would do so in roughly the way in which people might pay for clean water through a public-utility water company, with everybody having to pay for sewage and water purification regardless of how much water they used.)

Rawls regards the provision of public goods through this branch as a matter of efficiency rather than justice. Nonetheless, his system does have a place for such a mechanism within the background institutions that superintend and supplement the operations of the market. The only change that my analysis has introduced into the account that Rawls actually gives is that my analysis explicitly identifies social security insurance as a public good; and my analysis would not, incidentally, require that decisions about public goods—even within the Exchange Branch—be made only unanimously by a special representative body of the citizens (as Rawls requires) but instead would leave the decision to the normal legislative channels.[6]

I have, of course, emphasized the proviso that everyone (every worker, that is) is required to pay and therefore does, at some time, pay into the master social security fund from which the individual disbursements are made. Thus, children will pay into the fund once they're grown, and old people, now retired, did pay into it when they were working, and so on. The stipulation that everyone is required to pay is, I think, a leading feature of the provision of public goods. In the case at hand, the insurance fund is constituted by contributions that are made by workers during their productive adult years. Workers are here paying for something *they* want (i.e., social security when they are unable to work).

The case of people who are technologically unemployed is not so easily handled under the social security (or public goods) principle. Such people are not literally *unable* to work; it is simply that they cannot work at what they were trained to do. Their problem is not to find work but to find work at roughly the skill and income levels that they previously occupied—or at least to find it at a higher skill and income level than is currently available to them. It is not clear that workers would be willing to pay into a funding scheme that was specifically designed to provide unemployment benefits (in particular, long-term benefits) for this group. And if people are not willing to pay into such a scheme, let alone not willing to see everybody *coerced* to pay in, then we are really out of the province of public goods altogether. To put this point somewhat differently, it seems that the rationale required in order to cover persons in the technologically unemployed group is significantly different from the one advanced earlier (which concerned the sheer *inability* of people to work). Benefits for this group seem to open up a quite different set of issues from what was posed by social security insurance for those who are unable to work.

This can be brought out more clearly when we consider that there are actually two quite distinct problems for the technologically unemployed person: (1) the unemployment itself and (2) the cause of that unemployment—that is, the obsolescence of existing skills and the lack of suitable new ones. Now, it would make sense to deal with the fact of unemployment per se through an insurance scheme; but such a remedy, if taken as the *only* one, is unsuited to the problem as a whole and would very likely be resisted. Thus, I am not arguing that society would not cover the technologically unemployed under an insurance scheme but, rather, that it would probably make something other than insurance funds and unemployment payments its main line of remedy for technological (or "structural") unemployment.

Nevertheless, there is a significant ground of remedy, for the technologically unemployed, remaining in Rawls's theory. We can fall back on the theory of full employment. On the grounds that useful employment is here contemplated and that special job training is sometimes required so as to provide the opportunity for useful employment, a well-ordered society might be willing to set up, by legislative action, publicly funded job-training programs.

Let us briefly consider how the theory of full employment motivates such a solution. As I suggested earlier (in the first section of chapter 8), if a market system is to be just, constant readjustments by means of so-called background or nonmarket institutions are required in order (a) to supplement market distributions with difference principle–generated redistributions for the least-well-off group, even under conditions of perfect competition, and (b) to provide compensations to the least-well-off, again under the difference principle rubric, for market imperfections which are conceived as putting them at a competitive disadvantage and as further contributing to their disadvantaged status and to the lowering of their income levels. In case (b) the compensation need not take the form merely of income supplementation; rather, part of this compensation could be provided by full-employment policies (presumably of the standard Keynesian or fiscal sort).

The maintenance of full employment by governmental policy and action is conceived here as another governmental device for providing fair equality of opportunity, which in turn is a *precondition* of a market's being a fair procedure and, then, of market results being fair results. Thus, on this reading, even a "perfect" market would not be a fair procedure unless the full employment condition was met. (We assume, however, that the condition is met—

naturally or automatically—in a "perfect" market, since a perfect market is an efficient one.) But in an imperfect market (which is the normal case, in Rawls's view) we need to assume governmental full employment policy and *activity* as a standing background feature designed to provide fair equality of opportunity and, concurrently, to afford a form of compensation to the least-well-off—on the added ground that results in an imperfect market are not *fair* results.

And just as the imperfect market cannot deliver fair results, it cannot deliver efficient ones either. A policy of full employment, then, augments efficiency in an *imperfect* market by providing for the full use of at least one important resource—human effort.[7]

Clearly, full employment, as a necessary precondition of market fairness and as contributing to the full use of existing resources, is an idea that, insofar as it suggests that everyone work, is consistent with Rawls's earlier use of the notion of collective asset and of his heuristic principle of considering only the normal, able-bodied adult contributor in his argument for the difference principle. Rawls's commitment to the idea that the well-ordered society is a society of contributors, of persons who do contribute to the well-being of one another, requires a parallel commitment to full employment. No doubt, Rawls also believes that gainful or useful employment helps support the bases of self-respect, in that persons have need to think of themselves as solid contributors to the on-going life of their society.[8]

Now, let us fit these various parts of our analysis together. The ultimate rationale of most job-retraining programs is economic efficiency—the rationale that a market system is efficient only when all available resources are being used at their capacity. Job retraining, then, could be viewed as the shifting of a complex resource from one use, where it is no longer needed (due to the obsolescence of the relevant skill), to a new one, where it can be productively employed. (We presume that such shifting can be done intelligently.)

A program of job retraining on this basis is not, as such, an issue of fairness; a question of fairness (as given in the notion of fair equality of opportunity) arises only if the individual was seriously disadvantaged in terms of natural endowment or of initial social circumstances or was, presumably as a result of those factors, in the lowest income group. The rationale of fairness, then, could cover almost all primary job training (e.g., of disadvantaged youth) and some, but not all, *re*training. Nonetheless, a powerful rationale for such retraining is provided by the tie-in between full employment and economic efficiency. Accordingly, a society organized on Rawlsian principles could make legislative provision for publicly funded job-training programs (including programs to replace obsolescent skills).

By the same token, a society could, in a time of general economic recession, constitute the government as the employer of last resort, thereby creating a corps of people who could perform useful work on public projects at public expense. Thus, deep-seated and prolonged unemployment might be dealt with by using both of the remedies identified: an insurance scheme for unemployment payments (under the public goods principle) and a publicly funded job-training or work corps program (under the principle of full employment/efficient use of resources).[9]

The matter here is complex for two reasons. First, some of the cases that are under investigation in this section come under more than one rationale and thus can be handled by more than one of the available strategies. Second, the complexity here reflects, in turn, the fact that there are different ways or senses in which people can be said to be unable to work. Those who are unable to work by reason of economic recession or of technological unemployment are, strictly speaking, *able* to work; it is simply that there are not enough jobs or that the ones available are not of the right sort. Thus, job training or a work corps program (in addition to income supplementation) would make sense for persons in this group.

Now, since we have this variety of rationales and strategies and this complexity in the notion of inability to work, it might be useful to moderate our original argument somewhat. It could be contended that the difference principle is intended to range over the whole lives of people (over the lifetime expectations of representative persons). Thus, we ought to be able to accommodate the normal incidents of life—old age, illness and injury during working years, and childhood dependence—under it, because these are simply stages that representative working persons go through, or can be expected to. Let us grant this. Accordingly, we acknowledge that the difference principle could probably be designed to cover *some* of those who are unable to work (specifically, the first three classes mentioned at the beginning of section 2); thus, that principle would thereby authorize the appropriate legislative policies for them (including, most likely, a social security insurance fund). However, it is not likely that the difference principle would also cover satisfactorily those unable to work for reasons of technological unemployment or severe recession. These reasons do not identify incidents in the normal life of persons who work but, rather, incidents of a sophisticated technology for the production of goods and services and incidents of a market economy (especially where the ownership of productive property is in private hands). Or if the principle did cover them, we assume that more than income maintenance would be involved and that some program of job retraining would be instituted, on independent grounds, as well.

This leaves one important class as yet uncovered. For even where we allow the difference principle to cover some or even many of those who are unable to work, we are still left facing the problem of those who are *permanently* unable to work (for reasons of severe retardation or of critically disabling illness or physical handicap). The problem here is peculiarly difficult in that neither of the remedies already suggested would fit this case.

A social insurance scheme could not apply. It requires that workers pay into an insurance fund to cover certain foreseeable circumstances, but it is logically impossible that workers could be *permanently* unable to work. Hence, this particular circumstance could not come under such a scheme. (Recall that the provision of public goods—under a coercive, inclusive program of payments by everyone—operates under conditions of full knowledge of particular facts, unlike the case of choosing first principles of justice, which takes place behind a thick veil of ignorance.)

Nor would considerations of full employment policy under either of its guises (as economic efficiency or as fair equality of opportunity) have any weight in the case of those who are permanently unable to work. Both rationales presuppose the ability to work and, hence, are strictly inapplicable in the case at hand. Providing employment opportunities for persons in this group (persons who are completely and permanently unable to perform socially useful work) would be meaningless.

Accordingly, we need to seek out some other remedy in Rawls's system if we are to deal with the case of those who are permanently unable to work. Several possibilities are present; I will mention them only briefly. Let us begin with ones that I reject: mutual aid and paternalism.

We turn, first, to the Rawlsian natural duty of mutual aid.[10] This duty of justice is incumbent on all individuals and requires that they come to the aid of any individual who is in severe difficulty or peril. It is not clear whether this duty assumes reciprocation; for if it did, then those who are permanently unable to work would probably, for the same reason that made them unable to work, be unable to reciprocate the duty. In any event, natural duties hold only between individuals; they are, in this sense, personal duties, that is, duties of persons as individuals. If, however, we are looking for a basic structure or society-wide institutional solution to the problem of dealing with those who are permanently unable to work, then the doctrine of natural duties would do us no good, for we could not use any such duty to justify legislative policy or coercive governmental activity.

It has been suggested, second, that we turn to Rawls's discussion of paternalism for the outlines of the solution that we are seeking.[11] Rawls introduces his discussion of paternalism with the observation that, in some cases, "we must choose for others as we have reason to believe they would choose for themselves if they were at the age of reason and deciding rationally."[12] As the name implies, the theory of paternalism largely concerns the protection of the interests of children by parents, trustees, guardians, and assorted benefactors. Hence, it concerns a condition that is not permanent, that one can grow out of. Rawls also applies it specifically to those who, "through some misfortune or accident [, are] unable to make decisions for their good, as in the case of those seriously injured or mentally disturbed." Thus, it would cover victims of accident or injury (insofar as they were unconscious) and also persons who suffer from a mental disorder (insofar as they were rendered irrational, or nonfunctional).[13]

Even so, we must recognize that this principle, suitably construed, covers only a fraction of those in the class of persons permanently unable to work. We might grant that it covers the severely retarded—though I am uncomfortable with treating an extremely low degree of intellectual capacity as equivalent to irrationality (or even to inability to function). It does not, however, cover the large class of lifelong victims of physical injury or debilitating sickness or handicap who are, at the same time, conscious and able to reason. It is simply presumptuous to treat such persons as if they were children or mentally ill or severely retarded. We cannot presume, then, to act in their interest, nor can we confidently predict what their judgments about their own interests will be (as the tragic Bouvia case, in California, shows).[14] Rawls is, of course, guilty of no such presumption. And we are in no position to use the principle of paternalism as a general solution, in a well-ordered society, to the problem of those who are permanently unable to work.

We reach, then, the conclusion that the difference principle, as formulated in the original position, does not cover the class of such persons (as I argued in the first section of this chapter), that the institutional mechanisms of a well-ordered society are not constructed to include them, and that principles of mutual aid and of paternalism are not suited to deal with them. In sum, we have reached an impasse in which the deep moral judgment that society should provide for those who are permanently unable to work runs afoul of guidelines given in the developed theory of justice. The guidelines fail to cover, and hence mandate no solution for, a problem that conventional morality demands to be solved, and solved in the right way.

There is, in Rawls's theory, however, a standing mechanism designed to deal with precisely this sort of conflict. I refer to the Rawlsian idea of reflective equilibrium (discussed briefly in the first section of chapter 2 above). According to this notion, a principle generated in the original position (in this case the difference principle) is to be matched against certain considered judgments (either in the form of maxims or of paradigm cases) in an attempt to bring the main elements—the judgments, on the one hand, and the principle and its theoretical backdrop, on the other—into alignment.

Where adjustment through the mechanism of reflective equilibrium is required (and it is required when the problem cannot be resolved by devices already internal to the theory of justice), then something must change, something must at some point give way. If the alteration occurs on the side of the principle, then things would look something like this. In the simplest case, the explicit wording of the principle would be unchanged; but its interpretation and, hence, its extension—the kind of things or the class of persons covered—would be altered. Or in a somewhat more complex modification, both the wording of the principle and its extension would be changed.

In either event, though, a reflective equilibrium solution is not a weak procedure. In the case at hand it reflects both the claim that moral conviction requires income and services for those who are permanently unable to work and the claim that the difference principle—especially when considered in the light of its supporting argumentation—cannot require these things. These are strong claims, each intractable in the face of the other, and they require a hard solution: either we give up (or modify) the moral conviction, or we give up (or modify) the difference principle. There is no way to avoid such hard choices, given the way in which Rawls's whole theory has developed (in this case, in particular).

We might desire that the principles of justice could be so stated that they implicitly incorporated all settled and defensible moral convictions. But this is unlikely ever to happen given the restricted and nonhistorical character of the original position construct—with its demands for simplification, likeness of parties, severe restraints on usable knowledge, and high-order standards for decisions and for principle construction. Indeed, if it did happen, we would have no need for reflective equilibrium. But the very fact that Rawls's theory has a place for reflective equilibrium shows the somewhat tentative and provisional character of the principles reached and shows also Rawls's appreciation of the restricted and nonhistorical character of the reasoning in the original position.

We have, of course, in what Rawls calls "wide" reflective equilibrium the possibility of going around the original position to include other significant data, such as the concept of a person or the notion of a well-ordered society. But unless we believe that the *total* set of relevant initial considerations would give us a firm, comprehensive, and unshakeable array of justice principles, then we must accept that there will always be a need for the kind of matching, described here, between the principles of justice and their theoretical backdrop, on the one hand, and considered, defensible, socially located moral convictions, on the other. Sometimes there will be a need for such significant adjustments.

The method of reflective equilibrium is not ad hoc. What would be ad hoc is the suggestion that we state the difference principle in its original formulation (or interpret that formulation) so as to conform to conventional moral convictions. This suggestion has been resisted, however, in our turn to adjustments under a reflective equilibrium procedure.

How might such a procedure go? The difference principle, as I have tried to emphasize in this chapter, is not merely a principle; it is not something that is self-standing and remote, like an Aristotelian unmoved mover. Rather, it comes in as part of a characteristic train of reasoning, and it continues in that train throughout. The initial impulse that motivated this reasoning was the observation that the natural endowment of individual persons is undeserved, something that they can bear no responsibility for whatsoever. Some are less well endowed in their natural capacities and, predictably, end up (most of them) less-well-off in terms of realized income and wealth.

Surely, these observations apply to the case of those who are permanently unable to work. Their incapacity is, in the vast number of cases, something that they have not brought about and that they are in no way responsible for. They are certainly to be accounted among those who are least advantaged by their natural endowment or, if not that, by fortune. They would, moreover, in almost all cases, find themselves—as a result of their incapacity—in the very lowest income group. Indeed, they have no income at all, since they are permanently unable to work.

These considerations might not affect the formation of the difference principle itself. For the notion of the basic structure as a scheme of interaction, the heuristic principle of considering only normal cases, and the idea of a collective asset (as the master argument for the difference principle) together set it on a different course. But these considerations are strong enough to dispose persons in a well-ordered society to be receptive to the conventional moral conviction that we are here discussing. Such persons can see the point of the conviction, the thrust that it makes against the difference principle; for the conviction is not alien to the whole set of considerations that put that principle in motion. And it is, we presume, *their* conviction; so they are inclined to modify the difference principle, not the conviction.

Accordingly, the permanently disabled, those who are unable to work, are now to be treated as members of the class of the least-well-off and are thus admitted within the scope of the difference principle. The operation of that principle, then, would bring them up to the minimum level—as measured in income and in-kind services—of the representative member of that class, a level to be determined by the adjusted return on his contribution. For simplicity we could set that level at the median income for workers in the bottom quartile.

It is likely that such a level will not be enough for many of those who are permanently unable to work. For there are, we presume, special medical services needed and devices for helping them to cope with everyday life that are very costly and often go far beyond the money equivalent (in income and services) of the minimum level required to be made available to the able-bodied worker.

If this is so, then justice would have to be supplemented by beneficence. To take the difference principle beyond this point would be ad hoc; to fail to respond at all would be morally blameworthy. Two themes, then, provide the solution: One, a theme of general morality (be it conventional or critical); the other, a theme of justice.

I do not want, in saying this, to suggest that we know what the solution is (in all its infinite detail), for it is often the case with moral problems that we do not know how to develop concrete and satisfying answers. The problem we are concerned with, that of those who are permanently unable to work, has been rendered particularly acute by advances in modern medical technology and measures for public health. Certainly, the magnitude of the problem has been caused by these advances. Thus, there is and there will remain a serious problem in deciding about the percentage of national income and other resources that should be devoted to medical care and general maintenance, especially of the most extreme cases. And we cannot find an answer to this problem simply by turning to the principle of beneficence. What I want to suggest in my argument, instead, is that the problem takes us beyond principles of justice *alone* and to suggest that any acceptable solution will probably draw on the resources of principles *both* of justice and of beneficence.

But justice does have some role to play here, as I've tried to bring out. Indeed, insofar as it does, the matter actually is one of rights. For I argued (in chapter 6) that there is a basic right to a minimum level of income under the difference principle. Since those who are permanently unable to work have, through the procedure of reflective equilibrium, been brought into the group of the least-well-off and since any person, simply in virtue of being a member of that group, has a basic right to a specified level of income, it follows that those who are permanently unable to work have a basic right to income (in money and the provision of in-kind services) under the difference principle.

In chapter 6, I described the relevant right as the right to income *supplementation*. [15] This seemed to be the proper characterization; but it is not the way we can describe the basic right under the difference principle in the case of those we are permanently unable to work, for they have no income to supplement. Theirs is simply a right to income. To avoid undue complication and to reflect the difference in route by which this right to income has been arrived at, we might do well to identify *two* basic rights under the difference principle: a right to income supplementation for those who work but have substandard incomes and a right to income for those who are permanently unable to work.

The level of the adjusted income is identical in the two cases, but the absolute amount of money and in-kind services provided through the transfer branch would be less for working individuals (who have a base of earned income to start with) than for nonworking persons (who do not). And in cases where the needs of those who are permanently unable to work exceeded the level of income entitlement, as set by justice, principles of morality other than those of justice would have to be called upon to fill the gap. We must assume that a moral conviction strong enough to force revision of the difference principle is strong enough to lay the hand of obligation on individual persons and to motivate a well-ordered society, itself founded on morally accredited principles of justice, to public benevolence.[16]

### 3. Self-Respect: A Postscript

If this analysis is correct, then a second basic right under the difference principle will have to be added. Thus, the final version of the list of basic structure rights would look something like this:

1. rights to basic liberties and noninjuries under the first principle,
2. rights to certain economic liberties (e.g., free choice of occupation) under the fair equality of opportunity part of the second principle,
3. rights to certain other opportunites (e.g., to public schooling) under that same part, and
4. rights to transfer of income to persons in the difference principle–determined target class, the group of those least-well-off, as follows:
   a. a basic right to a certain level of income, as one's adjusted return on contributions, for those who work but who end up in the least-well-off group, and
   b. a basic right to a certain level of income and in-kind services for those permanently unable to work who end up in that lowest-income group.

Rawls seems to find the most secure base for self-respect in equal citizenship (essentially point 1 above).[17] My analysis goes well beyond that, however. In part the difference here is only semantic (for Rawls would, I believe, endorse all of the benefits listed in points 2–4). But if our concern is to delineate the main basis of self-respect, then the account I have offered seems to provide a much broader and more secure base. The account has accomplished this while retaining Rawls's focus on equal basic rights as fundamental. Furthermore, by including income distribution (at a certain minimum level) as a basic right, my account may actually strengthen Rawls's theory against its critics.[18]

At this point let me add a retrospective observation or two. In the course of the previous section one felt, no doubt, a temptation to turn to the good of self-respect as a way of solving the problem posed there. One would surely be inclined to argue that the basis of self-respect would be eroded for those who are permanently unable to work if they were not supported by society through the provision of income and services. We found in the end, though, that yielding to this particular temptation was unnecessary, since the problem could be resolved in another way.

Why is the solution that I proposed, which draws on the good offices of reflective equilibrium, preferable to one that relies on direct appeal to the notion of self-respect?

The Rawlsian theory of justice does not contemplate direct use of the good of self-respect in the construction of the preferred principles of justice. The theory holds, instead, that the good in question is achieved through the social upbuilding of the bases of self-respect—that is, of the other social primary goods. In short, the good of self-respect is a *result* of the theory of justice, on the basis provided.

The idea that the other social primary goods, then, are to be assigned to some people simply to serve, directly and independently, the good of self-respect requires the repudiation of this important and settled feature in Rawls's approach. I am reluctant to take such a tack, for I have followed throughout the principle that our job is not to redesign Rawls's theory of justice but, instead, to take it as far as possible on its own terms. Only then are we in a position to say what that theory comes to, and only then are we in a position to criticize it in any fundamental way.

Now, the idea that certain people are to be brought under a special principle, which covers some but not all people, is incompatible with the claim that the relevant principles of justice have been established for all under a sound decision procedure in the original position. It seems, then, that we should not create a special principle, constructed almost entirely out of considerations of self-respect, for those who are permanently unable to work.

Even if we merely interpret an existing principle, by using the good of self-respect, we are still isolating this one primary good from the basis provided in the general analysis and setting it apart from all the rest. There is no accredited or settled way *within* Rawls's theory of justice by which this can be done. In any event, if we were to install such a procedure prematurely—as we would have done were it to have been used to resolve the problem posed in the previous section—then we would not be letting the theory go to term, on its own devices.

Accordingly, I think that the method I have followed, where existing principles were modified (through the procedure of reflective equilibrium), is more in keeping with Rawls's theory of justice. Specifically, it is more attuned to Rawls's theory than would be any direct or independent reliance on the good of self-respect to fashion or interpret the principles of justice.

Indeed, it is not clear that the good of self-respect has any special role to play in the theory of justice at all. In Rawls's view, the *bases* of self-respect are provided in the normal course of things simply through the provision of the other social primary goods in the requisite amounts. Thus, individuals have the bases of self-respect in having liberties and opportunities, responsibilties and position, income and wealth in the amounts that are provided for under the two principles of justice. Self-respect as such does not directly enter this scheme; it is, rather, assumed to be supervenient on the social primary goods—specifically, on that peculiar amalgam of them which constitutes the social *bases* of self-respect.[19] In the account I have provided, the main element in that basis is the set or "family" of basic structure rights.

The supervenience of self-respect on the bases provided by the two principles is, then, a presumption of Rawls's theory of justice. Thus, if we stay with that presumption, then the tendency it sets up will carry us to the point we have reached. The presumption here is a rebuttable one, however; so it is useful to inquire whether this presumption is at all plausible.

Insofar as we regard self-respect as a moral notion, it probably is plausible. If we take self-respect as referring to such things as the dignity of persons and membership in the moral community (as defined by the notion of moral personhood), then the account that I have given seems to assure the moral sense of self-worth for everybody. No one would be merely a means to society's or anyone else's good. Each individual would be of infinite and intrinsic worth, an end in himself or herself.

But insofar as we regard self-respect as a psychological notion, the matter is not equally clear. We cannot say that a feeling of the worth of one's projects, a feeling of affirmation of one's character and other personal traits and of one's standing in comparison with other people will necessarily result when these bases are provided.[20] Perhaps, for most people in most social circumstances, a psychology of self-respect would ensue; but we cannot speak with confidence of such a result for *each* person in *every* social setting. In any event, the matter here is empirical, quite complex, and hard to decide. Thus, we would find it extremely difficult to measure the psychological good of self-respect, especially between persons, and well nigh impossible to establish viable standards in the matter, for example, for equality.

About all we can say with any confidence is that in a well-ordered society, a society ordered on Rawlsian principles, destructive envy is unlikely. I mean that persons in such a society would probably not be moved by spiteful feelings so great that such persons would act to make everyone less-well-off, themselves included, if only the inequality between them and others could be significantly reduced. Obviously such feelings would be incompatible with a Rawlsian well-ordered society. They would stem from a severe diminishment of self-respect. So we do require in the theory of justice that the bases of self-respect afforded in a well-ordered society should be sufficiently great to preclude destructive envy, so far as it is reasonably possible to do so. And we can presume, I have suggested, that this requirement will be met in a Rawlsian well-ordered society. But beyond this we do not attempt to answer the question of whether the psychological good of self-respect would flourish for each and every citizen in such a well-ordered society.

Now, the question at hand is an interesting one, but it remains interesting only so long as we retain a certain distance between the theory of justice, on the one hand, and the psychological good of self-respect, on the other. If we allowed the latter to have a direct hand in the theory, even to rearrange it, then, of course, the theory would serve the good of self-respect. It would have been tailor-made to do so. But the question that we began with would have lost interest. I do not think Rawls intended the theory of justice to include any such independent role for the psychological good of self-respect.[21]

In thus giving self-respect no *independent* role to play in the theory, it might appear that I am backing off from some fairly explicit claims in Rawls's texts. I do not think the record bears this out, however. One source of confusion in Rawls's theory is whether the primary good in question is self-respect or whether it is the *bases* of self-respect. His texts support both readings; but in his "final statement" of the two principles, he goes with "the bases of self-respect" version.[22] This same language is repeated, then, in the canonical lists of social primary goods found in his later writings.[23]

I do not mean to suggest here that self-respect is *not* a primary good, for it clearly is, in Rawls's view.[24] Rather, I want merely to suggest that the best way in which to characterize self-respect within the class of *social* primary goods is as the *bases* of self-respect. Thus, self-respect per se (as a psychological or even as a moral category) is not at the center of the deliberations about the principles of justice. In this respect it is like the *natural* primary goods (e.g., health, intelligence). These, though they are primary goods, are not said to be *social* primary goods, in that they are less amenable to social control. Thus, they are not the main objects distributed by the basic structure of a well-ordered society in accordance with the two principles.

The account that I have offered in this section is consistent with this reading. Both the account and the reading accord with the view that, in the end, one can leave undecided, within the theory of justice, the issue of whether a psychological sense of self-worth would supervene in a society that had successfully established the bases of self-respect.

One would like to think that a just society, a well-ordered one, is a social setting in which human beings flourish; one would like to believe that justice ultimately serves human well-being. Thus, we want a just society to be one in which people are healthy, in which the fine arts flower, in which science and technology together make for a better way of life for each person, and in which a psychological sense of self-worth is engendered for representative persons at the various levels.

We want justice and welfare to come together. If they do not, if justice

194

somehow thwarts or inadequately supports these other values, then we have ground for criticism. But if the supposition is sound that these other things will emerge in a society whose basic structure is well ordered, then we have independent confirmation of the goodness of justice.

To ask the question posed in this section about a psychological sense of self-worth, or to ask these other questions about welfare, takes us beyond justice. To try to answer these questions, in any fundamental way, marks a new beginning, a new mode of inquiry. Thus, a theory of justice ends at the very point we have reached.

# APPENDIX

Here, we will formally prove the equivalence of the two versions of the difference principle, as set out in chapter 5.

Consider a society that can be classified into $n$ groups of individuals according to their economic well-being. The economic well-being of an individual will be represented by a real-valued index (e.g., an index of primary goods) as a function of the individual's expected distribution of income, wealth, social position, and so on, over the individual's lifetime. Each of these $n$ groups will be represented by one hypothetical representative who is endowed with the average characteristics of the group that he represents. The *attainable set*, A, will then be the set of all feasible (practicable) distributions of expectations of these $n$ representatives under various basic structures that are consistent with the principles of equal liberty and fair equality of opportunity.

Without loss of generality, let group 1 consist of the most-favored individuals, group 2 consist of the next-most-favored individuals, and so on until group $n$ consists of the least-advantaged individuals. With this labeling of the groups, the attainable set A will satisfy the condition

$$A \subset \{x = (x_1, \ldots, x_n): x_1 \geqq x_2 \geqq \ldots \geqq x_n\}.$$

One should not interpret this condition to imply that, for example, the least-advantaged group is restricted so as to remain least advantaged under any feasible basic structure. Instead, since $x_n$ represents the expectation of the hypothetical representative of the least-advantaged group (regardless of the actual membership of this group), by definition $x_n$ will be smaller than the expectations of the representatives of other groups, and so on. Hence, the above condition does not constitute a restriction on the attainable set.

The Appendix is entirely the work of Prakash Shenoy. It is an expanded version of the appendix to our joint article "Two Interpretations of the Difference Principle in Rawls's Theory of Justice." I am very grateful to Shenoy for allowing the publication of the Appendix in its present form in this book.

Let the unique distribution favored by the maximin version of the difference principle (including the lexical version in case of nonuniqueness) be denoted by $a = (a_1, ..., a_n)$, i.e.,

(i) max $\{$min $\{x_i : i = 1, ..., n\} : x \epsilon A\} = a_n$;
(ii) max $\{$min $\{x_i : i = 1, ..., n-1\} : x \epsilon A, x_n = a_n\} = a_{n-1}$;

and so on until

(n) max $\{$min $\{x_i : i = 1\} : x \epsilon A, x_n = a_n, ..., x_2 = a_2\} = a_1$.

The set of all pareto efficient distributions in A will be denoted by P, i.e.,

P = $\{x \epsilon A$:there does not exist a distribution $(y_1, ..., y_n) \epsilon A$ such that $y_i \geqq x_i$ for each $i = 1, ..., n$ and $y_j > x_j$ for some $j = 1, ..., n\}$.

The combination of pareto efficiency and egalitarianism (with the lexical priority of the former over the latter) will lead to a unique distribution in A (see lemma 2 below). Let us denote this unique distribution by $b = (b_1, ..., b_n)$, i.e.,

(i) min $\{x_1 - x_n : x \epsilon P\} = b_1 - b_n$;
(ii) min $\{x_1 - x_{n-1} : x \epsilon P, x_1 - x_n = b_1 - b_n\} = b_1 - b_{n-1}$;

and so on until

$(n-1)$ min $\{x_1 - x_2 : x \epsilon P, x_1 - x_n = b_1 - b_n, ..., x_1 - x_3 = b_1 - b_3\} = b_1 - b_2$.

Before we prove the equivalence of the two versions of the difference principle, we need to prove two lemmas.

*Lemma 1:* The unique distribution $a$ that is favored by the maximin version of the difference principle is pareto efficient, i.e., $a \epsilon P$.
*Proof:* Suppose $a \notin P$. Then by the definition of P, there exists a distribution $e = (e_1, ..., e_n) \epsilon A$ such that $e_1 \geqq a_1, e_2 \geqq a_2, ..., e_n \geqq a_n$ and at least one of these inequalities is a strict inequality. If $e_n > a_n$, then we have a contradiction to statement (i) in the definition of $a$. If $e_n = a_n$ and $e_{n-1} > a_{n-1}$, then we have a contradiction to statement (ii) in the definition of $a$. Continuing in this fashion, we will always end up with a contradiction. Hence $a \epsilon P$.                    Q.E.D.

*Lemma 2:* The combination of pareto efficiency and egalitarianism (with the lexical priority of pareto efficiency over egalitarianism) will lead to a unique distribution in A.
*Proof:* Let $e$ be a distribution in A satisfying conditions (i) $-$ $(n-1)$ defining distribution $b$. Then we must have $e \epsilon P$ and $e_1 - e_n = b_1 - b_n, e_1 - e_{n-1} = b_1 - b_{n-1}, ..., e_1 - e_2 = b_1 - b_2$. If $e_1 > b_1$, then it follows that $e_i > b_i$ for $i = 1, ..., n$, and hence $b \notin P$, which is a contradiction. If $e_1 < b_1$, then it follows that $e_i < b_i$ for $i = 1, ..., n$, and hence $e \notin P$, which is a contradiction. Hence $e_1 = b_1$ which together with the equations above implies that $e_i = b_i$ for $i = 1, ..., n$, i.e., $e = b$.                    Q.E.D.

*Theorem 1:* If society can be classified into two groups, the more-favored group and the less-advantaged group (i.e., $n = 2$), then the distribution $a$, which is favored by the maximin version of the difference principle, will coincide with the distribution $b$, which is favored by the combination of pareto efficiency and egalitarianism (with the lexical priority of the former over the latter), i.e., $a = b$.
*Proof:* By the definition of $a$, $a_2 \geqq b_2$, and since $a \epsilon P$, then by the definition of $b$, $a_1 - a_2 \geqq b_1 - b_2$. Adding these two inequalities, we get $a_1 \geqq b_1$. Since $b \epsilon P$ (by the

definition of *b*), $a_1 \geqq b_1$ and $a_2 \geqq b_2$ together imply that $a_1 = b_1$ and $a_2 = b_2$, i.e., $a = b$ (because either $a_1 > b_1$ or $a_2 > b_2$ will imply that $b \notin P$).  Q.E.D.

To show the equivalence of the maximin difference principle with the combination of pareto efficiency and egalitarianism in the general case of *n* groups n > 2, we need a regularity condition called "chain connection."

According to Rawls, chain connection means that whenever the expectation of the least-advantaged group is increasing as a result of increasing the expectation of the most-favored group, the expectations of all other intermediate groups are also increasing.[1] Formally we will say that the attainable set A exhibits *chain connection* if and only if for any two distributions x, y∈A, if $x_n \geqq y_n$ and $x_1 \geqq y_1$, then $x_i \geqq y_i$ for each i = 2, ..., n − 1. Although Rawls never really defines chain connection very precisely, the above definition captures the essence of Rawls's discussion of chain connection.

In the general case of n > 2 groups, the equivalence of the maximin difference principle and the combination of pareto efficiency and egalitarianism can be shown if we assume chain connection. This is done in the following theorem.

*Theorem 2:* If the attainable set exhibits chain connection, then the maximin difference principle favors the same distribution as that favored by the combination of pareto efficiency and egalitarianism (with the lexical priority of the former over the latter), i.e., $a = b$.

*Proof:* Assume that chain connection holds. By the definition of *a*, $a_n \geqq b_n$, and since *a*∈P, then by the definition of *b*, $a_1 - a_n \geqq b_1 - b_n$. Adding these two inequalities, we get $a_1 \geqq b_1$. Since chain connection holds, we can then conclude that $a_i \geqq b_i$ for i = 2, ..., n − 1. Since *b*∈P (by the definition of *b*), we must have $a_i = b_i$ for i = 1, ..., n, i.e., $a = b$ (because $a_i > b_i$ for some i would imply that $b \notin P$).  Q.E.D.

Now let us consider the case where the attainable set does not exhibit chain connection. As discussed earlier, it is possible that in such cases, the distribution that is favored by the maximin version of the difference principle differs from the distribution favored by the combination of pareto efficiency and egalitarianism. Consider, for example, the case depicted in figure 13 on p. 200 ( = fig. 6 in chap. 5).

Using numbers, the alternatives *a* and *b* can be represented as shown in table 1.

TABLE 1

A NUMERICAL REPRESENTATION OF DISTRIBUTIONS *a* AND *b*
FROM FIGURE 13

| REPRESENTATIVES | DISTRIBUTION | |
| --- | --- | --- |
| | Alternative *a* | Alternative *b* |
| Most favored | 25 | 20 |
| Intermediate | 10 | 16 |
| Worst off | 7 | 6 |
| Inequality | 18 | 14 |

As seen in figure 13, distributions *a* and *b* are both pareto efficient. While the inequality in distribution *b* is smaller, the expectation of the worst-off representative is higher in distribution *a*. Rawls's maximin difference principle would prefer alternative *a* in cases where the combination of pareto efficiency and egalitarianism would favor

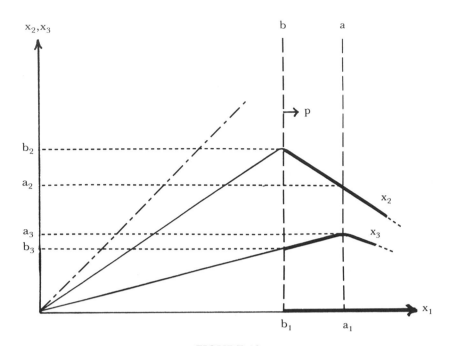

FIGURE 13

An attainable set that does not exhibit chain connection and in which the maximin principle differs from pareto efficiency and egalitarianism.

distribution *b*. However, note that favoring distribution *a* over distribution *b* is in direct violation of Rawls's mutual benefit principle which permits larger inequalities only if it is to *everyone's* advantage (see chap. 4 and, esp., 5 of the present book).

We will conclude this section by making two brief comments. In Social Choice theory, given a set of alternatives and a set of *n* members of a society each of whom has a preference profile on the set of alternatives, one question of interest is how should society aggregate these individual preferences in order to arrive at a societal preference profile. The maximin difference principle (stated by Rawls in the context of selecting a just basic structure arrangement of society) can be adapted to provide an answer to the above question. We will refer to such an adaptation as a maximin choice rule. In the context of Social Choice theory, Hammond (1976) and Strasnick (1976) have independently provided an axiomatic characterization of the maximin choice rule in terms of pareto efficiency and an egalitarianlike equity condition. A meaningful comparison of the approach taken in this paper with the approach of Hammond and Strasnick is not possible because of the different contexts and different assumptions made.

Regarding informational requirements needed in order to operationalize the maximin version of the difference principle, Rawls notes that only ordinal interpersonal comparisons of distributions of primary goods are required.[2] In other words, the basic structure that is specified by the maximin version of the difference principle remains invariant under an ordinal transformation of the index of primary goods. Although at first glance, the principle of egalitarianism seems to require cardinal and interpersonally comparable information, because of the result stated in theorem 2, if chain connection holds, then again the basic structure that is favored by pareto efficiency and egalitarianism remains invariant under an ordinal transformation of the index of primary goods.[3]

## NOTES

1. See *TJ*, 81–83.
2. See *TJ*, 90–95.
3. For further discussion see also Rawls, "Social Unity and Primary Goods," 159, 163, 174–75 (and 175n).

# NOTES

Throughout the notes, John Rawls, *A Theory of Justice* (Cambridge: Belknap Press of Harvard University Press, 1971), will be abbreviated to *TJ*. The numbers that follow *TJ* will be page numbers, unless otherwise indicated.

## Chapter 1
### The Background

1. See Jeremy Bentham, *Works,* ed. John Bowring, vol. 2 (Edinburgh: W. Tait; London: Simpkin, Marshall, 1843), p. 501. At an earlier point in the same work (*Anarchical Fallacies* [1791]) Bentham had described talk of such rights as mere "*bawling* upon paper*"* (p. 494). For interesting amplification see H. L. A. Hart, "Bentham and the United States of America," *Journal of Law and Economics* 19 (1976): 547-67.

The more important point here, though, is that for Bentham (a) rights attach to the qualified recipients of benefit-conferring obligations and (b) such obligations, in turn, are viewed as having been created by legal or other social sanctions attached to coercive rules. It follows from this that (c) there are no rights other than those given such social sanction. For (a) and (b) see Bentham, *Works,* 3:159, 181, 217-18; for (c) see also *Works* 3:221.

2. Dan W. Brock, "Recent Work in Utilitarianism," *American Philosophical Quarterly* 10 (1973): 241-76, at 268-69.

In the Preface, I have by and large cited references by giving just the author's name and the date of the piece cited, or sometimes a short title. This was a reasonable procedure to follow where there was no chance of confusion. But throughout the remainder of the book I will (as a more or less uniform practice) give first citations in the full form that the Brock reference has here, with subsequent citations in shortened form. Full bibliographical data on all items so cited, and such data on all Rawls's published writings subsequent to his book, will be found in the Selected Bibliography at the end of my book.

3. See H. L. A. Hart, "Utilitarianism and Natural Rights," *Tulane Law Review* 53 (1979): 663-80; "Between Utility and Rights," *Columbia Law Review* 79 (1979): 828-46.

4. I owe the formulation in this sentence to Robert Hall.

5. The idea of such a monopoly (and the term itself) I have taken from David Lyons. The term *welfare argument* is his as well.

6. In the next page or so, I will be drawing on recent work by Brandt and Lyons, as follows. Richard B. Brandt, "Utilitarianism and Human Rights," in *Human Rights,* ed. David Gruender (selected papers from the Tenth Inter-American Congress of Philosophy, forthcoming); this paper was originally given at the Tenth Inter-American Congress of Philosophy, in Tallahassee, in October 1981. David Lyons, "Mill's Theory of Morality," *Nous* 10 (1976): 101–20; "Human Rights and the General Welfare," *Philosophy and Public Affairs* 6 (1977): 113–29; "Mill's Theory of Justice," in *Values and Morals,* ed. Alvin. I. Goldman and J. Kim (Dordrecht, Holland: Reidel, 1978), 1–20; "Introduction," in *Rights,* ed. David Lyons (Belmont, Calif.: Wadsworth, 1979), 1–13; "Mill on Liberty and Harm to Others," in *New Essays on John Stuart Mill and Utilitarianism,* ed. W. E. Cooper, Kai Nielsen, and S. C. Patten (*Canadian Journal of Philosophy,* supplementary vol. 5, 1979), 1–19; and "Benovolence and Justice in Mill," in *The Limits of Utilitarianism,* ed. H. B. Miller and W. H. Williams (Minneapolis: University of Minnesota Press, 1982), 42–70 (this last item is a paper that was originally prepared in 1978 for a conference at Virginia Polytechnic Institute, in Blacksburg).

Brandt is conventionally regarded as a utilitarian; Lyons, in the works cited above, might better be regarded as a sympathetic interpreter of that tradition, one whose sympathies lie with Mill in particular. In this reconstructive account of utilitarianism I have tried to emphasize points that Brandt and Lyons have in common. It should be borne in mind also that Lyons has subsequently had second thoughts about the compatibility of utilitarianism and rights; I will turn to these later in the section.

7. The claim that it is a conceptual truth, for Mill, that morality is essentially a matter of obligations and rights is found in Lyons, "Introduction," 7 (also "Mill's Theory of Morality," 105, and "Mill's Theory of Justice," 7). The phrase "logic of the moral concepts" is from Lyons, "Mill's Theory of Justice," 5. And the claim that rules provide an appropriate generality is from Lyons, "Mill's Theory of Justice," 10.

Brandt does not accept the claim that the connection of morality to obligations and rights is, in any way, a conceptual or necessary truth. But he does, in his emphasis on a moral code and in his characterization of the typical content of such a code, accept the centrality of rules of obligation in morality.

8. See Lyons, "Mill's Theory of Morality," 113.

9. This particular feature of rights—the emphasis on *qualified* beneficiaries—I have taken from Lyons's earlier discussion of legal rights in Bentham (see David Lyons, "Rights, Claimants, and Beneficiaries," *American Philosophical Quarterly* 6 [1969]: 173–85, at 179 esp.). I have simply generalized the feature, as Lyons himself does, to cover moral rights as well.

10. See Lyons, "Mill's Theory of Morality," 115; he cites Mill, *Utilitarianism* (1863), chap. 2, last paragraph, and chap. 5, paragraphs 32–33, 37. The reply here represents my interpretation of Lyons's most cogent analysis of the relation of moral rules to utilitarianism (see Martin, "Justification of Rights," 164). For an alternative and less satisfactory interpretation of this relation, one that is more like the conventional rule-utilitarian answer, see "Justification of Rights," 164 also.

11. Both Lyons and Brandt regard the principle of utility as merely setting an end; and both treat expediency as identifying only what is desirable rather than what is required. The linkage of expediency—that is, the maximizing of utility—with *required*

conduct comes only at the point where morality is introduced; for it is only in morality, with its rules of obligation, that we can speak of conduct as being required.

For the claim that the principle of utility treats of ends only and is not concerned with conduct per se see Lyons, "Mill's Theory of Morality," 113; "Mill's Theory of Justice," 5, 8; "Human Rights and the General Welfare," 119.

12. David Lyons, "Utility as a Possible Ground of Rights," *Nous* 14 (1980): 17–28, at 26. This essay and the next one cited express Lyons's second thoughts, referred to earlier, about the compatibility thesis. See also Lyons, "Utility and Rights," in *Ethics, Economics, and the Law,* ed. J. R. Pennock and John W. Chapman, NOMOS 24 (New York: New York University Press, 1982), 107–38, esp. at 128, 136. I am indebted to Brandt's essay, "Utilitarianism and Human Rights," for helping me see the "gist" of Lyons's objection.

13. The idea of an "argumentative threshold" is from Lyons, "Utility and Rights," 111. Brandt has correctly pointed out (in "Utilitarianism and Human Rights") that Lyons's argument, if sound, would tell against all rule-governed rights, thus not merely against the legal rights (i.e., those having moral force) that Lyons is concerned with in these two articles.

14. See H. L. A. Hart, "Are There Any Natural Rights?" *Philosophical Review* 64 (1955): 175–91, esp. at 179n, 181–82. Interestingly, in his articles expressing his second thoughts, Lyons disputes the presumed conceptual connection (mutual entailment) between morality and obligations and rights; see Lyons, "Utility and Rights," 134–35.

15. For a discussion of the logic of the practical syllogism—or, as I would prefer to call it, practical inference—see my book, *Historical Explanation: Re-enactment and Practical Inference,* Contemporary Philosophy Series (Ithaca, N.Y.: Cornell University Press, 1977), chaps. 9 and 10. The crucial text in utilitarian theory from which this distinctive emphasis on practical inference could be derived is John Stuart Mill's *System of Logic* (originally published in 1843; 8th ed., 1872), bk. 6, chap. 12, esp. secs. 2 and 5–7.

16. I refer here to Lyons's views *before* his second thoughts. John Gray, in his book *Mill on Liberty: A Defence* (London: Routledge & Kegan Paul, 1983), has provided a useful summary of what he calls the "new wave of Mill scholarship" (p. 10). For his account of indirect utilitarianism see chaps. 1 and 2 in particular and also pp. 59, 63, 66, 111, 116, 121. For his citation of recent literature see n. 17 to chap. 1 (pp. 131–32), nn. 14 and 29 to chap. 2 (pp. 133–34). The idea of constraining the principle of expediency (or utility) so as to maximize utility is found at a number of points, in particular, pp. 65, 68, 94–95, 124. The important point about the conflict of rules or precepts occurs on p. 42.

Gray's argument is conveniently summarized in his earlier article "John Stuart Mill on Liberty, Utility, and Rights," in *Human Rights,* ed. J. R. Pennock and John W. Chapman, NOMOS 23 (New York: New York University Press, 1981), 80–116. The article is not only shorter but also much less congested than the book. For the theme of indirect utilitarianism see pp. 87, 91, 109, and also 106, 111; for citations of the literature see nn. 11 and 14 on pp. 113–15. Note also Gray's interesting assertion that Mill's position is "indistinguishable" from sophisticated forms of act-utilitarianism (pp. 90–91).

17. Mill, *Utilitarianism,* chap. 5, third paragraph from end. Mill is here quoting Bentham approvingly.

18. Hart, "Utilitarianism and Natural Rights," 670, also 664, 674, 676; and see Hart, "Between Utility and Rights," 829–30.

19. Barry Clark and Herbert Gintis, "Rawlsian Justice and Economic Systems," *Philosophy and Public Affairs* 7 (1978): 302–25, at 302–3.

20. *TJ,* 28 and 30 respectively; see also 159, 207, 211, 450.

21. *TJ,* 102.

22. Almost all of what I have said in the last several paragraphs is a paraphrase—I hope not too loose a one—of themes raised in Rawls's essay "The Basic Structure as Subject," in *Values and Morals,* ed. A. I. Goldman and J. Kim (Dordrecht, Holland: Reidel, 1978), 47–71. For Rawls's use of the term *cooperation* see, e.g., *TJ,* 58, and his article "Kantian Constructivism in Moral Theory," *Journal of Philosophy* 77 (1980): 515–72, at 528. He does, of course, also use the term in its more usual, more natural sense; see Rawls, "The Basic Liberties and Their Priority," in *The Tanner Lectures on Human Values,* ed. S. M. McMurrin, vol. 3 (Salt Lake City: University of Utah Press, 1982), 3–87, at 14. My emphasis on coercion is taken from Rawls, "Kantian Constructivism," 538–39, and on the idea that the basic structure constitutes a single system, from "Basic Liberties," 15.

23. *TJ.* 62; see also 303.

24. Rawls's own summary is given in *TJ,* 146–47; see also 126–27, 137.

25. *TJ,* 136 (italics added). In the next sentence he refers to this procedure as "pure procedural justice" (see also pp. 84–88.)

Pure procedural justice requires (i) that there be no independent standard or criterion for determining in advance a preferred (e.g., just) outcome. In such a situation, then, there could be no knowledge of what such an outcome should be nor, of course, any procedure for assuring such a result. Nonetheless, one could still reach an acceptable outcome if (ii) one can establish an impartial way or procedure to get to *some* outcome. Thus, under (i) and (ii), any determinate outcome within the established limits of the procedure would be regarded as having been arrived at fairly. Here the fairness of the procedure translates to the results. This, then, is Rawls's most general way of characterizing the decision procedure of the original position.

26. The point about ranking is found in *TJ,* 18; see also "Basic Structure," 61.

27. For the idea of a short list of competing principles of justice see *TJ,* 50, 52, 581, and "Basic Liberties," 8; also Rawls, "Reply to Alexander and Musgrave," *Quarterly Journal of Economics* 88 (1974): 633–55, at 637, 639. Rawls explicitly singles out Aristotle and Nietzsche as being examples of perfectionist theories (see *TJ,* 25, 325); I have added Plato (e.g., the *Republic*) as another appropriate instance.

For the two versions of utilitarianism see *TJ,* 162 and 22, 187–88 respectively. Rawls attributes (*TJ,* 162n) the theory of *average* utility to J. S. Mill, Knut Wiksell, J. C. Harsanyi, and, with qualification, R. B. Brandt. Arrow cites two names here: Harsanyi and W. S. Vickrey (see K. J. Arrow, "Some Ordinalist-Utilitarian Notes on Rawls' Theory of Justice," *Journal of Philosophy* 70 [1973]: 245–63, at 250).

28. See *TJ,* 60, 83, 250, and esp. 302–3 for his various statements of the principles. Rawls normally calls Principle 1 the Principle of Equal Liberty or Equal Basic Liberties; Principle 2a, the Principle of Fair Equality of Opportunity; and Principle 2b, the Difference Principle. The language in the text is a paraphrase of Rawls.

29. *TJ,* 42–44.

30. The phrase is Rawls's; see *TJ,* 12, 19, 169, and esp. sec. 24, pp. 136–42, for his discussion of the veil of ignorance. The veil is, of course, a metaphorical way of describing the constraints on knowledge that exist in the original position.

31. Rawls initially endorses deductivity as an ideal: "The argument aims eventually to be strictly deductive. . . . We should strive for a kind of moral geometry

with all the rigor which this name connotes" (*TJ*, 121; see also 119, 185). At a later point he repudiates this ideal quite explicitly when he says "the original position is not an axiomatic (or deductive) basis from which principles are derived" ("Kantian Constructivism," 572).

32. The doctrine of persons is developed in *TJ*, p. 211 and secs. 40, 77, 85; the special characterization of *moral* is found (in summary form) on p. 505. In his later writings, Rawls emphasizes the distinctive character of persons by frequently invoking the phrase "free and equal moral persons" (see, e.g., "Basic Structure," 57 and esp. 63; also "Kantian Constructivism," pts. 1 and 2). That developed conceptions of the good and plans of life can conflict—can oppose and even thwart one another—is also emphasized in his later writing (see, e.g., "Basic Liberties," 17).

33. See Rawls, "Kantian Constructivism," 548, and "Basic Liberties," 30.

34. Rawls, "Reply to Alexander and Musgrave," 638.

35. The theory of the well-ordered society is found at several points in Rawls's writings: *TJ*, sec. 69; "Reply to Alexander and Musgrave," sec. 1; "Fairness to Goodness," *Philosophical Review* 84 (1975): 536-54, at 547-51; "Kantian Constructivism," 521-22. I have emphasized two features in particular: (a) a public sense of institutional justice (see "Kantian Constructivism," 521, 537-38) and (b) the stability of a society with the preferred public sense of justice (see *TJ*, 454-58, 496-504; "Kantian Constructivism," 522, 534; "Basic Liberties," 31-32; and Rawls, "The Independence of Moral Theory," *Proceedings and Addresses of the American Philosophical Association* 48 [1974-75]: 5-22, at 13).

36. Rawls consistently gives a significant role, behind the veil of ignorance, to what he calls "social theory"—more conventionally called social science. (See, e.g., Rawls, "Distributive Justice: Some Addenda," *Natural Law Forum* 13 [1968]: 51-71, at 54; *TJ*, 137-38, 158-59, 176, 181; "Reply to Alexander and Musgrave," 637; and "Fairness to Goodness," 543-46.) Although he tends to emphasize their relevance to issues of motivation and stability, this is not the only role that the social sciences play in Rawls's theory.

On the particular point of relative stability, Rawls believes (as would be expected) that the two principles, when incorporated under the publicity condition, yield the most stable just society (see "Basic Liberties," 31).

37. See *TJ*, 139, 146.

38. Rawls restates both utilitarian positions so as to make them range over indexes of primary goods rather than over satisfactions or utilities (see *TJ*, 161-62, 175).

39. The idea of three "models" is found in "Kantian Constructivism," 520; for the original position as the mediating model see pp. 520, 533, and 566-67.

40. Rawls speaks of the desideratum of "grounding the theory of justice on weak stipulations" (*TJ*, 149). I have tried to provide a generalized (though perhaps partial) notion of such weakness in the account of nondeductivity.

41. I would like to call attention here to the article by Stephen Griffin, "Interpreting the Initial Situation," *Auslegung* 9 (1982): 50-66.

I am grateful as well to Jack Bricke for his helpful comments on this chapter.

## Chapter 2
## A Theory of Justice and Rights

1. I should make clear at the outset that I am concerned only with explicating and criticizing Rawls's theory of rights. I will make little effort to locate Rawls in

reference to other contemporary theories of rights. For those who are interested in a survey of the rights literature see my paper (with James W. Nickel, coauthor), "Recent Work on the Concept of Rights," *American Philosophical Quarterly* 17 (1980): 165–80. I would add simply that Rawls's theory has affinities at various points with ideas developed by Joel Feinberg and by Ronald Dworkin. Nor do I plan to discuss my own conception of rights and how *that* relates to Rawls. The closest I come to doing so is in the next section of the present chapter, where I develop an argument from some of my earlier papers as a way of interpreting Rawls.

2. See *TJ*, 62, 303.

3. For examples of the inclusion of rights among the primary goods see *TJ*, 62; also "Fairness to Goodness," 536; "A Kantian Conception of Equality," in *Property, Profits, and Economic Justice*, ed. Virginia Held (Belmont, Calif.: Wadsworth, 1980), 198–208, at 202; and "Social Unity and Primary Goods," in *Utilitarianism and Beyond*, ed. A. Sen and B. Williams (Cambridge: Cambridge University Press, 1982), 159–85, at 161.

4. For examples of where rights are *not* included in the Rawlsian list of primary goods see *TJ*, 303; also "Kantian Constructivism," 526, and "Basic Liberties," 22.

5. *TJ*, 302; see also 60, 250.

6. *TJ*, 302; see also 60, 83.

7. See *TJ*, 396.

8. "Basic Structure," 48. In an earlier version of "Basic Structure," Rawls had said "corrected" rather than "adjusted" (see "Basic Structure as Subject," *American Philosophical Quarterly* 14 [1977]: 159–65, at 159). These two papers constitute Rawls's main elaboration of his theory of the basic structure. All my references are to the later (1978) version, except where specifically noted.

9. See, e.g., *TJ*, 54, 58, 61, 84, 131.

10. See *TJ*, 61 and the argument of chap. 4 of that same book.

11. See *TJ*, chap. 8, pp. 505–6n.30.

12. See *TJ*, secs. 10, 14, 17, 18—esp. p. 112—38, 48, and 52.

13. The distinction between basic structure institutions (and their operation) and subsidiary institutions (and their operation) marks *the* main divide within Rawls's theory of justice. Note his reference to a "division of labor" between two kinds of social rules (see "Basic Structure," 54–55, 66, 68). I have followed Rawls's lead, as to this basic division of labor, at a number of points throughout my study of his theory.

14. Rawls discusses his method in *TJ*, esp. sec. 9 and also pp. 20–21, 111, 120, 182, 432; for his important endorsement of "wide" reflective equilibrium see Rawls, "Independence of Moral Theory," 7–8, 21. The argument in favor of wide reflective equilibrium would commend itself to anyone who found attractive my suggestion that the arguments developed in the original position must be progressively refined at subsequent stages.

15. See *TJ*, 313.

16. See note 3 above.

17. See chaps. 6 and 8 of the present book for further development of this argument (and for references to Rawls's texts see n. 14 of chap. 6).

18. The latter term is adapted from Ronald Dworkin (see his book, *Taking Rights Seriously* [Cambridge: Harvard University Press, 1977], 90–91). When we say a right is individuated we mean that the rights-justifying norm or principle "must define a class such that every member of the class is assigned the benefit" (see Martin and Nickel, "Recent Work on the Concept of Rights," 171–72).

19. For Rawls's emphasis on a guarantee see *TJ*, 169. Of course, there is a sense in which each of the social primary goods is guaranteed under the two principles of justice. But not all such guaranteed goods can be individuated. We are concerned, in the theory of rights, only with those that can be both individuated and guaranteed *as individuated*.

20. See, e.g., A. I. Melden, *Rights and Persons* (Oxford: B. Blackwell; Berkeley: University of California Press, 1977), 89–90, 103, esp. 112.

21. See *TJ*, 260–63.

22. Norman Bowie makes this point. See his article, "Some Comments on Rawls's Theory of Justice," *Social Theory and Practice* 3 (1974): 65–74, at 71.

23. In H. L. A. Hart, "Rawls on Liberty and Its Priority," in *Reading Rawls,* ed. Norman Daniels (New York: Basic Books, 1975): 230–52.

24. *A Theory of Justice* was translated into German as *Eine Theorie der Gerechtigkeit* (Frankfurt am Main: Suhrkamp, 1975). The "list" interpretation of the basic liberties is most clearly set forth in Rawls, "Basic Liberties," 5–6; see also "Kantian Conception of Equality," 202–3.

25. See *TJ*, esp. p. 61; also sec. 32.

26. For Rawls's clearest distinction of the original position from the state of nature see "Basic Structure," 68.

27. See *TJ*, 147; also "Basic Structure," 62.

28. My argument in this section draws on much more highly developed and detailed arguments which are found in my article "Human Rights and Civil Rights" and in my paper "T. H. Green on Natural Rights in Hobbes, Spinoza, and Locke," delivered at a conference at Balliol College, Oxford, in September 1982.

29. For examples, taken almost at random, of Rawls's pairing of (basic) rights and duties see *TJ*, 4–7, 10, 14, 54, 56, 58, 61, 63, 84, 131, 202.

30. I should add that I am not keen on putting the central contention in precisely this way. I would prefer to say that all rights imply significant normative direction of the conduct of second parties (with duties and obligations serving as a prime example of such direction).

For a discussion of the thesis, in contemporary rights theory, that rights imply duties (and for the argument in favor of saying, instead, that rights imply significant normative direction of the conduct of other persons) see Martin and Nickel, "Recent Work on the Concept of Rights," 165–67. In the present discussion I have used the terms *duty* and *obligation* interchangeably, as if no distinction existed; Rawls, of course, distinguishes them sharply (see *TJ*, secs. 18–19, 51–52, esp. pp. 114–15).

31. Evidence for saying that Rawls subscribes to the thesis that rights imply duties is found in *TJ*, 239 in particular (esp. n. 23), and also 112, 203, 236, 243.

32. I have analogized Rawls's account of legitimate expectations specifically to that of Joel Feinberg on valid claims. This procedure seems sound to me since Rawls tends to mix the terms *rights, claims,* and *legitimate expectations* and to use them, apparently on whim, more or less interchangeably (see, e.g., *TJ*, 84, 311, 313, 505n). For Feinberg's discussion of rights as valid claims see his book *Social Philosophy,* Foundations of Philosophy series (Englewood Cliffs, N.J.: Prentice-Hall, 1973), 64–67. Roughly the same discussion is found in Feinberg's paper "The Nature and Value of Rights," *Journal of Value Inquiry* 4 (1970): 243–57, at 253–57. See also Feinberg, "The Rights of Animals and Unborn Generations," in *Philosophy and Environmental Crisis,* ed. William T. Blackstone (Athens: University of Georgia Press, 1974), 43–68, at 43–44. For summaries and further discussions of Feinberg's views see Martin and Nickel, "Recent Work on the Concept of Rights," 167–69, and Martin,

"Justification of Rights," 154–59; my paper "The Development of Feinberg's Conception of Rights," *Journal of Value Inquiry* 16 (1982): 29–45, might also prove useful.

33. I do not want to imply that Rawls regards the liberty to travel as a *basic* liberty. (The matter is more complex than that; see chap. 4 of the present book.) I want to show here only what would be involved in calling the liberty to travel a right, specifically a human or natural right.

34. "[A]s a matter of fact men speak of their moral rights mainly when advocating their incorporation into a legal system" (Hart, "Are There Any Natural Rights?" 177). "Declarations of the Rights of Man did not include his right to be told the truth, to have promises kept which had been made to him, to receive gratitude from those he had benefited, etc. The common thread among the variety of natural rights is their political character" (Margaret Macdonald, "Natural Rights," in *Human Rights,* ed. A. I. Melden [Belmont, Calif.: Wadsworth, 1970], 40–60, at 52).

Human rights are explicitly represented, in the preamble to the United Nations' Universal Declaration, as rights to be secured "among the peoples of Member States"; they are enjoined on governments, in particular, as rights that "should be protected by the rule of law." In the two United Nations Covenants (1966, entered into force in 1976), one on economic and social rights and the other on civil and political rights, it is the States Parties, as they are called, that expressly undertake to do these things, as specified in the earlier Universal Declaration (1948).

35. See *TJ,* chap. 8, pp. 505–6n.30. The other main likeness to natural rights of such claims is, the note suggests, that such claims are not easily overridden. I will address this issue, specifically, in chap. 7. Even in this note, however, Rawls refers to the "protection" of these claims to basic liberties as being part of the function of natural rights. My argument has been designed to show that such liberties cannot be protected merely by their acknowledgment in the original position; rather, duties must be specified (and acknowledged) and institutions must be developed. In this way, natural-rights norms link up with the basic structure of a society and require the support of institutions there—a necessary requirement, indeed a conceptual one, if my analysis of natural rights is sound. And I take Rawls to be holding that the requirement is a necessary one.

36. The distinction of special/general rights is drawn from Hart ("Are There Any Natural Rights?" esp. 187–88). My discussion here is also indebted to William Nelson's analysis (in his "Special Rights, General Rights, and Social Justice," *Philosophy and Public Affairs* 3 [1974]: 410–30).

37. For Rawls's general perspective on this issue see *TJ,* 55–56, also 311. His characteristic emphasis is on the explicit formulation ("public recognition") of the basic liberties in particular (see pp. 544–45), though he does, of course, also mention institutions for their "protection" (see pp. 196–97).

38. *TJ,* 197; see also "Basic Liberties," 52, 54.

39. I have tried in this section to provide an interpretation of Rawls's idea of "embedding" as we find it, for example, in his claim that "an ideal conception of a just basic structure is embedded in the principles chosen in the original position" (*TJ,* 288; see also 160–61, 261–63, 288–89, 326–27).

I want also to call attention here to Scott Wasserman, "Rawls: On Rights" (senior honors thesis in philosophy, University of Kansas, 1982). I owe the idea that rights are *part* of the basic structure to him. "Rights are never distributed by a major social institution; instead, they *are* the institution. They are in the basic structure, not distributed by it" ("Rawls: On Rights," 12). It was also Wasserman who suggested to me the close connection between Rawls's analysis of rights (as legitimate expectations) and Feinberg's account of rights as valid claims.

40. It is important to see that the operation of the difference principle is in no way automatic; it is thus completely unlike Adam Smith's "invisible hand." Rather, as with constitutional rights and measures for fair equality of opportunity, the operation of the difference principle depends on explicit *political* mechanisms. Its application cannot outrun them. (For an example of the view that I am disputing here see Charles Frankel, "Justice, Utilitarianism, and Rights," *Social Theory and Practice* 3 (1974): 27–46, at 34.) Accordingly, we can say both that the difference principle must be embedded in the basic structure of a society and that it cannot, for all practical purposes at present, be globalized.

## Chapter 3
## Equal Basic Liberties

1. See *TJ*, sec. 31. The stages are (a) the original position, (b) the constitution, (c) legislation, and (d) judicial and administrative action and the conduct of individual citizens. There has been copious discussion of the original position, but relatively little has been written about the constitutional stage. For a discussion of the latter in particular see Ronald Moore, "Rawls on Constitution-Making," in *Constitutionalism*, ed. J. R. Pennock and John W. Chapman. NOMOS 20 (New York: New York University Press, 1979), 238–68.

2. See *TJ*, 197 esp., also 200, 206.

3. For Rawls's discussion of the representative citizen see *TJ*, pp. 204, 212, 220, 221, 231, 244, 246, and sec. 40, also pp. 547, 564, 566. This standpoint is further elaborated in the two "Kantian" essays: "Kantian Conception of Equality" and "Kantian Constructivism."

4. The list of basic liberties is from *TJ*, 61. For the point about productive property see "Basic Liberties," 12 esp. For further discussion of the ownership of productive property—and its status as a right—see the third section of chapter 8 of the present book.

Interestingly, the primary good involved here—in the list—is described by Rawls in his later essays as "the basic liberties" (and not simply as *liberties,* the term that he used in his book). See "Kantian Constructivism," 526; "Basic Liberties," 22; and "Social Unity and Primary Goods," 162. No important change in doctrine, however, is involved in this switch. It is merely that in his later writings, Rawls stresses the importance of the "model" of a person (i.e., the "Kantian conception") of persons as free and equal moral beings) as part of the background of the original position construct. The connecting of the model of the person with liberties, to get the *basic* liberties, is part of Rawls's overall strategy of connecting the Kantian conception with *each* of the so-called social primary goods. But even with this (slight) amendment, the crucial point is preserved: namely, that the basic liberties are those liberties which are *essential* to the status of being a person. It is this point that I have tried to bring out in the analysis here.

5. The analysis here of a liberty (the main elements of the analysis have been italicized) is drawn from G. C. MacCallum, "Negative and Positive Freedom," *Philosophical Review* 76 (1967): 312–34. Rawls follows MacCallum's account (see *TJ*, 202, esp. n. 4). I should add that Rawls simplifies MacCallum's analysis considerably and also omits mention of an important stipulation; nevertheless, since our concern is

with Rawls's own account, we will not pursue further the issue of his interpretation of MacCallum.

6. Rawls, "Kantian Constructivism," 525. Rawls's idea of the two highest-order interests is found in "Kantian Constructivism," 521, 525, 531, 543–44, 548–49, 567–68; and in "Social Unity and Primary Goods," 165. In "Basic Liberties," Rawls eschews talk of highest-order interests and instead addresses the issue straightforwardly in terms of the two fundamental moral powers (see, e.g., p. 16).

7. For the so-called higher-order interest (in the citizens' "protecting and advancing their conception of the good as best they can") see Rawls, "Kantian Constructivism," 525; and "Social Unity and Primary Goods," 165. The emphasis on revising (and on rationally grasping) one's conception of the good, so important to Rawls's overall position, is found in "Kantian Conception of Equality," 203; "Basic Structure," 63; "Kantian Constructivism," 544–45, 547–49; and "Basic Liberties," 27.

8. See "Basic Liberties," 47. Rawls's general program for dealing with the two fundamental cases (each identified with one of the two highest-order interests or moral powers) is set out on pp. 23–24, 47–51, esp. 47 and 50.

9. See Rawls, "Basic Liberties," 24–29, 47, 49–50. Technically, only freedom of conscience and of personal association are *primarily* governed by the highest-order interest (or moral power) of having, revising, etc., a determinate conception of the good. The other liberties and noninjuries mentioned in this paragraph come under *both* of the moral powers (see Rawls, "Basic Liberties," 50).

10. See Rawls, "Basic Liberties," pp. 24, 47–51, also secs. 10–12. For simplicity, Rawls normally arranges these liberties into two groups: (1) "freedom of thought" (i.e., freedom of political speech and assembly, freedom of the press) and (2) the political-participation or political-process liberties, such as voting.

11. *TJ*, sec. 33, esp. p. 206; also p. 211. I feel, however, that Rawls continues to give liberty of conscience (modeled on the idea of religious toleration) too central a place in his account of the basic liberties. (See, e.g., the references cited in n. 7 [above] on the importance of being able to revise a determinate conception of the good; also Rawls, "Basic Liberties," 24, 50.) Stephen Griffin suggested that I include more of Rawls's discussion of fundamental interests in my account of the basic liberties; I am grateful to him for this suggestion. Some of the points made, and even some of the formulations, I have taken from him.

12. Rawls's main discussions of equality are found in *TJ*, secs. 40, 77, 82, 85. See also his "Kantian Conception of Equality," esp. 205–6; "Kantian Constructivism," esp. 529, 532, 546–50; and "Basic Liberties," sec. 7.

13. Here I draw principally on his discussion in *TJ*, chap. 4.

14. See *TJ*, 224, 228–30.

15. Rawls allows for such restrictions; see *TJ*, 212–13, 246, esp. 215; see also "Basic Liberties," 70.

16. See *TJ*, 380–81.

17. See the discussion of "secondary guidance" in Martin and Nickel, "Recent Work on the Concept of Rights," 174. For further discussion of this issue see chapter 7 of the present book.

18. See Rawls, "Basic Liberties," 9.

19. Here I have simply applied Rawls's notion of rules as public practices (from his "Two Concepts of Rules," *Philosophical Review* 64 [1951]: 3–32) to his account of rights-rules. (And accordingly we presume, as we have throughout, that any such rule

is an operating or effective one and not a merely nominal rule.) See also Hart, "Rawls on Liberty and Its Priority," 236.

20. For Rawls's principal discussion of this point see *TJ*, 204–5, and "Basic Liberties," 44–45. I should add that after I had written this example, I came across a similar one in the recent book by Neil MacCormick (*H. L. A. Hart* [Stanford, Calif.: Stanford University Press, 1981], at 9).

21. This interpretation of Rawls is also advanced by Hart, "Rawls on Liberty and Its Priority," 236–37; and by Norman Bowie, "Equal Basic Liberty for All," 128. Rawls explicitly endorses this interpretation in "Basic Liberties," 40–41; see also 44–45. For a criticism of Rawls on this general point see Norman Daniels, "Equal Liberty and Unequal Worth of Liberty," 253–81, at 269–72. I should add that the political-participation liberties (voting, etc.) must adhere to a stricter standard even than this: for they are required by Rawls to be substantially equal in actual fact. I will take this issue up later in the present chapter.

22. *TJ*, 248. I should add that the arrangement specified here would not satisfy the constraints, required for justifiable inequality, set forth at the very end of the present chapter.

23. See *TJ*, secs. 36 and 37 and pp. 246–47.

24. See *Considerations on Representative Government* (1861), chap. 8. For an amusing proposal for plural voting see Nevil Shute, *In the Wet* (London: Heinemann, 1953), 102–8. I owe the reference to the Shute novel to Arthur Skidmore. I am also grateful, for help on this reference, to my son Justin.

25. For helping me refine the ideas expressed in this paragraph I am indebted to Christine Swanton.

26. See "Basic Liberties," sec. 7, esp. pp. 41–43; also pp. 75–78.

27. For these measures, in order, see "Basic Liberties," 75; *TJ*, 226 and 225 respectively; see also "Basic Liberties," 73.

28. See Rawls, "Basic Liberties," 43, 45–46; the phrase "limited space" is from p. 43. The point about coercion is found in *TJ*, 226 (see also 222, 225).

29. Rawls occasionally affords a respectful hearing to the idea that the political liberties are merely subordinate or instrumental to the more important, basic liberties but are not themselves basic liberties (see *TJ*, 230, 233, 247; and "Basic Liberties," 12–13). But he never, as I have tried to show, endorses such an idea (see esp. "Basic Liberties," 77).

30. I would not want to claim, by the way, that any significant idea of fair value for the political liberties is wholly absent from Rawls's book. But he himself admits that it was not played up there adequately. "While the idea of the fair value of the equal political liberties is an important aspect of the two principles of justice as presented in *TJ*, this idea was not sufficiently developed or explained [there]. It was, therefore, easy to miss its significance" ("Basic Liberties," p. 42n.34). Rawls then cites relevant references to the fair value of the political liberties in *TJ*, as found at 224–28, 233–34, 277–79, 356; and he adds that it should have been discussed, but wasn't, at 544–46 (see "Basic Liberties," pp. 32–33n.28).

31. "[A] less than equal liberty must be acceptable to those with the lesser liberty" (*TJ*, 302; see also 250).

32. Various phrasings of Rawls's motto can be found in *TJ*, 203–4, 214–15, 220, 244, 250 (repeated on 302); and "Basic Liberties," 9. Note also Rawls's remark that "the priority of liberty does not exclude marginal exchanges within the system of freedom" (*TJ*, 230). I should add that although the identified constraints are taken from Rawls, he nowhere gives them the explicit, systematic treatment and develop-

ment that they require. For a continuation and extension of the discussion of the limitation of liberty *by* liberty see chapter 7 of the present book.

## Chapter 4
## Fair Equality of Opportunity

1. This list is taken from *TJ*, 62. For Rawls's clearest interpretation of what he means by powers see "Fairness to Goodness," pp. 542–43n.8; he does not mean power over others (either politically or economically).

In his later writings, the list of primary goods is regularized (see "Kantian Constructivism," 526; "Basic Liberties," 22–23; "Social Unity and Primary Goods," 162). All three of these list "the social bases of self-respect" as a primary good. But I have not included this particular good in my list here. My reason is that Rawls tends to regard the adequate provision of the other primary goods (including basic liberties) as sufficient to provide the social *bases* of self-respect. Thus, these bases are an amalgam of the other social primary goods. For further discussion see chapter 9, third section.

2. See *TJ*, 62 and 303 respectively.

3. It is necessary to interpret the term *initially* as referring (1) to one's actual starting point in a particular society (as given by the reasonable lifetime expectations of one's representative position) and (2) to some "hypothetical initial arrangement in which all the social primary goods are equally distributed" in the basic structure of one's own society (see *TJ*, 62, also 65, 76, 80, 150–51, 497, 546; "Reply to Alexander and Musgrave," 635; "Basic Structure," 65; "Social Unity and Primary Goods," 173). Thus, what is required here is that the condition of improvement be satisfied for both (1) and (2).

4. Rawls is clearly willing to allow some trade-off of income and wealth (under conditions in which the two principles do apply) so as to achieve a more extensive and more secure system of equal basic liberties (see *TJ*, 244, 542–44, also 151–52). So, encouragement toward reading the *general conception* as concerned specifically with trade-offs is found in Rawls's own texts. Any criticism that I make of such a reading, then, has to be directed at Rawls himself.

5. For various statements of, and glosses on, the general conception see *TJ*, pp. 62, 83, 150–52, 303, and secs. 39, 82. There is, in my judgment, no significant mention of the general conception of justice in "Basic Structure," "Kantian Constructivism," "Basic Liberties," or "Social Unity and Primary Goods."

I think one important reason for this de-emphasis on the general conception in Rawls's own theory is that it has no real handhold there. A theory of justice, even to be applicable, requires certain objective preconditions, among which are the achievement of at least a subsistence level of economic well-being (see *TJ*, sec. 22.) Thus, where this and other reasonably favorable conditions obtain, as conditions for the application of a theory of justice, we are already in the domain staked out for the two principles of justice and its main competitors. And where these conditions do not obtain, it is doubtful that *any* theory of justice would be applicable, including the general conception. My discussion in what follows in this section should make clear that the Rawlsian account of the general conception has other problems as well.

6. See *TJ*, 62, 151, 541.

7. See *TJ*, 546; "Basic Liberties," 44.

8. One persistent point of confusion in Rawls's discussion of the general conception of justice is that, although the *explicit* deviation that is allowed for in the language of the general conception is deviation from equality, Rawls often talks about

deviations (trade-offs) between the amount available of one primary good as an exchange for the amount available of another. This latter way of talking is not really concerned with inequalities among individual persons but, rather, with whether persons would prefer, say, a greater amount of liberties and a lesser amount of wealth to other possible arrangements. These are not the same issue, and it is confusing to treat them under the same heading.

This confusion aside, I have tried to suggest that one way of reading the general conception—namely, as reasonable deviation from equality—makes sense (but as a principle of reasoning, not as a conception of justice per se). The other reading, as allowing trade-offs between primary goods, is suspect. In fact, this latter reading has a very dubious parentage. In one of his earliest writings on justice, Rawls first establishes a *presumption* of equal liberty and then a scheme whereby that presumption could be defeated (see "Justice as Fairness," *Philosophical Review* 67 [1958]: 164–94, at 165–67). But one could say that if the presumption were well established (as it is, presumably, in the first principle of justice as set forth in Rawls's book), then there is no real occasion to set it aside. Hence, the way in which the first principle can yield to the second (in "Justice as Fairness"), thereby allowing trade-offs even of liberty for wealth (p. 167), is not so much a feature of some "general conception of justice," as Rawls comes to call it later, as it is an inadequacy in his fundamental argument. And this defective beginning provides, I think, a very unpromising foundation for the general conception and leads, unfailingly, to the idea of trade-offs—an idea that is often found in Rawls's gloss on that conception. In reaching this conclusion, I am indebted to David Lyons's very perceptive reading of the early article (in his "Rawls and Utilitarianism," *Journal of Philosophy* 69 [1972]: 535–45, esp. at 537–38, 541).

9. For (a) see Rawls, "Distributive Justice," in *Philosophy, Politics, and Society,* ed. P. Laslett and W. G. Runciman, 3d ser. (Oxford: B. Blackwell, 1967), 58–82, at 67, 71; and "Basic Structure," 56. For (b) see Rawls, "Justice as Fairness," 173; "Distributive Justice: Some Addenda," 59; *TJ,* 78, 151, 164; "Basic Structure," 56. For (c) see *TJ,* 102, 151, 315, and for (d), 314–15. For (e) see Rawls, "Distributive Justice," 67 (but see also p. 74), and *TJ,* 78. For (f) see "Distributive Justice," 67.

Rawls tends to emphasize the incentive effect of inequalities (on those who have the advantage of the inequality). Presumably the ground of Rawls's emphasis is not some fact of human nature but, rather, certain general theoretical truths such as are to be found in "the laws of human psychology" and the "principles of economic theory." Such theoretical truths (or "general facts") are specifically allowed by Rawls to intrude behind the veil of ignorance (see *TJ,* 137).

10. The notion of specifying and *establishing* inequality is taken from *TJ,* 61.

11. Norman Daniels claims that Rawls is committed to a Productivity Principle according to which, in the filling of an economic office, "*overall* job performance is [to be] maximized"—in effect, a principle of the best person for the job (from the standpoint of the job's or, more broadly, of society's well-doing). (See "Meritocracy," in *Justice and Economic Distribution,* ed. John Arthur and William H. Shaw [Englewood Cliffs, N.J.: Prentice-Hall, 1978], 164–78, at 167; see also 166–68, 171, 174.)

12. "Kantian Constructivism," 526; also "Basic Liberties," 22–23, "Social Unity and Primary Goods," 162.

13. The liberties Rawls has in mind are very like those Adam Smith includes under the heading of "perfect liberty" (see Smith, *Wealth of Nations* [1776], bk. 1, chap. 7, par. 6 [from beginning] and par. 8 [from end]; and chap. 10, par. 1). Smith tended to emphasize free choice of occupation and the ability to shift (other) resources from one productive use to another. But in an age of lesser mobility, he put less

emphasis on freedom of movement (see here, in particular, *Wealth of Nations,* bk. 1, chap. 8).

14. Some of Rawls's remarks, to the effect that the societies under design in the original position and at the constitutional stage are "closed" (*TJ,* 8; "Kantian Constructivism," 524) or that "there is no entry or exit except by birth and death" ("Basic Liberties," 15), have been interpreted to mean that there is no right of emigration from a just society. Rawls does, of course, mean to suggest that, in the project of the original position and of constitutional design, societies are to be thought of as self-contained and as lifetime settings; it does not follow, however, that such societies would lack a right of emigration. Indeed, Rawls specifically provides for such a right (in "Basic Structure," 61). Given the strategic place of that liberty in his scheme, I think it should be added to his list of basic liberties.

15. For other references to these two key freedoms see *TJ,* 271, 272, 276, 281. Correspondingly, Rawls shows considerable animus against the "forced and central direction of labor" (*TJ,* 272, and also 276, 281).

16. See Rawls, "Basic Liberties," 79-80, 83. Interestingly enough, those freedoms indicated here are often called (in the language of constitutional adjudication) "commercial speech." Rawls specifically excludes, from consideration as one of the privileged types of commercial speech, advertising of products that is merely "market-strategic," that exists primarily to create a favorable brand image—often through irrelevant or tangential associations. Presumably, he had in mind on this point the sort of advertising that is characteristic of the Miller or Coors beer ads on television (see "Basic Liberties," 80-81).

17. *TJ,* 310; see also 270.

18. See *TJ,* 274-75.

19. I will try to provide the outlines of such an account in chap. 8 of the present book. It should be noted that some economic liberties characteristic of market societies under capitalist ownership are given no preferred status at all by Rawls in his theory of justice. He singles out two in particular: liberty of contract and free competition between unequals (see "Basic Liberties," 78). Presumably, even if these are liberties in some sense (e.g., in subsidiary relationships between associations or individuals), they are *not* privileged liberties under the second principle of justice.

20. For the record, freedom of movement and free choice of occupation do seem to be basic liberties in Rawls's scheme (see "Basic Liberties," 50); the freedoms associated with commercial speech are not (see p. 79). My point, though, is that this distinction is not weighty; it is irrelevant to the inclusion of these liberties as liberties appropriate to equality of economic opportunity and, hence, irrelevant to their status as rights, given that inclusion.

21. The phrase "careers open to talents" is found in *TJ,* 65, 66, 72.

22. For the phrase "system of natural liberty" see *TJ,* 65, 66, 72, 75. Adam Smith describes his own social ideal as a "system of natural liberty" (see, e.g., *Wealth of Nations,* bk. 4, chap. 9, next to last paragraph). I am indebted to Laurence Dickie for many helpful comments on Smith. Robert Nozick says that "Rawls comes closest to considering the entitlement system [the one Nozick himself prefers] in his discussion of what [Rawls] terms the system of natural liberty" (*Anarchy, State, and Utopia* [New York: Basic Books, 1974], 213; see also 204). Rawls's main direct discussion of Nozick's views is found in "Basic Structure," sec. 3.

23. For these examples see *TJ,* 73, also 101, 277-78; and "Basic Structure," 54. Under public education we would, of course, want to include vocational training at public expense as well (see chap. 9 of the present book).

24. The ideal that I have cited can be found in *TJ,* 73; see also sec. 12. It is instructive to compare the ideal of *fair* equality of opportunity with Rawls's statement of the ideal of the *fair* value of the political liberties (as discussed in chap. 3 of the present book). Rawls says that "citizens similarly gifted and motivated [should] have roughly an equal chance of influencing the government's policy and of attaining positions of authority irrespective of their economic and social class" ("Basic Liberties," 73; see also *TJ,* 225).

25. For the phrase "liberal interpretation" see *TJ,* 73.

26. See *TJ,* 72, 74, 75.

27. I am referring here to what Rawls elsewhere calls the primary *natural* goods (*TJ,* 62).

28. Interestingly, none of the examples of how to deal with natural inequalities is from Rawls himself. I have been unable to find a suitable example in his writings. The first example (of benevolent genetic engineering) is from Amy Gutmann, *Liberal Equality* (Cambridge: Cambridge University Press, 1980), 255n.27. Two of the examples are my own (prenatal care and measures for public health). The present example (of devices that aid the handicapped) is from Anthony Kronman, "Talent Pooling," in *Human Rights,* ed. J. R. Pennock and John W. Chapman, NOMOS 23 (New York: New York University Press, 1981), 59. Kronman here cites (p. 59 and p. 77n.4) the Architectural Barriers Act and the Rehabilitation Act (of 1973). The point about mathematical ability and computers was made to me by Dan Hausman.

29. Rawls's emphasis on the positive value of diversity is clearly stated in "Basic Liberties," 34-38, esp. 38. I am indebted to my wife's brother, David Mel Paul, for helpful comments on this point.

30. For the phrase "democratic interpretation" see *TJ,* 75. Technically, it is an interpretation of the entire second principle of justice, as I shall make clear shortly.

31. *TJ,* 511.

32. This is the account that I would offer of what Rawls calls "natural aristocracy" (*TJ,* 74-75). Natural aristocracy, in fact, constitutes a *fourth* interpretation of the second principle (see p. 65), but it is a peripheral one in Rawls's view. And I have dispensed with it in my discussion in the text. I think my account here is superior to Rawls's own. For he interprets natural aristocracy as combining *formal* equality of opportunity with the difference principle. But it is odd to think that in class societies such as an idealized feudalism (Rawls's own example), there would be a commitment even to this degree of equal opportunity. For such societies are characterized and properly understood as ones in which strong institutional and even legal barriers exist to maintain the distinctive character and rigid stratification of the classes. The ideal state in Plato's *Republic* is the exemplar of all such class societies. Where class membership is determined solely by birth, as it was *not* in Plato's republic, then the society is called a *caste* society. There is no *formal* equality of opportunity in class or caste societies.

33. My discussion in this section has, with considerable embroidery added, drawn on *TJ,* secs. 12-14, 16, 46. See also Rawls, "Distributive Justice: Some Addenda," secs. 3 and 4, for an important early statement of Rawls's three interpretations of the second principle of justice.

34. "[I]t is one of the fixed points of our moral judgments that no one deserves his place in the distribution of natural assets any more than he deserves his initial starting place in society" (*TJ,* 311). See also Rawls, "Distributive Justice: Some Addenda," 66-67.

35. *TJ,* 102; see also "Kantian Constructivism," 551.

36. See *TJ*, 137 esp.

37. The quoted terms are drawn from Rawls; see "Distributive Justice," 68; and *TJ*, 74, 75, 104.

38. For the first passage quoted see *TJ*, 179, also 101; for the second see 523. At this latter point in his book Rawls is discussing what he calls "social union" (see *TJ*, sec. 79, esp. p. 529 and pp. 523-25n.4.) *Social union* is a broader term than *collective asset,* and it is the term he normally employs in his later writings.

39. See Rawls, "Distributive Justice," 68, and *TJ*, 179, for the passages quoted and the point being made. For discussion of the motivational assumption of mutual disinterest (i.e., the assumption that individuals are naturally neither benevolent and altruistic nor egoistic) see the second section of chap. 1 of the present book. For amplification see Rawls, "Kantian Constructivism," 527, 531.

40. The idea that natural endowment is not *contrary* to desert is from David Gauthier, "Justice and Natural Endowment: Toward a Critique of Rawls's Ideological Framework," *Social Theory and Practice* 3 (1974): 3-26, at 15-16. Rawls at one point, mistakenly in my view, does associate fair equality of opportunity and the difference principle with redress (see *TJ*, 100-101; also Gauthier, "Justice and Natural Endowment," 16).

41. See Bernard Bosanquet, *The Philosophical Theory of the State* (London: Macmillan, 1899), chap. 8, sec. 5.

42. For Rawls's discussion of the family see *TJ*, esp. 301, 511.

43. See *TJ*, 302-3. On the important point about not sacrificing anyone's life prospects see also pp. 178, 180, 183.

44. I will provide examples of such measures in the first section of chap. 8 and in the first two sections of chap. 9 of the present book.

45. The development of and main argumentation for the collective asset idea is found in Rawls, *TJ*, 72-75, 101-4 (see also n. 38 above). To this main argumentation should be added "Basic Structure," secs. 5, 7, and 8, where Rawls attempts to address issues respecting natural endowment that are raised by David Gauthier; see also Rawls, "Reply to Alexander and Musgrave," 647-48. For further discussion of the relationship of the collective asset idea to individual desert see the second section of chap. 8 of the present book.

46. "We doubt seriously whether there is any necessary connection between the extent of talent and success or failure" (Robert Benne, *The Ethic of Democratic Capitalism: A Moral Reassessment* [Philadelphia, Pa: Fortress Press, 1981], 242; see also 229). Benne, believing that Rawls holds a necessary connection or deterministic view here, uses the idea that is quoted as a criticism of Rawls. The notion of a probabilistic connection, as advocated in the text, would both clarify Rawls's position and remove this particular ground of criticism. I should add that Rawls doesn't cite such a law, nor does he even see the need for one. (He does, however, allow laws such as these in the original position; see n. 9 above, par. 2.) I have, accordingly, supplied the law myself. I am indebted to Helen Butcher for asking the question that led me to conclude that such a law was required.

47. *TJ*, 275; see also 278.

48. Such a contention is offered by Gutmann, *Liberal Equality*, 133-34.

Chapter 5
The Difference Principle

1. Shenoy and I are indebted, for helpful comments, to Richard De George, Elizabeth Miller, A. K. Sen, and Michael Young.

2. See *TJ*, 84–85, 87. Rawls here associates fair equality of opportunity with what he calls pure procedural justice (the notion that organized the decision procedure in the original position). His idea seems to be that *no* distribution principle can be just unless it incorporates fair or equal starting points. The notion of fair equality suffices, then, in his view, to yield such starting points in matters of economic and social position and the income and wealth that derive from them.

3. See *TJ*, 76–80, 152–61; for his explicit description of it as a maximin principle see, e.g., "Reply to Alexander and Musgrave," 639ff.; "Basic Structure," p. 69n.4; and "Some Reasons for the Maximin Criterion," *American Economic Review* 64 (1974): 141–46, at 141–42. In case of nonuniqueness (i.e., the maximum expectations of the least advantaged are not affected in one way or the other by some changes in the expectations of the best-off, although these changes benefit others), Rawls expresses a more general principle that he calls the "lexical difference principle," as follows: in a basic structure with *n* relevant representatives, first maximize the welfare of the worst-off representative man; second, for equal—that is, unaffected—welfare of the worst-off representative, maximize the welfare of the second-worst-off representative man, and so on until the last case; here, for equal welfare of all the preceding $n - 1$ representatives, maximize the welfare of the best-off representative man (see *TJ*, 81–83, esp. 83.)

4. Examples of such criticism are Arrow, "Some Ordinalist-Utilitarian Notes on Rawls' Theory of Justice"; J. C. Harsanyi, "Can the Maximin Principle Serve as a Basis for Morality? A Critique of John Rawls's Theory," *American Political Science Review* 69 (1975): 594–606; Nozick, *Anarchy, State, and Utopia*, esp. 189–97; Douglas Rae, "A Principle of Simple Justice," in *Philosophy, Politics, and Society*, ed. Peter Laslett and James Fishkin, 5th ser., 134–54 (New Haven, Conn.: Yale University Press, 1979); and A. K. Sen, *Collective Choice and Social Welfare* (San Francisco, Calif.: Holden-Day, 1970), esp. 135–41. For a general discussion and survey of the literature see David H. Kaye, "Playing Games with Justice: Rawls and the Maximin Rule," *Social Theory and Practice* 6 (1980): 33–51.

5. Both figures 1 and 2 appear in *TJ*, 76; indeed, much of the material in this section is taken directly from that book, pp. 76–80. It is presented here in detail, especially the discussion of the attainable set and of indifference curves, partly for completeness and partly to facilitate the exposition of pareto efficiency and egalitarianism which follows in section two.

6. Included in the basic structure (as we saw in chap. 1 of the present book) would be a society's political system and its economic system. Each of these, in turn, would be made up of a set of structural elements or institutions. We would require in the political sphere, for instance, a constitution, a form of government, and modes of election; and in the economic, some form(s) of ownership of the means of production, specific sectors for determining capital investments, devices to provide "public goods" and to deal with externalities, and so on.

7. This definition of efficiency derives from Vilfredo Pareto (see his *Manual of Political Economy* [New York: Augustus M. Kelley, 1971], chap. 6, secs. 32–64, pp. 261–69; note esp. sec. 33, p. 261, and Appendix, sec. 89, pp. 451–52). Since we are using *pareto* as a technical term, rather than as a proper name, we will employ the lower-case *p* throughout.

8. See *TJ*, 70; also Rawls, "Distributive Justice: Some Addenda," 56–57.

9. For the claim just cited see *TJ*, 261, 565; and "Kantian Constructivism," 562. For the statement of Rawls's second priority rule see *TJ*, 302–3.

10. Rawls, "Reply to Alexander and Musgrave," 648. Here (p. 648n) Rawls cites E. S. Phelps, "Wage Taxation for Economic Justice," *Quarterly Journal of*

*Economics* 87 (1973): 331–54, esp. at 334–37; and A. B. Atkinson, "How Progressive Should Income Tax Be?" in *Essays in Modern Economics,* ed. M. Parkin (London: Longmans, 1973), 90–109, at 105–8; but neither one has, in our judgment, stated the point unequivocally.

11. Rawls, "Reply to Alexander and Musgrave," p. 648 (including n. 7); see also "Social Unity and Primary Goods," p. 173n.12. For additional discussion of the two-class situation see Rainer Stuhlmann-Laeisz, "Gerechtigkeit und Effizienz. Eine Untersuchung zum Verhältnis des Unterschiedsprinzips zu dem der Pareto-Optimalität in Rawls' Theorie der Gerechtigkeit," *Allgemein Zeitschrift für Philosophie* 6, no.1 (1981): 17–30.

12. Our suggested definition would, we think, be acceptable to Rawls; for he characteristically takes the well-being of the best-off class as the standard against which the well-being of the other classes, including the least-well-off, is measured (see the graphs in *TJ,* 81), while at the same time stressing the importance of minimizing the (necessary) inequality in a society (see Rawls, "Reply to Alexander and Musgrave," 647; and "Some Reasons for the Maximin Criterion," 145). Interestingly, Nozick, too, would measure the relevant inequality as that which holds between the best-off and the least-well-off classes (see *Anarchy, State, and Utopia,* 210–12). So, our definition is well motivated in light of the existing literature and, since it would be acceptable to Rawls, could justifiably be used in an explication of Rawls. Nor is the definition eccentric. For bear in mind that the classes identified are to contain equal numbers of persons. (Thus, if four income classes are identified, for example, then each would contain one-fourth of the relevant persons; five classes, each one-fifth; and so on.)

For purposes of completeness, we add the following to our definition. In case of nonuniqueness (i.e., where there are two or more distributions with the same minimum inequality $x_1 - x_n$) we will state a more general egalitarian principle that we call the "lexical egalitarian principle," as follows: in a basic structure with $n$ relevant representatives, first minimize the inequality $x_1 - x_n$; second, for equal value of the difference $x_1 - x_n$, minimize the inequality $x_1 - x_{n-1}$, and so on, until the last case, which is for equal value of all the preceding $n - 2$ differences $x_1 - x_n$, $x_1 - x_{n-1}$, ..., $x_1 - x_3$, minimize the inequality $x_1 - x_2$.

13. See *TJ,* 81–83, for a discussion of chain connection. Arrow ("Some Ordinalist-Utilitarian Notes on Rawls' Theory of Justice," 252) severely criticizes this condition, claiming that "on the face of it, it seems clearly false." However, Arrow's criticism is based on a misunderstanding of the chain connection condition (he also confuses chain connection with close-knitness, an assumption that Rawls makes to avoid nonuniqueness under the maximin criterion). Chain connection does not imply that as we raise the expectations of the more advantaged, the situation of the worst-off is continuously improved *all of the time.* In fact, Rawls (*TJ,* 158) is careful to qualify this statement with the statement that "each such increase is in the latter's interest, *up to a certain point anyway*" (emphasis added). Hence, Arrow's example of a reduction in the income tax for high brackets and, simultaneously, a reduction in welfare payments is not an example against the chain condition.

14. Rawls's comment that "given these special assumptions, the difference principle has the same practical consequences as the [principle] of average utility" (*TJ,* 82) and Arrow's concurrence "if it [chain connection] holds, there is no difference in policy implication between the maximin principle and the sum of utilities" ("Some Ordinalist-Utilitarian Notes on Rawls' Theory of Justice," 252) are both clearly wrong, as is indicated in figure 5. Perhaps both Rawls and Arrow intended to say only

that within the region of positive contributions (i.e., the region to the left of *a* in figure 5) there is a coincidence between Rawls's maximin criterion and utilitarianism.

15. *TJ*, 82.

16. *TJ*, 82. One reason for this, Rawls suggests, is that the operation of the fair equality principle tends, in particular, to make trained skills less scarce and to reduce their rewards through increased competition, etc. At the same time, the operation of that principle tends to favor a wide diffusion of these skills (together with improved prospects for income). Thus, "it seems plausible that if the least advantaged benefit so do others in between" (*TJ*, 82).

17. *TJ*, 104.

18. *TJ*, 105; see also 79, 81–82, 585.

19. *TJ*, 177–79; see also 510.

20. See the Appendix for a rigorous definition of chain connection. We shall not, however, attempt a proof of chain connection since that would be unnecessary for our purposes in the present chapter.

21. This statement is to be taken as an initial formulation. At the end of the third section we introduce the notion of relative pareto efficiency. The statement here, then, would have to be revised to include that notion. See note 24 below for our suggested reformulation.

22. See Rawls, "Distributive Justice: Some Addenda," 57. The principle relied on here is a special case of the one implicated in the idea of collective asset—the principle of mutual benefit. To bridge from mutual benefit to the present principle, one would have to resort to a scheme of lexical ordering (analogous to the one employed in note 3 above) in which the situation in which each group is benefited is preferred to (2) the case in which one group has its situation unchanged and all the other groups improve their situation, etc., on down to (n) the situation in which only one group improves its situation and all the others have theirs unchanged. Our point, then, is that (n) would be preferred to a situation of no improvement at all.

23. One of Rawls's clearest statements of this line of argument, stressing the equal status of participants in the original position, is found in "Kantian Conception of Equality," 205–6 in particular; see also *TJ*, 547; "Reply to Alexander and Musgrave," 637; "Some Reasons for the Maximin Criterion," 142–43; and "Kantian Constructivism," 529, 532, 546–50.

24. Thus, the (b) part of our principle, as stated at the end of the second section, would now read: "the resulting distribution of economic primary goods is pareto efficient (either absolutely or relatively)."

25. More generally, our contention is that where *g* and *f* could both be regarded as relatively pareto efficient (relative to each other), then the more egalitarian of the two is to be selected. A given set can actually include a large number of points that are relatively pareto efficient in this way; nonetheless, only one of them is the egalitarian point, the one that minimizes $x_1 - x_n$. This is the point that is to be chosen, according to our criterion.

26. Rawls, "Basic Structure," 65; see also *TJ*, 79, 81–82, 104–5, 585.

27. Such a distinction is carefully drawn by Rawls; see "Some Reasons for the Maximin Criterion," 141.

28. See *TJ*, 150–61, esp. 153–54 (and for his citation of the maximin rule, 152–53). The main arguments against computing risks and, as well, against using a principle of insufficient reason (to assign equal probability values to possible cases) is found in *TJ*, 165, 167–73, 175; see also "Reply to Alexander and Musgrave," 649. Rawls also argues that individuals, behind the veil of ignorance, are unaware of their

*personal* propensities for risk taking or risk aversion (see *TJ,* 172; also 152–57, 168, 530; and "Reply to Alexander and Musgrave," 649–50, 653; "Some Reasons for the Maximin Criterion," 143.) What he contends instead is that *all* individuals, as a matter of rationality, would be extremely risk averse under these conditions of extreme uncertainty (see esp. *TJ,* 172).

29. See Arrow ("Some Ordinalist-Utilitarian Notes on Rawls' Theory of Justice") and Harsanyi ("Can the Maximin Principle Serve as a Basis for Morality?"). See also Sen (*Collective Choice and Social Welfare,* 139–41) on this point; he writes: "[T]he link between the concept of 'fairness' and the two principles of 'justice' that identify the maximin rule lies in the belief that in a 'fair' agreement these two principles will be chosen. Is this argument acceptable? . . . Rawls's maximin solution is a very special one and the assertion that it must be chosen in the original position is not altogether convincing."

30. It has been argued, e.g., by Kaye ("Playing Games with Justice," 34, 41) and by Craig Ihara ("Maximin and Other Decision Principles," *Philosophical Topics* 12 [1981]: 59–72), that other rational decision strategies—such as minimax regret—would support Rawls's difference principle and that these other strategies would have as well the effect of ruling out utilitarian criteria as viable alternatives to that principle. (For the minimax regret strategy see William J. Baumol, *Economic Theory and Operations Analysis,* 4th ed. [Englewood Cliffs, N.J.: Prentice-Hall, 1977], 460–66, esp. 463–66.) Nonetheless, our point is that if the maximin strategy were thought to be unsound or inapplicable, then both Rawls (at least in his book) and his critics would regard the difference principle in its maximin version as unsupported.

31. See *TJ,* 152–57.

32. See Rawls, "Reply to Alexander and Musgrave," secs. 3 and 5 esp. and also p. 652; see also "Some Reasons for the Maximin Criterion," 142–43.

33. See Rawls, "Reply to Alexander and Musgrave," 647–48; see also "Distributive Justice: Some Addenda," 59, 69, 71.

34. See Rawls, "Some Reasons for the Maximin Criterion," 144–45. Rawls goes so far as even to *reject* the maximin interpretation of the difference principle as representing a philosophical "misunderstanding" (in "Social Unity and Primary Goods," p. 175n.15).

35. Technically, the second stage of the two-stage argument is directed against the principle of maximizing average utility (for the primary goods of income, wealth, and position) where that principle is subject to the further constraint that a *suitable social minimum is to be maintained for these goods* (see, e.g., *TJ,* sec. 49). I have neglected to mention this further constraint for two reasons: first, it is not material to the basic argument being conducted, and second, the constraint actually favors the competing principle (2b). Hence, omitting mention of it tends to strengthen the principle of maximizing average utility in this competition.

As I have said, the principal argument *for* 2b is derived from the collective asset idea. The general argument *against* the undiluted principle of maximizing average utility, where the social minimum constraint is omitted, remains the one summarized in note 28 above. Rawls would probably want to strengthen this argument, however, by adding in considerations of publicity (public recognition) as well. In my judgment a decisive argument favoring 2b over utilitarianism cannot be deployed until the considerations developed in the second and third sections of chapter 6 have been introduced.

36. Rawls, "Distributive Justice," 66; see also "Distributive Justice: Some Addenda," 59, and *TJ,* 78–79, 319.

37. The "final statement" of the difference principle speaks of "the greatest benefit of the least advantaged" (*TJ*, 302). At other points, Rawls speaks quite comfortably and naturally in the "improving" idiom (e.g., in *TJ*, 75, 103; in "Fairness to Goodness," 553; in "Basic Structure," 64–65; in "Social Unity and Primary Goods," 171–72; these examples could be multiplied).

It is important to note again that Rawls's justification of inequality (in income, wealth, social position) presupposes that representative members of the least-well-off group are better-off under either emphasis, the maximizing one or the improving one, than they would be under "a hypothetical initial arrangement in which all the social primary goods are equally distributed [which would include that] income and wealth are evenly shared" (*TJ*, 62).

## Chapter 6
## The Priority of Liberty

1. For the doctrine of the priority of liberty see *TJ*, pp. 63, 93, 150–52, 542–43, 563, and esp. sec. 82; also "Some Reasons for the Maximin Criterion," 142–43; "Kantian Constructivism," 562; "Basic Liberties," 13, 23, 26, 39, 83; and "Social Unity and Primary Goods," 162, 168, 183. Rawls's discussion of "marginal significance" is found in *TJ*, 542–43. The argument from marginal significance is one of two main arguments that Rawls presents in *TJ*, sec. 82, in favor of the priority of liberty. The other argument asserts the priority of certain fundamental interests (see *TJ*, 543, 563 esp.). I will take up the argument from fundamental interests (as determined by the two highest-order interests) later in this section.

2. See Rawls, "Basic Liberties," p. 87 (esp. n. 83). This repudiation is a further consequence of Rawls's denial that there is a priority to liberty as such, an idea with which it is intimately connected (see "Basic Liberties," 5–6, 56).

3. Rawls, "Basic Liberties," 83–84, also 4; and see "Social Unity and Primary Goods," 166.

4. "Kantian Constructivism," 525. For the main discussion by Rawls of the two highest-order interests, see the references in n. 6 to chap. 3 above.

5. See "Kantian Constructivism," 521, 525, and esp. 527–29, 531, 534, 548–49, and 567–68; "Basic Liberties," 4, 21–23, and esp. 22 and 86; "Social Unity and Primary Goods," 159, 164–65, 167, 170n, and esp. 166. The idea is also expressed, though less clearly, in "Basic Structure," 61.

6. Rawls says that "the parties in the original position . . . are moved in the first instance by their highest-order interests in developing and exercising their moral powers; and the list of primary goods, and the index of those goods, is to be explained so far as possible by reference to these interests" ("Kantian Constructivism," 531). Earlier, he had marked this very point ("making the account of primary goods rest upon a particular conception of the person") as an important revision in his theory—from what he had said in his book—and expressly denied that "the list of primary goods is [to be] regarded as the outcome of a purely psychological, statistical, or historical inquiry" ("Kantian Constructivism," 527; see also "Basic Liberties," 22).

7. This argument is drawn from "Basic Liberties," sec. 9. It is a composite argument; I trust that I have put it together without distorting Rawls's intent or meaning. The passages quoted can be found in "Basic Liberties," 51, 52, 53, 52, and 52 respectively; see also *TJ*, 199.

8. I should add that education is *not* regarded in American constitutional law as a "fundamental right" for purposes of equal protection analysis under the Fourteenth

Amendment to the U.S. Constitution. See the controlling decision in *San Antonio* (Texas) *Independent School District* v. *Rodriguez,* 411 U.S. 1 (1973). The majority opinion was written by Justice Lewis Powell; see also the important dissenting opinion by Justice Thurgood Marshall. For additional discussion see Kenneth S. Tollett, *The Right to Education,* Publication of the Institute for the Study of Educational Policy (Washington, D.C.: Howard University, 1983), sec. 2. One important reason for the Supreme Court's stance, I'm sure, is that education is not explicitly treated in the U.S. Constitution at all, and where it is found, in the constitution of most states, it appears as a requirement on government to provide that particular service rather than as a constitutional right of citizens to have it provided. These facts do not in any way challenge my claim that public schooling is a basic structure right in the U.S. and in other contemporary societies. Moreover, I think it is clear from the argument of chapter 4 in this book that Rawls would concur in calling it a basic structure right.

9. I am indebted to Paul Schumaker for pointing out to me, in general outline, this Rawlsian analysis. The term "nature of the policy process" is his. Since Schumaker endorses the Rawlsian argument here, my criticism of that argument is directed as well against his view that the argument is a cogent one. Rawls's analysis is susceptible to my argument. Especially when he says that the sequence of constitutional/legislative/judicial action is intended as "a schema for working out a conception of justice and guiding its principles to the right subject in the right order" and is not "a description of any actual political process" ("Basic Liberties," 55).

10. The list is deliberately something of a rag bag. Some authors would regard only some of these items—e.g., clean air and water—as pure cases of public goods in the economic sense. These are certainly paradigm examples. National defense is often cited as an example and, indeed, is so cited by Rawls himself (*TJ,* 266–67). A few thinkers would include others of the things from this list. For example, William Riker argues cogently that public safety (police protection) is a public good; see his paper, "Public Safety as a Public Good," in *Is Law Dead?* ed. Eugene V. Rostow (New York: Simon & Schuster, 1971), 370–90.

11. See *TJ,* 24, 26.

12. A public good has, Rawls says, "two characteristic features: indivisibility and publicness. That is, there are many individuals, a public so to speak, who want more or less of this good. . . . [But] the quantity produced cannot be divided up as private goods can and purchased by individuals according to their preferences for more and less" (*TJ,* 266; see also 267–70, 366). In order to be provided to all, public goods have to be provided publicly or at large. They must be provided for everyone—regardless of whether the good is needed or can be used by every single individual—and they must be provided for everyone without regard to any one person's willingness or ability to pay. They are paid for, then, by the public: either by government or on the basis of some cooperative, nonvoluntary arrangement (e.g., a home owners' agreement or a manufacturers' code or an insurance policy which goes with the "territory" and binds all relevant persons). For this reason, public goods are said to represent market failures. Rawls's footnote to p. 266 adds, "For a discussion of public goods, see J. M. Buchanan, *The Demand and Supply of Public Goods* (Chicago, Rand McNally, 1968), esp. ch. IX. This work contains useful bibliographical appendixes to the literature."

13. For Rawls's emphasis on ideal theory (sometimes called strict compliance) see *TJ,* 8–9, 145, 241–42, 245–46, 351, and 391. Thus, *ideal* in this sense refers to what would be the case in a well-ordered society, one that conforms without defect, in the appropriate way and at the appropriate level, to the two principles of justice.

14. The argument presented here is an elaboration of one presented earlier in chapter 2 (section 1) of this book. The argument derives from Rawls himself. In particular I attribute to him the view that the difference principle does not yield determinate results for particular, given individuals. Thus, any criticism that I make of this argument (as I do, for example, in the next section) is intended as a criticism of Rawls's own views. The main sources for the view that I attribute here to Rawls are *TJ*, sec. 14, esp. p. 88; also pp. 274-75, 304; and his article "Justice as Reciprocity," in *Utilitarianism [by] John Stuart Mill, with Critical Essays*, ed. S. Gorovitz (Indianapolis, Ind.: Bobbs-Merrill, 1971), 242-68, at 247 (esp.), 267.

15. Rawls has not specified clearly which of two readings of the distributional principle in question is the preferred one: whether the goal is a certain *level* of income, as set by the income of the representative person in the target class, or whether the goal is a certain set *amount* of income supplementation for all members of the target class, as determined by the increment of income that is required in the case of the representative person by the redistributive operation of the difference principle. In neither case, however, is this a troubling indeterminacy, because determinate and usable results can be attained under either reading. I would add, for the record, that Rawls seems to be inclined to some sort of *levels* reading. I base my judgment on characteristic language of his, found at various points. Thus, we find reference to an "adequate minimum" (*TJ*, 175), a "social minimum" (265, 275, 284-85, 316-17), and a "minimum stipend" (Rawls, "Reply to Lyons and Teitelman," *Journal of Philosophy* 69 [1972]: 556-57, at 556).

16. In *TJ*, 542-43 esp.

17. "Basic Liberties," 72, 74; see also *TJ*, 204, 230, 243-44, 506n. In his book the preferred term is "system," not "family."

Chapter 7
On the Conflict of Rights

1. For general discussion see Martin and Nickel, "Recent Work on the Concept of Rights," sec. 2.

2. For a statement of the apparent dilemma that is posed for a system of rights by the practice of punishment, and for an attempted resolution, see the paper "Punishment and Rights," which I delivered at the Eleventh World Congress of the International Association for Philosophy of Law and Social Philosophy, in Helsinki in August 1983.

3. For Rawls's assertion that basic rights are inalienable see "Basic Liberties," 81-82; and "Social Unity and Primary Goods," 171n. For his use of the term "imprescriptible" see *TJ*, 217. Rawls contrasts his view here with that of Nozick, who does regard basic rights as alienable. Presumably Rawls had particularly in mind Nozick's argument in *Anarchy, State, and Utopia*, chap. 9. For general discussion of the notion of inalienability (and for references to the literature) see Martin and Nickel, "Recent Work on the Concept of Rights," sec. 3. And for discussion of Rawls in particular see Diana T. Meyers, "The Rationale for Inalienable Rights in Moral Systems," *Social Theory and Practice* 7 (1981): 127-43, at 138-40.

4. Robert's compendium of rules, originally published in 1876, codifies and adapts the rules of the U.S. House of Representatives for general use. Rawls had such rules of order specifically in mind; see "Basic Liberties," 10-11.

5. The key ideas developed here can be found in Rawls, "Basic Liberties," as follows: (a) the distinction of regulating/restricting, 9-10, 71; (b) the notion of the

central core or range of a right, 9, 11, 12, 26, 56–57, 63, 71, 74; and (c) the idea that a right is "self-limiting" at its central core, 56, 71–72. For (b) see also Rawls, "Reply to Alexander and Musgrave," 640.

6. See Rawls, "Basic Liberties," 69, for the two passages quoted and for discussion. Rawls's analysis here is consistent with the argument that I developed in chapter 3. Indeed, the entire argument in chapter 7 should be read in conjunction with that in chapter 3, for it presupposes and draws on it.

7. The main Supreme Court sources of the "clear and present danger test" are Justice Holmes's decisions, for a unanimous court, in *Schenk* v. *United States,* 249 U.S. 47 (1919), and *Debs* v. *United States,* 249 U.S. 211 (1919). The first uses of the test to attempt to *protect* freedom of political speech are found in the dissenting opinions of Justices Holmes and Brandeis, in *Abrams* v. *United States,* 250 U.S. 616 (1919). For Rawls's discussion see "Basic Liberties," sec. 11.

The constitutional right of habeas corpus is interesting in this regard. The U.S. Constitution expressly asserts (I.9.ii) that persons can be held only when charged and allows writs to that end "unless when in Cases of Rebellion or Invasion the public safety may require [suspension of the privilege of such writs]." The test here invoked, a weighting test, is rather more like the one that Rawls had in mind with his talk of a "constitutional crisis of the requisite kind." It also casts a shadow on Rawls's rather sanguine remark that if the U.S. Civil War did not constitute such a crisis, then such a crisis was unlikely ever to occur (see "Basic Liberties," 70–71). Rawls correctly notes that elections continued to be held throughout the war; but he fails to note that the right to writs of habeas corpus was, in fact, suspended during the war and even after.

8. See Rawls, "Basic Liberties," p. 57, for the two passages quoted and for the discussion. See sec. 9 for the discussion.

9. Rawls, "Basic Liberties," sec. 7 and pp. 10–13, has been my main source for the discussion of the right to liberty of political speech and the press in this section. All the distinctions drawn (in the various partitionings, etc.) are his, except the exclusion of obscene and libelous speech; these are drawn directly from American constitutional law. I am also indebted to the very helpful article by Alan Fuchs, "Taking Absolute Rights Seriously," in *Filosofia del derecho y filosofia politica,* vol. 2 of Memoria del X Congresso mundial ordinario de filosofia del derecho y filosofia social (Mexico City: Universidad nacional autonomia de Mexico, 1981), 107–21 (esp. at 113 and, for the graphics, at 120–21).

10. The *constitutional* stage is emphasized by Bowie, "Equal Basic Liberty for All," at 117, 121, 123, 129; the emphasis on the *legislative* stage is found in Fuchs, "Taking Absolute Rights Seriously," at 119. I should add that I have also drawn on an earlier version of Fuchs's paper, presented at the Conference on the Moral Foundations of Public Policy: Rights, meeting at Virginia Polytechnic Institute, in Blacksburg, Va., in May 1980.

11. The informational or knowledge constraints in the four stages are summarized and discussed in *TJ,* 197–200, also 206. For the point that the representative legislator "does not know the particulars about himself" and hence cannot consult his own particular interests see p. 198; for the point about the complete access of the judiciary (and administrators) to all the facts see pp. 199–200. I am indebted to Helen Butcher for pointing out both the unsatisfactory characterization of the legislative stage in Rawls's book and the "big jump" that this entailed.

12. See Rawls, "Reply to Lyons," 557.

13. This idea is stated most clearly by Rawls in "Basic Liberties," 55; see also *TJ,* 200. I am indebted to Lye Yee for having suggested the idea to me in the first place.

14. "By moving back and forth between the stages of the constitutional convention and the legislature, the best constitution is found" (*TJ*, 198). Moore expresses dismay at the permeability between these stages in Rawls's account ("Rawls on Constitution-Making," 261). There is, I think, considerable confusion at this point.

15. See 424 U.S. 1 (1976). The decision was delivered per curiam. Rawls also cites, in connection with the *Buckley* case, the Court's decision in *First National Bank* v. *Bellotti,* 435 U.S. 765 (1978). The latter case concerned a Massachusetts law that prohibited expenditures by banks and corporations with the purpose of influencing the vote in certain referendums. The decision in *First National Bank* was written by Justice Lewis Powell.

16. For Rawls's discussion of the *Buckley* case see "Basic Liberties," 74–79. The idea of the fair value of the political-participation liberties is discussed in chapter 3 of this book.

17. Rawls's explicitly endorses the institution of judicial review in "Basic Liberties," 54. There he calls attention, as "a valuable discussion of judicial review in the context of the conception of justice as fairness," to Michelman's article, "In Pursuit of Constitutional Welfare Rights" (see esp. pp. 992–96, 998–99, 1002, 1005–10).

18. Thus the Swiss Civil Code (of 1907):

> Art. 1: The Code governs all questions of law which come within the letter or the spirit of any of its provisions.
>
> If the Code does not furnish an applicable provision, the judge shall decide in accordance with customary law, and failing that, according to the rule which he would establish as legislator.
>
> In this he shall be guided by approved legal doctrine and judicial tradition.

I owe this reference to Francis Heller and Philip Kissam. I have generalized the principle that is involved (in statutory construction) to cover constitutional interpretation as well.

I have left aside, as posing no special problem, the third main area in which courts can be said to be lawmaking bodies. I mean their making of rules in common-law adjudication (and their continual revision of such rules through the "distinguishing" of cases and, sometimes, their sheer overthrow of one rule supported by accumulated precedent in favor of another such competing rule).

19. There has been little discussion by Rawls directly on the work of courts in constitutional interpretation or statutory construction. Such matters are virtually untouched in the secondary literature on Rawls (with the exception of the Michelman article cited in note 17 above). For an interesting programmatic discussion see Richard B. Parker, "The Jurisprudential Uses of John Rawls," in *Constitutionalism,* ed. J. R. Pennock and John W. Chapman, NOMOS 20 (New York: New York University Press, 1979), 269–95.

20. See H. L. A. Hart, "Rawls on Liberty and Its Priority," esp. 241–44, 248, 251–52.

21. One source of the present section is a paper that I delivered at the American Philosophical Association Western Division meeting, in Milwaukee in April 1981. I am indebted to Alan Fuchs and G. C. MacCallum for helpful comments on this paper.

22. Rawls specifically repudiates the "most extensive scheme" or mere quantitative extent criterion in "Basic Liberties," 46. He has been at pains there and elsewhere to assert that justice as fairness does not *maximize* anything, not even the array of liberties; see "Basic Liberties," 47–49, 56n, and *TJ*, 220 and 509.

23. For Rawls's revised statement of the first principle see "Basic Liberties," 5. Interestingly, in "Primary Goods and Social Unity" (published in the same year but written earlier) he uses the old formulation.

24. Rawls, "Basic Liberties," 48; see also 7, 10, 50, 72. The two moral powers, we might recall from our discussion in chapter 3, are an individual's capacity to advance a determinate conception of the good (subject to the provision that any such conception is revisable) and his capacity to be actively guided by a determinate sense of justice.

25. The passages quoted came from "Basic Liberties," 48 and 46 respectively; see also 56, 63, 72, and *TJ*, 231.

26. For Rawls's explicit endorsement of assigning weight as one device for reducing or eliminating conflict of rights, see "Basic Liberties," 50–51.

27. The use of scope drawing (definitional balancing) as a way wholly to avoid conflict of rights is advanced, as an interpretation of Rawls, by Dworkin, Fuchs, and Bowie. Here I base my view as to Dworkin on an important footnote in Hart (see "Rawls on Liberty and Its Priority," p. 245n.12). For Fuchs see "Taking Absolute Rights Seriously," esp. 113; and for Bowie, "Equal Basic Liberty for All," esp. 117.

My account differs from theirs in holding that Rawls also included the idea of *weight* in his system and, hence, did allow one right justifiably to override another on a given occasion. Thus, if we have regard not to scope limitations alone but also to zones of overlap, where conflict is possible, we can see the point of Rawls's remark that, contrary to Dworkin et al., "basic liberties are bound to conflict with one another" ("Basic Liberties," 9; see also 71–72). The point even here, though, is that these conflicts can, in Rawls's view, be controlled by precise assignments of weight; thus, there is no need ever for what Rawls calls "indeterminate and unguided balancing" ("Basic Liberties," 10).

28. Thus, Rawls says, "For practical purposes, . . . in a well-governed democratic society under reasonably favorable conditions, the free public use of our reason in questions of political and social justice would seem to be absolute" ("Basic Liberties," 71; see also "Basic Liberties," 11, and *TJ*, 213–15). The interpretation that all of the basic liberty rights in Rawls's system are absolute has been advanced by Fuchs (in the article cited in note 27 above). This interpretation is inadequate for several reasons. It takes no account of the factor of weight, as I said in that note, and hence gives no credit to Rawls's idea that one right can justifiably override another. It also ignores Rawls's important qualification as to "reasonably favorable conditions." My discussions in the next sections provide additional reason for rejecting Fuch's account. One other point is worth making. So far as I can tell the passage cited above in the present note is the *only* place in all Rawls's writings where he says that a given basic right could be absolute. I have quoted the passage here for the record and, also, as evidence for saying that Rawls did think that conflict of rights (in the sense described in note 27 above) could be eliminated in principle. For, where no *single* basic right was absolute, the only way in which such rights could *each* be absolute, under "favorable conditions," would be to make them nonconflictable.

29. The idea that rights "of the *same* kind" can conflict is drawn from Joel Feinberg, *Social Philosophy*, 95. He emphasizes, in particular, that rights to liberties (the kind of right that Rawls is especially concerned with) are not *internally* "nonconflictable" (see pp. 95–96 and, for further general discussion of possible conflicts of rights, chap. 5 of Feinberg's book). Unfortunately, Feinberg's examples of internal conflict are not good ones, and therefore I have had to supply one of my own.

30. I have here capsulized Dworkin's well-known "rights thesis"; see his *Taking Rights Seriously,* chap. 4 in particular. My argument in the present section would pose a serious problem for Dworkin's thesis.

31. One source of the present section is the paper identified in note 21 above. Another is a paper that I delivered at the meeting of the Society for Philosophy and Public Affairs, in Columbus, Ohio, in April 1982. I am grateful to Carl Wellman and Bernard Gert for their helpful comments on this paper.

32. The term 'incumbent' is taken from Feinberg (see *Social Philosophy,* 80ff.). I mean by it roughly what he meant: a right is incumbent when it has been previously (and expertly) partitioned, its scope adjusted in relation to other rights, and its competitive weight assigned by the relevant bodies.

33. See Rawls, "Basic Liberties," 9, also 74.

34. The basic liberties—or, as I would say, basic rights—"have an absolute weight with respect to reasons of public good and of perfectionist values" (Rawls, "Basic Liberties," 8).

35. This particular reading is, I think, closer to Rawls' own view. In the concluding sentence to a long footnote on natural rights and the weight of such rights, he says, "Although specific rights are not absolute, the system of equal liberties is absolute practically speaking under favorable circumstances" (*TJ,* 505–6n.30; see also "Basic Liberties," 72 esp. and 74).

## Chapter 8
## Rawlsian Economic Justice

1. For the point about practical coordination see *TJ,* 310; for the point about efficiency see 271–72 and also 274, 276.

2. *TJ,* 88; see also 66, 84–85, 87, 274–75, 282, 304, 545; Rawls, "Distributive Justice: Some Addenda," 54, 56; and "Basic Structure," 64.

3. *TJ,* 270–74, 304–10; see esp. 310 and also "Basic Structure," 64.

4. Adam Smith's discussion of natural price is found in *Wealth of Nations,* in particular, in bk. 1, chap. 7. Karl Marx, who cites Smith's account approvingly, discusses natural price in his 1865 address *Value, Price and Profit,* ed. Eleanor Marx Aveling (Chicago: Charles Kerr, n.d.), at pp. 66–68. See also *TJ,* 271.

5. See "Basic Structure," 53.

6. "[The] overall result of separate and independent transactions is away from and not towards background justice. We might say: in this case the invisible hand guides things in the wrong direction and favors an oligopolistic configuration of accumulations . . ." (Rawls, "Basic Structure," 54; see also 66). The term 'invisible hand' is, of course, taken from Adam Smith. Rawls's idea that the competitive market is inherently unstable differentiates him not only from classical liberals, such as Adam Smith (what with his Newtonian idea of a "natural system" in economic life) or such as contemporary advocates of equilibrium theory, but also from libertarian philosophers such as Robert Nozick (see *Anarchy, State, and Utopia,* 179, 182).

7. Public goods are defined and are identified as market "failures" in nn. 10 and 12 to chap. 6 above. See also *TJ,* 272.

8. Following the lead given by R. A. Musgrave, Rawls discusses these matters under the heading of the "four branches" into which the background institutions can be divided (see *TJ,* sec. 43, pp. 275–79 esp., for the sketch that Rawls provides). In my account the main goals or policies that are served by the background institutions have been emphasized.

9. See *TJ*, 276; and esp., "Basic Structure," 65–66 (for the point about antitrust regulation), and *TJ*, 275 (for the point about measures for fair equality of opportunity).

10. *TJ*, 585.

11. There is, Rawls argues, no return to good moral character as such; economic earnings don't *correspond* to moral goodness (see *TJ*, 311–12).

12. See Rawls, "Basic Structure," secs. 5, 7–8; also see *TJ*, 314, and "Kantian Constructivism," 551–52. In the text I refer to the notion of desert as *moral*. I do so in the following sense. Even if we could specify the exact proportion that an individual's initiative and effort make to his overall contribution, it does not follow from that fact alone that he *should* receive an economic return that reflects this proportion in some suitable way. To say that he should is to make a normative claim of some sort, and this is what I meant by *moral*. For instances of such normative claims (e.g., that a worker *should* be compensated in accordance with his marginal contribution to production), see *TJ*, secs. 47, 48.

I should add that I do support the claim that individuals contribute something—some appreciable degree—to the development of their own talents. And I do endorse the principle that when people have contributed more to that development, then *ceteris paribus* (and when due account is taken of the market and of the other relevant institutions in the basic structure), they will properly receive more in the way of returns. These are rather loose, commonsensical maxims, and I will try, in what follows, to fill in behind them and to make their bearing more precise.

13. Rawls does think that we as individuals "have a right to our natural abilities . . ." ("Basic Structure," 65). This endorsement of the notion that individuals are *entitled* to their natural assets serves to bring Rawls closer to Robert Nozick and at the same time to mitigate the force of much of Nozick's criticism (see Nozick, *Anarchy, State, and Utopia*, 213–31).

14. For the argument, which Nozick calls "acceptable," see *Anarchy, State, and Utopia*, 225. The three steps and the conclusion in the text are quoted directly from him. He adds (pp. 225–26) a second sentence in conclusion: (5) "If people are entitled to something, then they ought to have it (and this overrides any presumption of equality there may be about holdings)." I have omitted this sentence from the text; it is not germane, since Rawls makes no such presumption. After I had written the paragraph in the text, I came across a paper that Rawls had written (for a Liberty Fund conference in June 1984). In it he states Nozick's argument, step by step, provides a similar gloss at individual points, and asserts the coincidence of his views and those of Nozick on the matter of individual entitlement.

15. The mousetrap example, I have subsequently noted, is used with roughly the same intent by Michael Walzer (see his *Spheres of Justice: A Defense of Pluralism and Equality* [New York: Basic Books, 1983], 109).

16. See Rawls, "Justice as Reciprocity," 247 esp. and also 267 (for points made in the previous paragraph); and "Basic Structure," 59–62 (for points made in the present one).

17. Thus, we can expect significant differences in income to emerge for individuals in a well-ordered society. Rawls believes, though, that the gap in income shares "tends to close" in such a society through the concomitant operation of fair equality of opportunity and the difference principle (see *TJ*, 307).

18. It is, of course, not improper for me to cite the difference principle in this particular version. That version is, as was argued in chapter 5 and proven in the Appendix, mathematically equivalent to the preferred way of stating the difference

criterion: that is, as the result given in a basic structure characterized by pareto efficiency (either absolute or relative) constrained by egalitarianism, under the chain connection condition, in a well-ordered society.

19. See *TJ*, 270–71, 310.

20. Whether ownership of productive property should be private or public, Rawls says, is to a great extent a circumstantial matter (see *TJ*, 273–74; also 258, 271, 280–82; "Distributive Justice: Some Addenda," 56; "Fairness to Goodness," 546).

21. See *TJ*, sec. 42 (esp. p. 266) and p. 284; also "Basic Liberties," 80.

22. Rawls's discussion of management per se is sparse; as to *social* management see *TJ*, 280.

23. By regulating economic "offices," the difference principle helps to determine the structure of holdings (owning, managing, profiting) of productive property in a society. It could also be used to help decide upon a pattern of public goods, to justify the control of externalities (unwanted side effects of a process of production or distribution), or to underwrite allocative and investment decisions within an industry, or a whole society (see *TJ*, sec. 42, for an elaboration of these topics; also see p. 87 and "Social Unity and Primary Goods," 163.)

24. See, in particular, "Basic Liberties," 53–54. We assume that in a Rawlsian well-ordered society the legislative and judicial decisions would reflect the relevant factors identified in this section and, hence, be justifiable.

25. See Rawls, "Basic Liberty," 12, 53–54.

26. See Rawls, "Reply to Alexander and Musgrave," 640, and "Kantian Conception of Equality," 203.

## Chapter 9
## Justice and Welfare

1. "The theory of primary goods is an extension of the notion of needs, which are distinct from aspirations and desires. One might say, then, that as citizens the members of a well-ordered society collectively take responsibility for dealing justly with one another founded on a public and objective measure of (extended) needs, while as individuals and members of associations they take responsibility for their preferences and devotions" (Rawls, "Kantian Conception of Equality," 204); see also Rawls, "Reply to Alexander and Musgrave," 643; "Basic Structure," 67; "Fairness to Goodness," 554; "Kantian Constructivism," 546, 550; "Basic Liberties," 40; and "Social Unity and Primary Goods," 172–73, 183.

2. The primary characterization of income and wealth as "all-purpose means (having an exchange value)" is from Rawls, "Basic Liberties," 23; see also "Social Unity and Primary Goods," 166. The idea of including in-kind goods and services as a part of income and wealth is a notion that I have added. Such an idea can also be found in Gutmann, *Liberal Equality*, 126; and in Benne, *Ethic of Democratic Capitalism*, 171. For considerations that might tell against the inclusion of in-kind goods and services see Michelman, "In Pursuit of Constitutional Welfare Rights," esp. 980, 1011n. I should add that, for the most part, Michelman reaches conclusions that are roughly similar to those I reach in this chapter—even though the perspectives within which we operate are quite different. His concern is to develop a theory of justiciable or constitutional welfare rights; mine is to determine what view of welfare and of welfare rights is internal to Rawls's theory.

3. *TJ*, 309. For Rawls's discussion of the transfer branch see *TJ*, 276–77.

4. Rawls says that his theory, in the original position, starts from "the conception of persons as capable of being normal and fully cooperating members of society . . . over a complete life" ("Basic Liberties," 52; see also 15, 48). Since he assumes normal capacities, Rawls says that he will not consider "special health and medical needs" ("Social Unity and Primary Goods," 168, incl. n. 8, and 178n; see also Rawls, "Reply to Alexander and Musgrave," 640; "Some Reasons for the Maximin Criterion," 142; "Basic Structure," 57, 70n.9; and "Kantian Constructivism," 546).

5. It is, of course, possible that in a well-ordered society, pregnancy (and the at-home nurture of very young children by their parents) or the various forms of rehabilitation (including self-rehabilitation) following disabling sickness or injury could be regarded as productive work and be remunerated (though not through market processes). Even so, it is unlikely that people while they are sick or injured can engage in socially useful work; accordingly, there will probably always be *some* people in this category in a well-ordered society.

6. For Rawls's discussion of the exchange branch see *TJ*, 282–84. Rawls says there that the principles of this branch are those of efficiency and general benefit rather than of justice. I should add that, although Rawls conceives some public goods (e.g., national parks) as coming under this branch, it is unlikely that he would bring them all under it. (National defense, for example, would probably not be handled by the exchange branch.) Thus, some public goods are conceived by him as falling, from the beginning, within the province of the legislature (rather than the exchange branch), and it is likely that social security would be of this nature for Rawls. It is likely, too, that the legislature would enact some sort of insurance scheme of the sort that have I described. However, no fundamental change in my basic argument would be required if these last two points were granted.

For the reasons given—namely, that such goods are decided in the legislative stage and under conditions of full knowledge—there are no basic structure rights to such public goods in Rawls's theory.

7. Over and beyond the exchange branch (mentioned in note 6), Rawls refers to four basic "branches" or goals of governmental economic policy and activity (*TJ*, sec. 43). He says: "The stabilization branch . . . strives to bring about reasonably full employment in the sense that those who want work can find it and the free choice of occupation and the deployment of finance is supported by strong effective demand" (*TJ*, 276). The two main objects of full employment policy, as mediated through the Rawlsian notion of pure procedural justice (see *TJ*, 85–87, 89, 274–75, 310), are (a) fair equality of opportunity (see 87) and (b) efficiency (see 87, 276).

8. See *TJ*, p. 303 and sec. 67; also Rawls, "Basic Liberties," 32–34, 52, 85.

9. I realize that full employment, as that idea is conceived in political economy, is compatible with the fact that *some* are unable to work. For full employment is defined by reference to those who are able and willing to work. Moreover, the legislative definition of full employment (in the United States and Britain, at least) allows a margin of some actual unemployment (for it never sets the full employment target amount at exactly 100% of those who are able and willing to work). My use of the notion of full employment has assumed these two definitional constraints throughout; moreover, it is important to recognize that what is contemplated under the heading of full employment is, not make-work, but socially *useful* work. (On this last point see *TJ*, 290.) For reasons why full employment is not a right see my paper "The Human Right of Inmates to Work with Just Compensation," *Journal of Social Welfare* 9 (1983): 41–60, esp. at 45–47.

10. The Rawlsian duty of mutual aid is discussed in *TJ*, secs. 19 and 51 (see esp. pp. 330–39).

11. For Rawls's discussion of paternalism see *TJ*, sec. 39 (esp. pp. 248–50); also pp. 209, 510.

12. *TJ*, 209.

13. For the matter quoted above see Rawls, *TJ*, 249. Elsewhere Rawls adds, "But those more or less permanently deprived of moral personality may present a difficulty. I cannot examine this problem here . . ." (*TJ*, 510). This passage suggests to me that those who are permanently comatose probably are not intended to be covered by Rawls's principle of paternalism.

14. Elizabeth Bouvia, stricken with cerebral palsy since birth, suffering severe pains from arthritis, confined to a wheelchair and almost wholly dependent on others for care and feeding, has despaired of this lifelong dependency and requested that officials at the Riverside General Hospital desist from force-feeding her and allow her to die. Her lawyer, who is also a medical doctor, said that he thinks she is making the wrong decision but that, as regards the control of her own medical treatment, it is her decision to make.

15. The sources of income for those who are able to work are (a) market income earned, (b) benefits from available public goods, and (c) difference principle–derived transfers (see *TJ*, 304, also 285). The sum total of those (along with any further adjustments required) would be, in the language of the previous chapter, the adjusted return on their contribution.

16. I want to thank, for helpful comments and suggestions on this section and the previous one, Richard De George, Susan Daniel, Robert Hall, Dan Hausman, Diana Meyers, and Alan Fuchs (who suggested, among other things, the turn to paternalism as a possible solution).

17. See *TJ*, 544–46, also 234; and "Basic Liberties," 32–34, 50.

18. Stephen Griffin suggested the main lines of what I have said in this paragraph. One criticism I have specially in mind is the Marxist criticism that Rawls has sharply separated politics from civil society (i.e., social and economic life). See, for example, Russell Keat, "Liberal Rights and Socialism," in *Contemporary Political Philosophy: Radical Studies,* ed. Keith Graham (Cambridge: Cambridge University Press, 1982), 59–82, at 67–68. The approach that I have suggested, which ranges basic rights throughout the social primary goods, would go some way toward meeting this criticism.

19. Rawls makes the point about supervenience in "Reply to Lyons," 557.

20. For Rawls's discussion of what I have called the psychological sense of self-respect or self-worth see *TJ*, secs. 67, 80, and 81; also pp. 178, 224–27, 265, 277, 338, 543–46; "Basic Structure," 66; and "Basic Liberties," 33.

21. Rawls recognizes that at some point it might become necessary to afford self-respect an independent weight in figuring the index of social primary goods, but he adds that he would regard this as an "unwelcome complication" (see *TJ*, 546). In one of his latest writings he indicates that no such index has been developed in his theory (see "Social Unity and Primary Goods," 162–63).

22. See *TJ*, 303.

23. See "Kantian Constructivism," 526; "Basic Liberties," 23; and "Social Unity and Primary Goods," 162, for the lists. See also Rawls, "Kantian Conception of Equality," 202; and "Basic Liberties," 33.

24. See *TJ*, 440 esp.

# SELECTED BIBLIOGRAPHY

Until recently the principal bibliographical sources on Rawls were J. H. Wellbank, "A Bibliography on Rawlsian Justice: 1951–1975," *Philosophy Research Archives* 2 (1976), unpaginated, a total of 20 pages, including a two-page appendix to bring the bibliography up through 1976; Robert K. Fullinwider, "A Chronological Bibliography of Works on John Rawls' Theory of Justice," *Political Theory* 5 (1977): 561–70, and "Bibliography," pp. 495–517 in Blocker and Smith (see below). Now, a comprehensive bibliography on Rawls has been published by Wellbank and others (see below).

For items by Rawls published before his 1971 book, *A Theory of Justice* (below), see that book's preface (pp. vii and x). The important items that have been published by Rawls since his book, including everything cited in *Rawls and Rights,* are listed in the present bibliography.

Most of the items I have written (or coauthored) that are relevant to this study are listed in the Preface; a few additional items have been cited in individual notes. These items are not repeated here. Nor are books written before the turn of the century, all adequately cited in individual notes, listed again in this bibliography. Nor are the court cases and laws mentioned in the the text. With these exceptions, all of the things that are cited in the present study are listed in the bibliography below.

Arrow, K. J. "Some Ordinalist-Utilitarian Notes on Rawls' Theory of Justice." *Journal of Philosophy* 70 (1973): 245–63.

Atkinson, A. B. "How Progressive Should Income Tax Be?" In *Essays in Modern Economics,* edited by M. Parkin, 90-109. London: Longmans, 1973.

Barry, Brian. *A Liberal Theory of Justice.* Oxford: Clarendon Press, 1973.

Baumol, William J. *Economic Theory and Operations Analysis.* 4th ed. Englewood Cliffs, N.J.: Prentice-Hall, 1977.

Benne, Robert. *The Ethic of Democratic Capitalism: A Moral Reassessment.* Philadelphia, Pa.: Fortress Press, 1981.

Blocker, H. G., and E. H. Smith, eds. *John Rawls' Theory of Social Justice: An Introduction.* Athens: Ohio University Press, 1980.

Bowie, Norman. "Equal Basic Liberty for All." In *John Rawls' Theory of social Justice,* edited by H. G. Blocker and E. H. Smith, 110–31. Athens: Ohio University Press, 1980.

———. "Some Comments on Rawls's Theory of Justice." *Social Theory and Practice* 3 (1974): 65–74.

Brandt, Richard B. "Utilitarianism and Human Rights." In *Human Rights,* edited by David Gruender. Selected papers from the Tenth Inter-American Congress of Philosophy, forthcoming.

Brock, Dan W. "Recent Work in Utilitarianism." *American Philosophical Quarterly* 10 (1973): 241–76.

Buchanan, J. M. *The Demand and Supply of Public Goods.* Chicago: Rand McNally, 1968.

Clark, Barry, and Herbert Gintis. "Rawlsian Justice and Economic Systems." *Philosophy and Public Affairs* 7 (1978): 302–25.

Daniels, Norman. "Equal Liberty and Unequal Worth of Liberty." In *Reading Rawls,* edited by Norman Daniels, 253–81. New York: Basic Books, 1975.

———. "Meritocracy." In *Justice and Economic Distribution,* edited by John Arthur and William H. Shaw, 164–78. Englewood Cliffs, N.J.: Prentice-Hall, 1978.

———, ed. *Reading Rawls: Critical Studies of a Theory of Justice.* New York: Basic Books, 1975.

Dworkin, Ronald. *Taking Rights Seriously.* Cambridge: Harvard University Press, 1978.

Feinberg, Joel. "The Nature and Value of Rights." *Journal of Value Inquiry* 4 (1970): 243–57.

———. "The Rights of Animals and Unborn Generations." In *Philosophy and Environmental Crisis,* edited by William T. Blackstone, 43–68. Athens: University of Georgia Press, 1974.

———. *Social Philosophy.* Foundations of Philosophy series. Englewood Cliffs, N.J.: Prentice-Hall, 1973.

Frankel, Charles. "Justice, Utilitarianism, and Rights." *Social Theory and Practice* 3 (1974): 27–46.

Fuchs, Alan. "Taking Absolute Rights Seriously." In *Filosofia del derecho y filosofia politica.* Vol. 2, pp. 107–21. Memoria del X Congresso mundial ordinario de filosofia del derecho y filosofia. Mexico City: Universidad Nacional Autonomia de Mexico, 1981.

Gauthier, David. "Justice and Natural Endowment: Toward a Critique of Rawls's Ideological Framework." *Social Theory and Practice* 3 (1974): 3–26.

Gray, John. "John Stuart Mill on Liberty, Utility, and Rights." In *Human Rights,* edited by J. R. Pennock and John W. Chapman, 80–116. NOMOS 23. New York: New York University Press, 1981.

———. *Mill on Liberty: A Defence.* London: Routledge & Kegan Paul, 1983.

Griffin, Stephen. "Interpreting the Initial Situation." *Auslegung* 9 (1982): 50–66.

Gutmann, Amy. *Liberal Equality.* Cambridge: Cambridge University Press, 1980.

Hammond, Peter J. "Equity, Arrow's Conditions, and Rawls' Difference Principle." *Econometrica* 44 (1976): 793–804.

Harsanyi, J. C. "Can the Maximin Principle Serve as a Basis for Morality? A Critique of John Rawls's Theory." *American Political Science Review* 69 (1975): 594–606.

Hart, H. L. A. "Are There Any Natural Rights?" *Philosophical Review* 64 (1955): 175–91.

———. "Bentham and the United States of America." *Journal of Law and Economics* 19 (1976): 547–67.

———. "Between Utility and Rights." *Columbia Law Review* 79 (1979): 828–46.

———. "Rawls on Liberty and Its Priority." In *Reading Rawls*, edited by Norman Daniels, 230-52. New York: Basic Books, 1975. Reprinted from *University of Chicago Law Review* 40 (1973): 534-55.

———. "Utilitarianism and Natural Rights." *Tulane Law Review* 53 (1979): 663-80.

Ihara, Craig. "Maximin and Other Decision Principles." *Philosophical Topics* (formerly *Southwestern Journal of Philosophy*) 12 (1981): 59-72.

Kaye, David H. "Playing Games with Justice: Rawls and the Maximin Rule." *Social Theory and Practice* 6 (1980): 33-51.

Keat, Russell. "Liberal Rights and Socialism." In *Contemporary Political Philosophy: Radical Studies*, edited by Keith Graham, 59-82. Cambridge: Cambridge University Press, 1982.

Kronman, Anthony. "Talent Pooling." In *Human Rights*, edited by J. R. Pennock and John W. Chapman, 58-79. NOMOS 23. New York: New York University Press, 1981.

Lyons, David. "Benevolence and Justice in Mill." In *The Limits of Utilitarianism*, edited by H. B. Miller and W. H. Williams, 42-70. Minneapolis: University of Minnesota Press, 1982.

———. "Human Rights and the General Welfare." *Philosophy and Public Affairs* 6 (1977): 113-29.

———. "Introduction." In *Rights*, edited by David Lyons, 1-13. Belmont, Calif.: Wadsworth, 1979.

———. "Mill on Liberty and Harm to Others." In *New Essays on John Stuart Mill and Utilitarianism*, edited by W. E. Cooper, Kai Nielsen, and S. C. Patten, 1-19. *Canadian Journal of Philosophy*, supplementary vol. 5, 1979.

———. "Mill's Theory of Justice." In *Values and Morals*, edited by Alvin I. Goldman and J. Kim, 1-20. Dordrecht, Holland: Reidel, 1978.

———. "Mill's Theory of Morality." *Nous* 10 (1976): 101-20.

———. "Rawls and Utilitarianism." *Journal of Philosophy* 69 (1972): 535-45.

———. "Rights, Claimants, and Beneficiaries." *American Philosophical Quarterly* 6 (1969): 173-85.

———. "Utility and Rights." In *Ethics, Economics, and the Law*, edited by J. R. Pennock and J. W. Chapman, 107-38. NOMOS 24. New York: New York University Press, 1982.

———. "Utility as a Possible Ground of Rights." *Nous* 14 (1980): 17-28.

MacCallum, G. C. "Negative and Positive Freedom." *Philosophical Review* 76 (1967): 312-34.

MacCormick, Neil. *H. L. A. Hart.* Stanford, Calif.: Stanford University Press, 1981.

Macdonald, Margaret. "Natural Rights." In *Human Rights*, edited by A. I. Melden, 40-60. Belmont, Calif.: Wadsworth, 1970. Originally published in *Proceedings of the Aristotelian Society* 47 (1946/47): 225-50.

Mack, Eric. "Rawlsian Economic Rights versus Pure Procedural Justice: A Comment on Martin." In *Ethical Issues in Government*, edited by Norman Bowie, 133-42. Philadelphia, Pa.: Temple University Press, 1981.

Melden, A. I. *Rights and Persons.* Oxford: B. Blackwell; Berkeley: University of California Press, 1977.

Meyers, Diana T. "The Rationale for Inalienable Rights in Moral Systems." *Social Theory and Practice* 7 (1981): 127-43.

Michelman, Frank I. "In Pursuit of Constitutional Welfare Rights: One View of Rawls' Theory of Justice," *University of Pennsylvania Law Review* 121 (1973): 962-1019. Reprinted, with some revisions, as "Constitutional Welfare Rights and *A Theory of Justice,"* in *Reading Rawls,* edited by Norman Daniels, 319–47. New York: Basic Books, 1975.

Moore, Ronald. "Rawls on Constitution-Making." In *Constitutionalism,* edited by J. R. Pennock and John W. Chapman, 238–68. NOMOS 20. New York: New York University Press, 1979.

Nelson, William N. "Special Rights, General Rights, and Social Justice." *Philosophy and Public Affairs* 3 (1974): 410–30.

Nozick, Robert. *Anarchy, State, and Utopia.* New York: Basic Books, 1974.

Pareto, Vilfredo. *Manual of Political Economy.* Translated by Ann S. Schwier; edited by Ann S. Schwier and Alfred N. Page. New York: Augustus M. Kelley, 1971. This book is a translation of a French version (Geneva, Switzerland: Librairie Droz, 1927). The book originally appeared as *Manuel d'economie politique* (Paris: Giard & Brière, 1909); that book is described on its title page as "translated from the Italian edition by Alfred Bonnet and reviewed by the author."

Parker, Richard B. "The Jurisprudential Uses of John Rawls." In *Constitutionalism,* edited by J. R. Pennock and J. W. Chapman, 269–95. NOMOS 20. New York: New York University Press, 1979.

Phelps, E. S. "Wage Taxation for Economic Justice." *Quarterly Journal of Economics* 87 (1973): 331–54.

Rae, Douglas W. "A Principle of Simple Justice." In *Philosophy, Politics and Society,* edited by Peter Laslett and James Fishkin. 5th ser., pp. 134–54. New Haven, Conn.: Yale University Press, 1979.

Rawls, John. "The Basic Liberties and Their Priority." In *The Tanner Lectures on Human Values,* edited by S. M. McMurrin, vol. 3, pp. 3–87. Salt Lake City: University of Utah Press, 1982.

———. "The Basic Structure as Subject." *American Philosophical Quarterly* 14 (1977): 159–65.

———. "The Basic Structure as Subject." In *Values and Morals,* edited by Alvin I. Goldman and J. Kim, 47–71. Dordrecht, Holland: Reidel, 1978. This essay is a considerable revision of the previous entry; secs. 2 and 3 are new.

———. "Distributive Justice." In *Philosophy, Politics and Society,* edited by P. Laslett and W. G. Runciman. 3d ser., pp. 58–82. Oxford: B. Blackwell, 1967.

———. "Distributive Justice." In *Economic Justice,* edited by E. S. Phelps, 319–62. Baltimore, Md.: Penguin, 1973. This entry includes all of the previous entry, as secs. 1–4 and 11–14, and most of the next entry, as secs. 5–10.

———. "Distributive Justice: Some Addenda." *Natural Law Forum* 13 (1968): 51–71.

———. "Fairness to Goodness." *Philosophical Review* 84 (1975): 536–54.

———. "The Independence of Moral Theory." *Proceedings and Addresses of the American Philosophical Association* 48 (1974/75): 5–22.

———. "Justice as Fairness." *Philosophical Review* 67 (1958): 164–94.

———. "Justice as Reciprocity." In *Utilitarianism [by] John Stuart Mill, with Critical Essays,* edited by S. Gorovitz, 242–68. Indianapolis, Ind.: Bobbs-Merrill, 1971. This article is basically the same as the previous entry; but it contains some interesting new language and some interpolated examples drawn from economics.

———. "A Kantian Conception of Equality." In *Property, Profits, and Economic Justice,* edited by Virginia Held, 198–208. Belmont, Calif.: Wadsworth, 1980. This essay is reprinted, slightly revised, from an essay of the same name in *Cambridge Review,* Feb. 1975, pp. 94–99; it has also been reprinted, under the title "A Well-Ordered Society," in *Philosophy, Politics and Society,* edited by Peter Laslett and James Fishkin. 5th ser., pp. 6–20. New Haven, Conn.: Yale University Press, 1979.

———. "Kantian Constructivism in Moral Theory." *Journal of Philosophy* 77 (1980): 515–72. A published version of three lectures given as the John Dewey Lectures, at Columbia University, 14–16 Apr. 1980.

———. "Reply to Alexander and Musgrave." *Quarterly Journal of Economics* 88 (1974): 633–55.

———. "Reply to Lyons and Teitelman." *Journal of Philosophy* 69 (1972): 556–57.

———. "Social Unity and Primary Goods." In *Utilitarianism and Beyond,* edited by A. Sen and B. Williams, 159–85. Cambridge: Cambridge University Press, 1982.

———. "Some Reasons for the Maximin Criterion." *American Economic Review* 64 (1974): 141–46.

———. *A Theory of Justice.* Cambridge: Belknap Press of Harvard University Press, 1971. Translated into German as *Eine Theorie der Gerechtigkeit.* Frankfurt am Main: Suhrkamp, 1975, 1979.

———. "Two Concepts of Rules." *Philosophical Review* 64 (1951): 3–32.

Riker, William. "Public Safety as a Public Good." In *Is Law Dead?* edited by Eugene V. Rostow, 370–90. New York: Simon & Schuster, 1971.

Schaefer, David L. *Justice or Tyranny? A Critique of John Rawls's "A Theory of Justice."* Port Washington, N.Y.: Kennikat Press, 1979.

Sen, A. K. *Collective Choice and Social Welfare.* San Francisco, Calif.: Holden-Day, 1970.

Shenoy, Prakash P. "Efficiency, Egalitarianism and the Difference Principle in Rawls's Theory of Justice," presented at the Second Seminar on Game Theory and Mathematical Economics (held in Hagen and Bonn, Federal Republic of Germany, 7–10 Oct. 1980), mimeographed.

Shute, Nevil. *In the Wet.* London: Heinemann, 1953.

Strasnick, Steven. "The Problem of Social Choice: Arrow to Rawls." *Philosophy and Public Affairs* 5 (1976): 241–73.

Stuhlmann-Laeisz, Rainer. "Gerechtigkeit und Effizienz: Eine Untersuchung zum Verhältnis des Unterschiedsprinzips zu dem der Pareto-Optimalität in Rawls' Theorie der Gerechtigkeit." *Allgemeine Zeitschrift für Philosophie* 6, no. 1 (1981): 17–30.

Tollett, Kenneth S. *The Right to Education.* Publication of the Institute for the Study of Educational Policy. Washington, D.C.: Howard University, 1983.

Walzer, Michael. *Spheres of Justice: A Defense of Pluralism and Equality.* New York: Basic Books, 1983.

Wasserman, Scott. "Rawls: On Rights." Senior honors thesis in philosophy, University of Kansas, 1982.

Wellbank, J. H.; Denis Snook; and David T. Mason, eds. *John Rawls and His Critics: An Annotated Bibliography.* New York: Garland Publishing Co., 1982.

Wolff, Robert Paul. *Understanding Rawls: A Reconstruction and Critique of A Theory of Justice.* Princeton, N.J.: Princeton University Press, 1977.

# INDEX

*Abrams* v. *United States*, 226
Adjudication, Theory of, 129-30, 139-41, 145, 147, 149-54, 227, 229
—judicial review (Rawls), 53, 140, 227
Affirmative Action (and Anti-discrimination Policy), 40, 84-85, 161
Archimedean Point, 28-29, 57. *See also* Ideal Theory
Aristotle, 15, 39, 206
Arrow, Kenneth, 102, 206, 219, 220, 222
Association, Liberty of, 50, 112, 146
Atkinson, A. B., 220

Basic Structure, 1, 12-14, 17, 20-21, 23-24, 30, 42-45, 59, 89-91, 112, 117, 157, 163, 173, 180, 206, 208, 219. *See also* Basic Structure Rights; Well-ordered Society
Basic Structure Rights, 1-4, 21, 22, 24-25, 27-28, 31-32, 35-41, 52, 69, 82-83, 113, 125, 131, 139, 173. *See also* Rights—natural
Baumol, William J., 222
Benevolence (also called Beneficence), 180, 190-91
Benne, Robert, 218, 231
Bentham, Jeremy, 2, 3, 5, 8, 19, 203, 204, 205
Bill of Rights (and Rights in the Written Constitution), 24, 39-40, 112-14
Bosanquet, Bernard, 218
Bowie, Norman, 137, 139, 209, 213, 226, 228

Brandt, Richard, 204, 205, 206
Brock, Dan, 2, 203
Buchanan, J. M., 224
*Buckley* v. *Valeo*, 139, 140, 227

Chain Connection, 88, 94-97, 101, 122, 199, 220-21
—close-knitness, 220
Clark, Barry, 206
Coherence Criterion (Rational Interests of the Representative Equal Citizen), 143-48, 151, 154. *See also* Rights—harmonizing of
Collective Asset, Idea of, 76-81, 97-98, 102-3, 106, 110, 131, 144, 163, 165-66, 169-70, 177-78, 180, 184, 189, 218, 221
—social union, 131, 218
Conflict of Rights, 129-31, 148, 155, 228
—internal conflict, 148-52, 154, 228
—resolution through adjustment of scope and weight, 130-37, 140, 145-49, 151-54 (core of a right, 131, 133-35, 147, 149, 152, 153, 226)
—*See also* Rights—harmonizing of
Conscience, Liberty of, 47, 50-51, 68, 112, 123, 149-50, 175
Constitutional Stage, 45, 82, 84, 111-14, 123, 137-41, 143, 147, 154, 211, 226-27. *See also* Basic Structure; Original Position—sequence of stages
Contract Tradition, 11, 31-32, 45, 209
Contribution, 169-73, 178-79, 181, 184, 230. *See also* Justice—in earnings

Daniels, Norman, 209, 213, 215
*Debs* v. *United States*, 226
Desert. *See* Entitlement
Difference Principle, 43–44, 87–88, 115,
119–20, 124–27, 159, 161, 170, 172–73,
175–80, 185, 187, 189, 197, 211, 223, 225,
230
—argument for (collective asset), 79–80,
97–98, 102–4, 106, 110, 144, 170, 177–78
—maximin argument, 102–4, 221–22 (criticism of, 104–6)
—maximin version, 88–91, 93–94, 102–4,
197–200, 219, 222
—mutual benefit, 75, 80, 97–98, 101, 104,
106, 169, 200
—normal operation of the difference principle, 91, 95–96, 105
—pareto efficiency and egalitarianism, 88,
91–101, 104–6, 115, 122, 160, 163, 170,
198–201 (and relative pareto efficiency,
99–101, 221)
—rights under the difference principle, 23,
27, 107, 120–25, 127, 129, 143, 155, 168,
189–91
—supplement to fair equality of opportunity,
74–75, 85, 87–88, 158–60, 183
—and the worth of liberty, 55, 59, 119, 160
—*See also* Second Principle of Justice; Two
Principles of Justice
Disability, Permanent, 179, 181, 186–91
Dworkin, Ronald, 2,
129, 150, 208, 228, 229

Efficiency, 66, 70, 115, 183–85
—pareto efficiency, 70, 91–92, 198
—*See also* Difference Principle—pareto efficiency and egalitarianism
Employment, Full, 161, 171, 183–86, 232
Entitlement (and Desert), 157, 162–69, 217,
230. *See also* Justice—in earnings
Envy, 193
Equal Basic Liberties, 28, 38, 45, 104, 117,
121, 163
—argument for (fundamental interests of the
representative citizen), 45–52, 60, 109–10,
143–44, 147
—equality, 46, 52–61, 63, 121
—noninjuries, 47–48, 121, 124
—personhood (and the idea of basic liberties), 37, 45–52, 56, 58, 60, 109–11, 131,
211
—as rights, 29–32, 41–44, 61, 125, 191
—*See also* Fair Equality of Opportunity—
includes (economic) liberties; First Principle

of Justice—list of liberties; Liberty; Political Participation Liberties
Equality and Egalitarianism, 64, 66, 89,
93–94, 98–99, 101, 104–5, 122, 198, 200,
214–15, 218, 220–21, 223. *See also* Difference Principle—pareto efficiency and
egalitarianism; Equal Basic Liberties—
equality; Fair Equality of Opportunity;
Original Position—equality; Second Principle of Justice—inequality
Equal Opportunity, Conceptions of, 67–70,
158
—democratic, 72–75, 78–79, 80 (*see also* Fair
Equality of Opportunity)
—liberal, 71–72 (criticism of, 72)
—natural liberty (Smithian), 70 (criticism of,
71)
—other, 75, 217

Fair Equality of Opportunity, 16, 43–44, 55,
70–75, 77–79, 87–88, 104, 158–59, 161,
163, 184, 217, 219, 221
—argument for, 66–67, 76–81, 144
—includes (economic) liberties, 67–70, 125,
136, 143, 145, 191, 215–16
—rights under, 68–69, 82–85, 104, 113, 120,
124–25, 136, 143, 191
—supplemented by difference principle,
74–75, 85, 87–88, 158–60, 183
—*See also* Equal Opportunity, Conceptions
of; Second Principle of Justice; Two
Principles of Justice
Family (and Fair Equality of Opportunity),
79, 218
Feinberg, Joel, 208, 209, 211, 228, 229
*First National Bank* v. *Bellotti*, 227
First Principle of Justice (Rawls), 15, 23–24,
28–31, 142–43, 227–28
—as itself a right, 23, 28–32, 41, 142
—as a justification of rights, 24–25, 142
—list of liberties, 29, 46–47, 141, 209
—*See also* Equal Basic Liberties
Frankel, Charles, 211
Fuchs, Alan, 137, 139, 226, 227, 228, 233
Full Employment, 161, 171, 183–86, 232

Gauthier, David, 218
General Conception of Justice (Rawls),
63–65, 78, 117, 214–15
—inequality, 64, 66
—as a principle of reasoning, 65
—special conception, 64–65
—trade-offs, 64, 65, 214–15

—*See also* Two Principles of Justice
Gintis, Herbert, 206
Gray, John, 9, 205
Griffin, Stephen, 207, 212, 233
Gutmann, Amy, 217, 218, 231

Habeas Corpus, Writ of, 226
Hammond, Peter J., 200
Harsanyi, J. C., 102, 206, 219, 222
Hart, H. L. A., 2, 6, 10, 29, 31, 141, 203, 205, 209, 210, 213, 227, 228
Hobbes, Thomas, 31

Ideal Theory (also called Strict Compliance), 118–19, 224
—normal operation of the difference principle, 91, 95–96, 105
—a "perfectly just" society, 105
—*See also* Archimedean Point; Well-ordered Society
Ihara, Craig, 222
Inequality. *See* Equality and Egalitarianism
Interaction (and Cooperation), 13, 24, 101, 170, 175, 180, 189
Interests. *See* Coherence Criterion; Equal Basic Liberties—argument for; Persons—two powers

Judicial Review. *See* Adjudication, Theory of—judicial review
Justice
—in earnings, 162–69, 175, 233
—as fairness, 15, 93
—global, 21, 41–44
—a "perfectly just" society, 105
—(pure) procedural justice, 87–88, 158–59, 161, 183, 206, 219
—and rights, 39
—and welfare, 175, 194–95
—*See also* General Conception of Justice; Two Principles of Justice

Kant, Immanuel, 11
Kaye, David H., 219, 222
Keat, Russell, 233
Kronman, Anthony, 217

Lexical Order (or Priority), 15–16, 81, 87–88, 92–93, 98, 107–20, 124–26, 138,

140, 144–45, 147, 153–55 (criticism of, 118–19). *See also* Difference Principle; Rights—priority of
Liberty
—concept of, 47, 211–12
—liberties (mere), 46, 108, 223
—"perfect liberty" (Adam Smith), 70
—priority of, 107–14, 118, 126
—restrictions on, 61, 213–14
—value (or worth) of, 55–56, 119, 122, 160
—*See also* Equal Basic Liberties; Fair Equality of Opportunity—includes (economic) liberties; First Principle of Justice—list of liberties
Locke, John, 31
Lyons, David, 9, 204, 205, 215

MacCallum, G. C., 211, 212, 227
MacCormick, Neil, 213
MacDonald, Margaret, 210
Market (Supply/Demand), 116, 157–65, 167–69, 171, 183–85
—competition, 158–63, 229
—market goals or values, 158–60, 162, 171, 229
—*See also* Basic Structure
Marx, Karl, 158, 229
Maximin. *See* Difference Principle—maximin argument *and*—maximin version
Melden, A. I., 209, 210
Meyers, Diana T., 225, 233
Michelman, Frank I., 227, 231
Mill, J. S., 1, 3, 4, 5, 8, 19, 40, 57, 204, 205, 206
Moore, Ronald, 211, 227
Morally Valid Claims, 38–39, 41, 209. *See also* Rights
Musgrave, R. A., 229
Mutual Aid, 186–87

National Security, 53–54, 61, 115, 134–36, 139, 148
Needs (and Welfare), 174–78, 180–91, 231
Nelson, William, 210
Nickel, James W., 208, 209, 212, 225
Nietzsche, Friedrich, 15, 206
Nozick, Robert, 167, 179, 216, 219, 220, 225, 229, 230

Original Position, 1, 15–19, 23, 25, 26, 30, 43, 52, 56, 71, 76–77, 117, 142, 146–47, 154, 166, 168, 178–80, 192, 232

—equality, 17, 52–53, 56, 71, 98–99, 221
—knowledge conditions, 15, 18, 46, 137–38, 140, 179, 200–201, 236
—nondeductivity, 16, 20, 22, 206–7
—ranking of principles, 15–16, 18, 206
—sequence of stages, 13–14, 20, 21, 45–47, 137–41, 143, 147, 211, 224
—contrasted with state of nature, 31, 209
—*See also* Persons; Well-ordered Society
Ownership of Property, 47, 51, 68, 127, 157, 170–74, 178, 185, 219, 231
—social ownership of the means of production, 171–73, 231

Pareto, Vilfredo, 219
Parker, Richard B., 227
Paternalism, 186–87
Perfectionist Theories, 15, 117, 206
Persons (Moral), 16–17, 19, 48–52, 60, 109–11, 147, 166, 207, 211
—two powers, 48–51, 109, 143, 146, 212, 228
Phelps, G. S., 219
Plato, 15, 206
Political Participation Liberties, 47, 51, 53–54, 56–58
—fair value, 58–60, 83, 139–40, 160, 217, 227
—majority vote (restrictions on), 53–54
—plural voting, 57–60
Powers (as Social Primary Goods), 63, 214.
*See also* Primary Goods—social
Primary Goods, 21, 197, 201, 207, 214, 223
—natural, 14, 22, 194, 217
—psychological (self-respect), 193–95, 233
—social, 14, 16, 19, 22–23, 26, 49–50, 110–11, 175, 192–93, 233 (and rights, 22–23, 26, 27, 30, 208)
Privacy, Right of, 40, 130, 133
Public Accommodation, 146
Public Goods, 115, 117, 160, 182–83, 186, 219, 224, 231–32
Punishment (and Rights), 25, 130–31, 225

Rae, Douglas, 219
Reflective Equilibrium, 25–26, 187–89, 192, 208
Rights (in Rawls's Theory), 11, 21–31, 39, 208
—absolute, 148, 155, 228–29
—concept of, 26–30, 32–35, 39–41, 69, 82–83, 119–20, 125–26, 144

—harmonizing of, 141–48, 153–54
—moral (as contrasted to natural rights), 35–36, 210
—natural, 2, 21, 24, 31–32, 35–39, 40–41, 44–45, 52, 164, 173, 210
—priority of, 107, 114–20, 125–26
—subsidiary, 21, 24–26, 31, 168–69
—system of (also called family of rights), 60–61, 114–20, 124–27, 129, 143–48, 153–55, 193, 225
—*See also* Basic Structure Rights; Bill of Rights; Conflict of Rights; Equal Basic Liberties—as rights; First Principle of Justice; Political Participation Liberties; Punishment; Second Principle of Justice—rights under the second principle; Utilitarianism
Rights, Moral and Constitutional. *See* Basic Structure Rights; Rights—moral *and*— natural
Riker, William, 224
Rousseau, J. J., 11

*San Antonio* (Texas) *Independent School District* v. *Rodriguez*, 224
*Schenk* v. *United States*, 226
Schooling (Public), 82–84, 112–13, 120, 121, 123, 125, 161, 191, 216, 223–24
Second Principle of Justice (Rawls), 15, 23, 75, 80–81, 88, 97, 112, 144, 157
—inequality, 63, 66, 68, 80–81, 170
—rights under the second principle, 23, 27, 68–69, 82–85, 104, 107, 113, 120–25, 127, 129, 136, 143, 155, 168, 173, 189–91
—*See also* Difference Principle; Fair Equality of Opportunity
Self-respect, 175, 184, 191–95, 214, 233. *See also* Primary Goods
Sen, A. K., 208, 218, 219, 222
Shenoy, Prakash, 87, 197, 218
Shute, Nevil, 213
Sidgwick, Henry, 8
Slavery, Liberty from, 25, 39, 50, 56, 58
Smith, Adam, 70, 75, 114, 158, 171, 211, 215, 216, 229
Social Security Insurance, 181–83, 185–86
Speech, Assembly, and Press, Liberty of, 47, 51, 53–55, 61, 68, 125, 130, 131–36, 139, 146, 148, 226
—"clear and present danger" test, 135, 226
—commercial speech, 68, 135–36, 216
Strasnick, Steven, 200
Stuhlmann-Laeisz, Rainer, 220

Tollett, Kenneth S., 224
Travel, 34, 58, 210
—economic, 67
—emigration, 67, 216
Trial (Fair), Right to, 35–36, 120–22, 130, 133–36
Two Principles of Justice (Rawls), 21, 23, 64, 102–3, 115, 161–62, 173, 175, 180
—special conception, 64–65
—*See also* First Principle of Justice; General Conception of Justice; Second Principle of Justice

Utilitarianism, 1–11, 19–20, 95, 102–3, 115–17, 206
—average, 15, 103, 206, 221–22
—indirect, 3–9, 204–5 (criticism of, 5–9)

—Rawls on, 11–12, 106
—and rights, 1–4, 9–11, 22, 203–4 (contrasted with Rawls's theory of rights, 69, 126, 152–53)

Vickery, W. S., 206

Walzer, Michael, 230
Wasserman, Scott, 210
Well-ordered Society, 17–19, 59, 96–97, 115, 139, 147, 154–55, 163, 173, 179, 184, 207
—public sense of justice, 17–18
—stability, 18
—*See also* Basic Structure; Ideal Theory
Wiksell, Knut, 206